LIVING LOW-CARB

Also by Fran McCullough

The Low-Carb Cookbook

Best American Recipes 1999 (with Suzanne Hamlin)

Great Food Without Fuss (with Barbara Witt)

Great Feasts Without Fuss (with Barbara Witt)

Classic American Food Without Fuss (with Barbara Witt)

LIVING LOW-CARB

The Complete Guide to Long-Term Low-Carb Dieting

BY FRAN MCCULLOUGH

LITTLE, BROWN AND COMPANY
BOSTON   NEW YORK   LONDON

First Edition

The author wishes to thank the following for permission to reprint their recipes: Zucchini Posing as Fettuccine in Lemon Cream by Susan Simon. Published in *The Nantucket Table*. Copyright © 1998 by Susan Simon. Reprinted by permission of Chronicle Books; Chocolate Climax and Zucchini Vichyssoise by Rozanne Gold. Published in *Recipes 1-2-3 Menu Cookbook*. Copyright © 1999 by Rozanne Gold. Reprinted by permission of Little, Brown and Company; Flourless Chocolate Cake by Michael Roberts. Published in *Parisian Home Cooking*. Copyright © 1999 by Michael Roberts. Reprinted by permission of William Morrow and Company, Inc.; Voluptuous Cauliflower by Anne Rosenzweig. Published in the *New York Times*. Reprinted by permission of Anne Rosenzweig.

Library of Congress Cataloging-in-Publication Data
McCullough, Frances Monson.
    Living low-carb : the complete guide to long-term low-carb dieting / Fran McCullough — 1st ed.
        p.   cm.
    Includes bibliographical references.
    ISBN 0-316-55768-4
    1. Low-carbohydrate diet.   I. Title
RM237.73.M386 2000
613.2'83 — dc21   99-057132

10 9 8 7 6 5 4 3 2 1

Q-FG

Book design by H. Roberts Design

Printed in the United States of America

Contents

Part Six
Recipes

Author's Note

Before beginning this or any other diet or nutritional program, you are advised to consult with your physician. In particular, if you are pregnant or have any special condition requiring medical attention, or if you are taking or have been advised to take any medication, you should consult regularly with your physician.

The information provided in this book is based on sources that the author believes to be reliable. All information regarding specific products and companies is current as of January 2000.

Acknowledgments

My first thanks go to my should-be-sainted husband David, who's not only endlessly long-suffering but endlessly supportive — and always willing to raise his fork to taste the latest little surprise from the kitchen.

I still had my A-team for the writing of this book, the fantastic group of people who were behind *The Low-Carb Cookbook*: my agent Irene Skolnick, my editor Rick Kot, and Rick's lieutenant Michael Liss. Special thanks to Jennifer Josephy, who guided this book through the publication process. I'm incredibly lucky to have all of you. And part of my luck is Irwyn Applebaum, the godfather of all my low-carb books.

I'm also fortunate to have great friends, who have contributed their expertise in various fields and let me pick their brains and bounce ideas off them and talk to them incessantly about this fascinating (to me, not always to them) subject. A huge thank-you to Bruce Aidells, Janet Bailey, Jo Bettoja, June Biermann, Carver Blanchard, Catherine Brandel, Dr. Louis Buzzeo, Dana Carpender, JoAnn Clevenger, Darian Cork, Warren Cork, Susan Costner, Robert Crayhon, Marion Cunningham, Drs. Mike and Mary Dan Eades, Susan Fischer, Linda and Fred Griffith, Christopher Gross, Suzanne Hamlin, Diana Kennedy, David King, Niloufer Ichaporia King, Pat Klinkhammer, Wendy Lane, Mark Lindner, Maggie McCarthy, Dr. Larry McCleary, Ben McCullough, Katy McCullough, Deborah Madison, Patty O'Neill, James O'Shea, Gene Opton, Pat Puglio, Dr. Donald Robertson and Carol Robertson, Dr. Ron Rosedale, Lorna Sass, Lindsey Shere, Martha Rose Shulman, Alan Silverstein, Nina Simonds, Brian Termini, Barbara Toohey, Charles VanOver, Eileen Weinberg, Faith Heller Willinger, Barbara Witt, Paula Wolfert, Diane Rossen Worthington, and Rob Wynne.

Introduction

It took me many years to realize that I am unable to properly metabolize carbohydrates. This became most painfully clear at the dawn of the low-fat era, when I was told by expert after expert that it was fat that made me fat, and I could eat all the carbohydrates I wanted and still lose weight. But I continued to gain weight, and whenever I managed to lose a pound or two after a huge effort, it would come right back in spades after one restaurant dinner.

I began to recognize something was wrong, basically wrong, with the approach I had chosen. But I was afraid to return to the Atkins diet, the only diet I'd ever both felt good on and lost weight on, because I was sure it would kill me, given the medical opinion of the time. And I couldn't simply give up dieting, either, because left to my own predilections I'd typically gain between 15 and 20 pounds a year, just eating whatever appealed to me. At that rate, I'd add on 150 to 200 pounds a decade, and end up weighing over 400 pounds by the time my kids graduated from college.

As I've written in *The Low-Carb Cookbook,* my saviors appeared in the form of Drs. Mike and Mary Dan Eades, who more or less fell into my lap when I became their enthusiastic editor. Their book *Protein Power* convinced me that there was a solution to my problem. I credit the Eadeses not only with whittling my size down by more than 60 pounds but with saving my life. Today, in fact, I got the results of my latest blood tests: perfect cholesterol, perfect triglycerides, and perfect blood pressure. (My homocysteine* level was not perfect, though that's easily corrected by taking 800mcg of folic acid a day.)

My weight isn't yet perfect, but that's not the fault of the low-carb regime. My professional life revolves around great food: I'm constantly tasting it and testing it and being treated to extraordinary meals and samplings that only a fool (or a very wise person) would pass up. I'm still working on passing up at least some of it, though.

In my family I'm known as the Pleasure Maniac, the one who insists on the constant little daily pleasures — espresso, flowers, real silver on the table — as well as the big ones. That tendency very much informs my dieting habits and to some degree it informs this book. I want to responsibly enjoy as much as I possibly can: to eat as well as I can and still lose or maintain; to find the secret weapons that will allow me that pleasure; to test the boundaries without losing my balance.

Because I've had a life-threatening illness (a major blood clot) and because my older sister has had a massive stroke from which she will probably never recover, I'm also determined to be as healthy as I possibly can be. That's why you'll find regular notes throughout this book on little or large details of general health.

No one diagnosed my blood clot but me; I had to go to four doctors (who told me I was wrong) and finally to a vascular surgeon before my original hunch was confirmed. As the surgeon told me, I could have died at any point along the way. That experience has convinced me that we're all responsible for our own health, for listening to our bodies and heeding what they tell us.

What my body tells me on the low-carb regime is that all's well: I have great energy, I don't catch every passing flu anymore, and my bloodwork confirms the value of this regime for me. But low-carb dieting may not be as worthwhile for you — or perhaps some variation of it may be what works for you. We're all amazingly different biochemically, and each person has to figure out what's right for him- or herself.

---

*This amino acid is always present in our blood, but at high levels it can damage the cells lining the blood vessels, which leads to plaque buildup.

You may be lucky enough to find a doctor to guide you, but don't take it for granted that that will be the case.

I have no doubt that at some point someone will come along with a better version of low-carbing or another system entirely that will address the same problems in a better way. We're still just at the beginning of understanding all the mechanisms involved. As David King, a research biochemist at the University of California, Berkeley, says, "Less is known about human nutrition than any other field of human endeavor, with the possible exception of sociology and psychology." And the more it's unraveled, the more complicated it gets. But until we know much more, this is the best way I've found to lose weight, improve general health, and give yourself a shot at a dynamic long life.

When I wrote *The Low-Carb Cookbook* in 1997, I was basically writing it for myself, so that I'd have an arsenal of delicious low-carb recipes to keep me happy on the program I suspected I'd be following for the rest of my life. I thought other low-carb dieters might also be interested, but I was completely unprepared for the avalanche of correspondence I received. The book was greeted as the low-carb cooking bible, the essential guide to eating your way to success without giving up good food in the process. Since then, the letters have only increased, and the refrain is always the same: Thanks so much for writing this book, and please write another one. I've been incredibly touched and inspired by this mail, as people share their frustrations and their triumphs, their health challenges and their joy at having finally found a way of eating that works.

Like many of the fans of *The Low-Carb Cookbook,* I've come to discover that I now need "more" myself. I know for certain that I'm in the low-carb world for the long haul, or at least until something much better is discovered. And I've learned a huge amount in the last few years that goes beyond recipes, important as recipes are. *Living Low-Carb* is intended for long-term low-carbers, people whose health or weight problems require a serious, extended commitment. It integrates low-carb eating into ordinary life, discussing both practical concerns — including issues like travel and holidays — as well as more subtle ones, such as the little emotional roller-coasters we all find ourselves riding.

It also explores the pros and cons of various elements of the diet and suggests ways for you to devise your own version — which, in the end, will be the only diet that really works for you.

Because I wish I'd known some of these things when I first started, I've featured some material that beginners will find useful, as well as many recipes that are extremely low-carb, for early stages of the diet. For readers who have been low-carbing for a while now, and have eased up a little on their carb budget, *Living Low-Carb* has many recipes that use those extra carbs deliciously. In addition, almost everyone on a low-carb diet has encountered the same roadblocks or discovered that some pieces to the low-carb puzzle are missing. I hope you'll find some of the answers here — as well as some inspiration and some great food to keep you happily on track.

PART ONE

Why Are We Doing This, Anyway?

The Basic Idea

The objective of all low-carb diets, which date back at least to the early nineteenth century, has always been weight loss. Although plenty of low-fat advocates continue to insist that it's only water that's lost on a low-carb regimen, many patients using it have lost over 100 pounds in short order. Among the many formerly obese, it's pretty well agreed that low-carb is the most effective, most enjoyable, and most successful over the long term of all the various diets. Despite our government's dictate that we load up on carbs to maintain our health, low-carb books have consistently topped the bestseller charts for nearly a decade. Literally millions of people have followed these diets with no reported ill effects so far. Although low-carb diets are still controversial within the health establishment, they have never been vulnerable to charges like the deaths that have been associated with fen-phen or liquid diets. The theoretical argument will continue to rage, and it's extremely unlikely that any definitive studies will be done anytime soon to settle it.

Why do these low-carb diets work so well when almost nothing else does? For a long time the exact mechanisms weren't clearly understood, but when Drs. Michael and Mary Dan Eades (authors of *Protein*

Power) went back to their basic biochemistry texts, they discovered not only the weight-loss mechanism but also the huge number of health benefits that can accrue to many who follow the low-carb path. These include dramatically lowering high blood pressure, levels of the dangerous blood fats called triglycerides, and LDL (bad) cholesterol; controlling diabetes; supplying extra energy throughout the entire day with no up-and-down swings; increasing concentration and focus; enhancing lean body mass with loss of excess body fat; improving immune function; eliminating gout and esophageal reflux; and many other benefits, such as a reversal of inflammatory conditions.

All this happens, the experts in the area now agree, because restricting carbohydrates — sugar and starch in whatever form, from Popsicles to baked potatoes — puts the brakes on insulin, the hormone that's responsible not only for storing fat (and worse, keeping it stored) but also for raising blood pressure, damaging blood vessels, and wreaking other bits of havoc throughout the body for those of us who are genetically predisposed to obesity, diabetes, and heart disease. Incoming sugars and starches require insulin — the more sugar you consume, the more insulin is needed to process it at the cellular level. After an individual has been on a steady high-sugar diet over a number of years, the insulin receptors on his or her cells may become resistant, in which case even more insulin is required to handle the sugar load. Such a person usually develops insulin resistance, sometimes called Syndrome X or hyperinsulinemia, which usually leads to Type II (adult-onset) diabetes. An insulin-resistant person usually has an increased waist-to-hip ratio, high blood glucose levels, high uric acid, high triglycerides, and low HDL (the good cholesterol). There seems to be a genetic propensity to have problems with insulin. If your family tends to gain weight easily, especially in the abdominal area, you probably have this syndrome, and are therefore at risk for the related health problems (if you don't already have them) unless you change your diet.

The only way to cut back on this outpouring of insulin is by reducing your intake of carbohydrates. Since you always need the same amount of protein, no matter what diet you're on — about 0.5 gram for every pound of your ideal weight — you'll obviously eat more fat on a low-carb diet. (Remember, there are only three food groups to choose from: protein, fat, and carbohydrate.) A number of low-carb diets feature enormous amounts of steak, cheese, butter, and cream, and many anecdotal tales tell of people consuming up to 3,000 calories a day on such a regime and still continuing to lose weight. Other low-carb diets limit the consumption of fats, or vary the ratios of the kinds of fats consumed.

So, do calories not count? They do and they don't. If you don't have insulin problems and have a normal metabolism but simply eat too much, you can go by the standard advice: Cut calories and you will lose weight. But if you do have genetic insulin problems, as you probably do if you're from an overweight family, you may not fare as well on a reduced-calorie diet unless you also cut the carbs very far back. Except for the amazing tales of the 3,000-calorie dieters, though, there's no free lunch on a low-carb diet: If you want to lose a substantial amount of weight, you still need to create a caloric deficit, though perhaps not such a dramatic one as if you weren't concentrating on cutting carbs.

Many people who aren't actually overweight adopt a low-carb diet for health reasons. Some of them are skinny but diabetic; others would prefer to attempt to control their cholesterol or blood pressure without dangerous and expensive medications. The muscular guys you see at the gym eat low-carb to build their lean body mass and minimize fat. Many children with epilepsy have for decades now been given a very successful treatment that involves a no-carb, high-fat diet — not only has their epilepsy been controlled when medication has failed, they've suffered no ill effects from such a drastic regime.

The nutritional establishment's thinking on the subject of dietary fat has begun to change, partly because the low-fat prescription has had fairly unhappy results, such as continuing rampant obesity throughout the population and childhood diabetes increasing by 20 percent in the last decade. Fertility levels have fallen, which may also be a result of our not eating enough fat, and leading researchers such as Dr. Walter Willett of Harvard have started arguing that it's the *kind* of fat, not the total fat consumed, that makes the difference in weight gain. Willett is comfortable with a diet that's as high as 40 percent fats, as long as those fats are mainly unsaturated.

The fact is, we don't really know very much about human nutrition and metabolism, despite experts' having made claims for "the perfect diet" since the beginning of time. What our species actually evolved to eat, though, is quite like the low-carb diet: protein and fat from small animals and sea creatures and birds, small amounts of carbohydrate from plants and berries and seeds and nuts, and the occasional feast on a major animal. Dairy products are quite recent additions to the human diet, as are agricultural products, which we've had for only 10,000 years — a minuscule amount of time, from an evolutionary stand-point. Many of us may simply not have adapted biologically to this rel-atively "new" diet, which may be one reason we feel so good and flourish so well on a low-carb plan.

Needless to say, there are many theories within the low-carb camp, and many different low-carb regimens. If you're seriously thinking about eating this way for the rest of your life — as you should be if you have the insulin problem — you ought to take a look at all of them and choose the one that seems best suited to you.

The Theories

Paleolithic Diet. This regime, also known as the Stone Age diet, is probably the purest form of low-carb eating, and it's extremely restric-tive. Its premise is that you're not supposed to eat anything your an-cestors wouldn't have eaten, say, 40,000 years ago. I'm filled with admiration for paleodieters, but I'm too much of a pleasure eater to subsist on game and berries. To learn more about this theory, read Ray Audette's *Neanderthin: Eat Like a Cave Man to Achieve a Lean, Strong, Healthy Body.*

Dr. Atkins. Although there were many low-carb diet proponents before him, among them Gaylord Hauser, Dr. Robert Atkins is the main popularizer of this regimen for our time. He has gained a reputation for being an outlaw, partly because he sneers at the health establishment, which has tried very hard to vilify him, and partly because he has only recently begun to explain the biochemistry of his regime — it just works, he says, so do it. His diet puts you in ketosis (see page 29) initially, then moves on to a more generous maintenance carb level. No coffee is allowed in the restrictive stage of Dr. Atkins's diet.

Protein Power and *The Protein Power Lifeplan.* These are the thinking person's low-carb diet books, developed by real doctors, the Eadeses, and full of elegant explanations of how it all works plus various strategies for success, including planned indulgences. You can drink alcohol and have coffee on the Protein Power plan, and it doesn't require ketosis. The Eadeses are strongly against aspartame.

Carbohydrate Addicts. The creators of this diet, Rachael and Richard Heller, pose in white coats on their book jackets, but they aren't actually medical doctors. They stress the addictive nature of carbs but they're also enablers: They allow dieters a grace meal once a day with all the carbs they can eat within a certain time frame. They also identify trigger foods that tend to launch carb binges. This strategy works for some, not for others (and not for me). Success may depend on the degree of your insulin resistance.

Sugar Busters. This book might be thought of as *Protein Power for Dummies.* If you're having trouble grasping the entire concept, take a look at *Sugar Busters,* which allows more carbs than most of the other plans. This plan comes out of New Orleans, where they know a thing or two about good food, and was devised by a bunch of real doctors.

The Zone. Barry Sears's popular program isn't strictly speaking a low-carb diet; it's just a lot lower-carb than most other regimens, especially low-fat diets. Sears is a researcher who developed his program for elite athletes seeking maximum performance and endurance. Some people lose weight on the Zone, others just maintain. There are a number of Zone clones on the market, such as Carol Simontacchi's *Your Fat Is Not Your Fault.*

Dr. Bernstein's Diabetes Solution. This is a radical approach — although it used to be the standard one — to treating both types of diabetes (juvenile and adult onset) by controlling carbohydrates to achieve normal blood sugars. Richard Bernstein is a hero in the alternative-medicine world, and his book is definitely worth reading even if you're not diabetic. As Dr. Ron Rosedale, the author of the forthcoming *Cap-*

turing the Fire of Life, notes, we're all basically diabetic anyway, and we should all be eating as if that were the case.

The GO-Diet, by Jack Goldberg and Karen O'Mara. This is a variation on the Protein Power diet, with an emphasis on monounsaturated fats, live-culture fermented milk products, and lots of fiber. One glass of alcohol per day is allowed. The carbohydrate level is relatively low, and saturated fats are kept below 40 grams a day. The GO-Diet was developed by a clinical biochemist and an intensive-care specialist, and tested in a Chicago community hospital with a small number of patients who lost an average of 20 pounds in 12 weeks. You can download the diet from go-diet.com free of charge.

Suzanne Somers' Get Skinny on Fabulous Food. You remember Suzanne, if not from her part as the ditz in *Three's Company,* then for her hustling the ThighMaster and AbRoller on infomercials. Her newest book has a medical introduction by Dr. Diana Schwarzbein lauding its low-carb elements but declining to comment on Somers's other diet essential: food combining. Dr. Schwarzbein is very pro low-carb (and has published her own book on the subject), but if you combine foods the way the book suggests, you can end up eating very many carbs — starting out with Grape-Nuts (23 grams before you add milk) for breakfast.

If this plan works for you, great — you can eat a lot more foods this way — but not sugar, starch, caffeine, or alcohol. You eat fruits alone, with a time window between them and other foods. If you eat carbs, you eat them with vegetables, not protein or fat.

Some correspondents on the Amazon.com reader response list did very well on the diet, as did many readers whose cases Somers cites in this book. Others actually gained weight. The difference may be a function of the degree of insulin resistance these people have. Once again, if it works for you, it works. If not, you'll still find some very good low-carb recipes in this book.

The Montignac Diet. This slightly goofy French version of a low-carb diet is highly entertaining — and can be highly successful. Michel Montignac is a layman who more or less stumbled on his theories: There are good and bad carbs, based on the Glycemic Index (a French version, which lists beer at its pinnacle as the most glycemic ingestible of all). He also likes a bit of food combining — you can have fruit, but only in isolation. And you can have bread, but only at breakfast. You can have a little bittersweet chocolate and up to half a liter of wine a day. And don't bother exercising. When you've run through all the other low-carb diets and you're nearing the end of your rope, Montignac may be just what you need.

The Careful Carb Diet. In *How I Gave Up My Low-Fat Diet and Lost 40 Pounds!* author Dana Carpender (yes, she's the Dana in "Real Life Stories," page 31) describes her weight-loss experience and also offers an interesting version of the low-carb regime, the Careful Carb Diet. It uses moderate but adequate amounts of protein, is relatively low-fat, and allows certain carbs that supposedly don't raise blood sugar levels — which means, of course, you can have many more carbs, including super-premium ice cream, peanut M&Ms, beans, and two fruits a day — plus a glass of wine. Not at all a bad deal, and although it doesn't work for Dana, because she's too insulin resistant, it does work for a lot of her fans.

Carpender's is a sassy, tell-it-like-it-is book that's a great low-carb companion, and it has terrific lists of things like low-carb vegetarian foods and supplements, plus notes on medical studies.

If you're like most long-term low-carb dieters, you'll work your way through one or several of these different approaches until you come up with your own plan, one that is successful for you and feels comfortable. Remember, biochemically we're all unique individuals, so there's no one-size-fits-all program, and you owe it to yourself to do a little experimenting, with guidance from the medical experts.

Another Way of Looking at the Puzzle

You may have heard about the glycemic index, an effort to measure the blood sugar effects of various foods. This research, which came out of the University of Toronto in 1981, provoked a lot of interest, even though it tested only 47 foods. These were evaluated by their capacity to raise blood sugar as measured against the action of white sugar. (Potatoes, for instance, were right up there with white sugar.) In theory, at least, the glycemic index would give you an accurate picture of what the insulin response to a given food would actually be.

Not all low-carb experts are enchanted with this idea; Dr. Richard Bernstein, the low-carb diabetes guru, thinks it's irrelevant and pays no attention to it. Dr. Michael Eades (*Protein Power*) points out that it doesn't tell you what the actual insulin response is, and certainly not what the glucagon response is — the crucial element in whether you store or burn fat. If the subjects had been typically insulin-resistant types, that might be significant information, but of course they were the very people least likely to have problems, healthy young men. And foods are almost never eaten in large amounts by themselves; as part of a meal, they may have completely different effects.

One of the leading advocates of glycemic information is Dr. Ann DeWees Allen, a biomedical researcher and inventor who works with Olympic competitors and other elite athletes like Mr. Universe, Ms. Galaxy, and the NFL. Dr. Allen is still living in the low-fat world, so some foods don't make her acceptable list even though they might be low on the glycemic index — coconut oil, for instance, falls under the old bad-tropical-oils axe. Along with some products, such as sweeteners, Dr. Allen also sells a booklet giving not specific numbers for various foods, as in her earlier research, but lists of acceptable and unacceptable foods according to whether they quickly or slowly raise blood sugar.

In some ways this is a very appealing way of looking at carbs. You can eat all sorts of things you never imagined you could, from pasta to sweet potatoes to most beans. Also on the acceptable list are bulgur, barley, kasha, Special K cereal, whole wheat tortillas, and Fig Newtons (though dried figs are, oddly enough, unacceptable). You can eat raw Old-Fashioned Quaker Oats, but not oatmeal. Watermelon is out, and so are turnips, but that seems a small price to pay for some great new food options. Remember, though, that other experts say sugar is sugar is sugar, from whatever source — and that carbs do really count. And it requires the same amount of insulin, over a short period or a longer period, to handle it.

A popular treatment of this approach is *The Glucose Revolution* by Jennie Brand-Miller, Thomas M. S. Wolever, Stephen Colagiuri, and Kaye Foster-Powell. This book comes with raves from Jean Carper and from Andrew Weil, who was thrilled to discover he can have sugar and pasta in his life again. *The Glucose Revolution* collates the available studies on glycemic indexes (GI) of 300 foods and drinks. The glycemic index measures how fast blood sugar rises (not insulin levels, but the presumption is that high blood sugar requires lots of insulin) after consuming a particular food.

The Glucose Revolution is not a low-carb book; on the contrary, it advocates a low-fat approach, recommending the USDA pyramid with low-GI foods and a level of carbs that is anywhere from 200 to 330 grams a day. You can eat a lot of fruit on this regime.

There are some huge surprises: Peanuts are rated only 14g for ½ cup; all yogurt, even sweetened yogurt, has a very low GI. Fettuccine and vermicelli are quite low, lower than many protein sources such as fish.

The low-carb diet is dismissed in a couple of sentences with the argument that it won't help you lose weight, because your body can't convert its fat to glucose, so it has to use its muscle protein instead. (That's assuming you ate no protein, of course.) Then, having carefully explained that potatoes are higher than glucose on the scale, literally off the scale, the authors go on to recommend potatoes for dinner, on the grounds that they're good sources of vitamin C and potassium.

The lists in *The Glucose Revolution* can be helpful; certainly, anything that's both low-carb *and* low-GI is a good thing, and you may want to play around with some of the other low-GI foods such as pasta. See what works, but be careful with this diet if you're seriously insulin-resistant.

A major study published in 1997 did get the low-carb world's attention by testing the actual insulin response to a few foods — though not, unfortunately, chocolate. Since we're most of all interested in this insulin response, these numbers are much more relevant, at least theoretically. There were several ways in which insulin response differed from the glycemic index response. Perhaps the most striking was that pasta is even lower on the insulin index than it is on the glycemic index, and significantly lower than either beef or fish. Peanuts have only two-thirds the insulin-raising effect of eggs, and oatmeal (not allowed on Dr. Allen's list) is lower than cheese or beef. French fries are lower than white rice, ice cream is right up there with cookies, and jelly beans (that low-fat diet staple) are the absolute worst of all. Beef and fish are about the same as potato chips, lentils, apples, oranges, and brown rice.

What should we make of all this confusing information? Could we have some potato chips for dinner instead of fish? As with almost everything else on the low-carb diet, you'll have to figure it out for yourself. Try one of these foods — pasta, say — and see what happens. Do you keep losing weight, if that's what you're trying to do? Do you have the typical carb-OD symptoms of great thirst, puffiness, fatigue, brain fog? If you're a little more curious, you can test your own blood with a glucometer (see pages 46–47) and see how the pasta really affected your blood sugars.

See what you can get away with, both in terms of blood sugar elevation, weight loss, and the effect on your general health several months down the road. (I.e., have your physician test your blood for triglycerides, cholesterol breakdown, glucose level, and so on.) If you can expand your dietary choices, great. If not, go back to square one and consult with your doctor. But maybe you'll discover there really is free lunch . . .

Is This Diet Right for Everyone?

One of the problems with diet books is that the authors always insist theirs is the Only Way, the one truth that solves all mysteries that have heretofore baffled mankind. Obviously they can't all be right, and sorting out which elements of which ones are right for you can be a full-time job.

In theory, at least, low-carb eating is indeed suitable for everyone, because it's the diet the first humans ate, before we left the forest and moved up the evolutionary ladder to the Industrial Revolution — and sugar. The more addicted to sweets you are, the more appropriate this regime is for you — unless you have no weight or health problems as a result of your sweet tooth.

A low-carb diet definitely *isn't* for you if you have serious kidney problems, which is why it's important to have bloodwork done by a doctor before you begin. According to Dr. Louis Buzzeo, a kidney specialist, kidney damage, like liver damage, is silent; you can lose as much as 90 percent of your kidney function without being aware of it — and at that point, the damage is irreversible. Any kidney problems will show up in standard blood testing, however, both in the urinalysis and in the Bun/Creat factors. If your bloodwork's okay, your kidneys are okay. If not, avoid this diet. (Dana Carpender's book, however, details a case of extremely successful low-carb dieting for a kidney patient; see Bibliography.)

The diet may also not be for you if you're a vegetarian — see page 89. Many vegetarians successfully eat low-carb, but it requires a huge effort, especially if you're a vegan (someone who shuns eggs and diary products as well as meat).

Dr. Leo Galland feels that pear-shaped people do best on high carbs, whereas apple-shaped people will flourish on low carbs, especially those with low HDL. If you feel strong after eating a steak and tired after eating pasta, low-carb is your diet.

Some low-carb dieters don't have the usual high energy on this diet and instead feel foggy and full of lassitude. If that state persists for more than three weeks and you're following a low-carb regime faithfully, you probably need more carbs to function well. Remember: If you don't feel great on a low-carb diet, don't pursue it. Your body is sending a message you should acknowledge.

If you're trying to lose weight and nothing happens — and again, you're absolutely sure you're following one of the regimes to the letter — consider switching to another low-carb plan. If that doesn't work either, drop the low-carb approach and consider trying something more traditional, like calorie restriction.

If after several months of low-carbing, your cholesterol values actually increase, which is rare, you need to change the ratio of fats in your diet. A good place to start is the GO-Diet; see page 8.

If you're scheduled for surgery, pregnant, or nursing, you should up your carbs to at least 100 grams daily, more if you don't have a weight or health problem. Obviously, you should tell your doctor about your diet and ask his or her advice.

JAN, 50

Jan's always been very healthy, but found herself with more weight than she wanted when she suddenly had to prepare for a nationwide publicity tour. In the two months she had before the tour, she wanted to lose 20 pounds — and chose to do it low-carb after meeting Mike and Mary Eades (*Protein Power* authors) through a mutual friend.

The pounds disappeared and they've stayed off, but that's because Jan has adopted a careful lower-carb way of eating. She weighs herself once a week and makes a point of looking at her waistline in the mirror every time she exits the shower — those fat cells have no chance of filling up again.

For Jan, the big secret is portion control. She stopped serving meals family style and instead just makes up plates that look full and inviting. She eats salad first, then the main course — and if she's feeling peckish, she pops a few olives while she's cooking so she won't dive into the meal. She's learned that you can indeed take just one almond for a snack, and then go back to the kitchen for another one, making a conscious decision to do so and not just mindlessly dip your hand into the nut jar again and again.

Snacks have been a bit of a problem, since Jan works at home and the kitchen is always beckoning. The stretch between lunch and dinner tends to be the worst time, and she's solved it by making an afternoon mini-meal with extra protein cooked the night before. She'll slice leftover meat thinly and spread it with a fancy mustard, with a pickle on the side. She makes an appealing plate of it, and sits down to eat it and enjoy it.

If cravings or hunger intrude through the day, she grabs a little bottle of water, which usually does the trick. If not, she'll have olives, especially the ones stuffed with garlic, or a few almonds toasted with garlic or cayenne.

Jan tries hard to keep no sweets in the house; if she's yearning for sweets, she indulges in a Swiss Miss Fat-Free Cocoa after dinner. Bread is a special craving, but a couple of fancy crackers usually satisfy it — or sometimes a paper-thin slice of French bread will do the trick.

For breakfast, she has a fruit smoothie — frozen strawberries, milk, nonfat vanilla yogurt, chocolate protein powder, an ice cube or two, all churned up in the blender. Or it might be a cottage cheese sundae, with fruit and nuts and yogurt.

Amazingly, Jan has come to prefer a burger without a bun — as long as it's smothered in sautéed onions and mushrooms. And although she eats a lot of red meat, her cholesterol level is perfect. Now that she's lost the pounds, she can indulge in more carbs, of course — but she's vigilant about her weight, and the minute it goes up, she's back on the path.

So What *Can* You Eat?

Now that all of America has internalized the low-fat edict, it's really hard for most of us to conceive of food in an entirely new way, one that requires us to think in terms not of fat grams or calories, but of the basic metabolic effect food has on our bodies. That task is complicated by the fact that each of the many low-carb systems now available puts a slightly different spin on the basic message. Most long-term low-carb dieters have been on several if not *all* of these diets, and then settled for one, with some individual modifications.

Here's a simplified, general plan that will allow you to jump on the low-carb diet. If you're just starting, have some beef broth or bouillon on hand to drink if you feel a bit faint or tired — you may need the potassium while your body's adjusting. Using Morton's Lite salt, which has extra potassium, will also do the trick.

A Basic Low-Carb Plan

1. Drink 8 to 12 eight-ounce glasses of water a day. Seriously. If you don't do this, you won't lose as much weight and you won't flush the toxins that are released when you burn your stored fat. Drink 2 glasses before breakfast and you're well on your way.

2. Get enough protein at every meal. This means about 0.5g pro-

tein daily for every pound of your ideal weight, somewhere from 60 to 85g unless you're very large or very small. For weight loss, keep the carbs low — close to zero if you're on the Atkins diet and trying to get into ketosis; 20 to 30g daily if you're just trying to lose weight in a not-so-rapid way. Don't worry about fat grams.

3. Eat whole foods, organic if possible, and raw ideally. The more fiber, the better. Read labels carefully on prepared foods and note that you can subtract the fiber grams from the total carb count — which means you can have more vegetables and low-carb fruit.

4. A good general rule is to avoid everything white — especially flour, sugar, potatoes, popcorn, and rice. (Technically complex carbohydrates, potatoes and rice act as simple sugars in the body.) Milk is fairly high-carb, so limit it. But do eat turnips, cauliflower, and giant white radishes (daikon).

5. Eat fruit at breakfast, if at all, and stress low-carb fruits: berries, melon, peaches, kiwi. Half a banana or a finger banana is your maximum.

6. Be prepared. Stock up on canned tuna, sardines, celery, hard-cooked eggs, cheese, nuts, green vegetables. On the road, take along low-carb protein bars or other portable low-carb foods.

7. Choose your fats wisely. Good fats include cold-pressed olive oil, nut oil, avocado, nuts, sesame oil, and peanuts. Bad fats are processed oils, partially hydrogenated fats, and margarine. Don't go wild with the fat if you're trying to lose weight. If you save the rich cheese and butter and cream for treats, you'll not only lose weight faster, you may be doing your health a favor, too (see page 56).

8. If you're trying to lose weight, weigh yourself no more than once a week; once a month is better.

9. Have dinner early, and make it minimal — just protein and salad or vegetables — if you're trying to lose weight. A little exercise after dinner is also a great idea.

10. If you fall off the wagon, savor what you're eating but jump right back on at the very next meal. Don't blow a whole day; chances are you may see no ill effect whatsoever if you don't compound the problem by splurging again right away.

It's amazing how quickly the low-carb program becomes second nature. You'll feel especially energetic, you'll look really good, and you'll be losing weight, toning your body, and boosting your level of general health dramatically.

What a great diet! So why isn't everyone in America on it and getting lean and healthy? The fact is, although it's very easy in one sense it's hard in another — it tends to be boring, and you have to give up some favorite foods, at least in any quantity. For those of us who are completely hooked on sugar and starch, it's difficult. I'm no exception; because my work revolves around food, I'm always being invited on fantastic trips to exotic food destinations (this month, it's the Piedmont district of Italy, where the pasta and risotto will be practically in my bed). I'm constantly tempted — and I frequently succumb. My laxity isn't good for my general health profile and certainly not good for weight loss; in fact, I spend about half of each year just losing weight I've recently gained on these pilgrimages. I get a little more resistant to the carb devils as I struggle through this eternal Groundhog Day of gaining and losing, and I'm hopeful that eventually I'll just be able to resist them all. I'm entirely sympathetic with readers who find themselves snatching the french fries off their dining partners' plates.

When I'm on the straight and narrow for weeks at a time, though, I tend to get bored, and that's another situation where temptation has an easy time with me. The only solution to that is to cook your way out of it, to make interesting food that makes you eager to sit down to a low-carb meal (see Part Six, Recipes).

Throughout the book, you'll find stories from other successful low-carb dieters, with their own solutions to the what-to-eat problem. Here's how I cope with low-carbing myself on weekdays when I'm not cooking something special and I have no time to think about what I'm eating.

Breakfast
Fruit, preferably low-carb
Cottage cheese with active live cultures
    OR
Low-carb protein bar

OR

Protein shake with a finger banana blended in

OR

Eggs and sausage or bacon with low-carb toast and low-carb jam

OR

Smoked salmon on low-carb toast with sprouts

OR

Low-carb cereal

Lunch

Egg salad on low-carb toast or Wasa Fiber Rye Crispbread

Green salad or cherry tomatoes and cucumbers

OR

Tuna salad on greens or low-carb toast

Green peppers or celery stuffed with cream cheese

Dinner

Soup and salad

OR

Protein (fish/poultry/meat) with green vegetable and salad

OR

Chef's salad

Why You Don't Have to Worry About . . .

A number of low-carb myths keep coming up over and over again, many of them perpetuated by the low-fat nutritional establishment — despite ample evidence to refute them. You may hear these myths from your friends, in the press, or, worst of all, from your doctor, and of course they can cause you a lot of anxiety if you don't know the actual facts. Here are some of the major recurring scare stories, along with the other side.

None for Me, Thanks

I don't need to tell you how thrilling sugar is in its many seductive forms — bread, pasta, sweets, potatoes, we love it all. But before you decide to indulge, or just fall into indulging without even bothering to make a decision, try to remember these little factoids, which go above and beyond the insulin-raising factor we know so well.

- Unlike all other cells in your body, which feed off oxygen and a little sugar, cancer cells require lots and lots of sugar.
- Sugar depresses your immune system, almost immediately.
- Sugar, especially fructose, has a caramelizing effect in the body called glycation — these "caramelized" cells are a major cause of wrinkling and other signs of aging.

So if you'd like to look old, fat, and sick, sugar is just the ticket.

Eggs

The egg hysteria has now almost entirely passed, thanks to a major investigation from the University of Arizona that evaluated 224 studies of 8,000 participants over 25 years. Their conclusion? Eggs present no cholesterol problem. This comes as no surprise to readers of alternative medical literature (and students of biochemistry), who have known for decades that most cholesterol is made in the body itself, as a response not to eating actual cholesterol, but to eating carbohydrates to excess. As Dr. Ancel Keys, the father of the Mediterranean Diet, said in *Eating Well* (March/April 1997), "There's no connection whatsoever between cholesterol in food and cholesterol in the blood. None. And we've known that all along."

In fact, eggs probably *lower* cholesterol. An American Cancer Society study found that egg-eaters have fewer heart attacks and strokes than egg-avoiders.

So where did this egg-phobia come from? It began with the Cereal Institute, which conducted an egg/cholesterol study back in the 1940s. Its results were actually correct, though its subject was wrong: The study used dried egg yolk powder, which is oxidized or trans fat, the most dangerous kind.

The egg is, in fact, a superior nutritional product at a bargain price. Organic eggs from free-range chickens are best of all, a delicious, affordable luxury that's really good for you. At the natural foods store — and some supermarkets — you can find eggs high in omega-3 oil, from chickens whose chow includes flaxseeds. Eggs also contain sulfur, generally missing from our modern diet.

Fat, Meat, and Dairy Products

A natural consequence of our obsession with lowering our fat intake is that animal products have been so demonized, it has become difficult to unself-consciously consume a steak or a piece of brie in public. You may also have your own anxieties about these products; after all, it's hard to fly in the face of the government's dictates on what you should be eating and, more important, *shouldn't* be eating.

But evidence in favor of fat, even saturated fat, is beginning to come in, and even diehard low-fat advocates like the *New York Times*'s Jane Brody and Marian Burrows (both of whom have written bestselling low-fat books) have recently come out in favor of more fat in the diet.

The charges against fat made by the government and the nutrition establishment are that (a) it makes us fat; (b) it is associated with cancer; and (c) it can lead to heart disease. In fact, recent research points in the opposite direction for this entire range of health problems; they're all to some degree actually promoted by excessive consumption of carbohydrates, not fat.

Breast cancer has consistently been associated with high fat consumption, but in fact, as the Harvard Nurses Study shows, women who ate the least fat (15 percent of their total diet, almost as low as

Dean Ornish recommends) had the highest incidence of breast cancer. A huge study of 90,000 women reported in the *Lancet* showed no relationship whatsoever between fat consumption and breast cancer. In these same women, excessive consumption of carbohydrates raised their breast cancer risk by a whopping 39 percent. (The one caution is that women who like well-done meat have five times the breast cancer risk of those who prefer it rarer.)

One possible explanation of the cancer finding is that cancer cells actually feed off sugar (glucose). This may also be one reason that vegetarians — who usually eat high-carb and low-fat — have a higher cancer risk than meat-eaters.

There's also good news about fat and cardiovascular disease. According to a Japanese study (of men only), the more fat you eat, the lower your risk of stroke. The Nurses Study showed that total fat consumption had no effect on heart disease. However, those at highest risk for heart disease did consume the most trans fats (altered fats that are in margarine and vegetable shortening, commercially fried foods, and junk foods). There's no longer any question that trans fats are dangerous, but if you stick to whole foods, you won't have any trans fats in your diet in any case.

Too little fat can be a serious problem. Low-fat diets don't contain enough RRR-a-tocopheryl, an essential nutrient used by every part of the body. This nutrient is stored for only 12 hours, and is fat-soluble, so fat needs to be consumed on a daily basis to supply it. Dietary fat is also what makes your hair gleam, your eyes shine, your skin look supple, your hormones work, and your immune system flourish.

But of course, there are fats, and there are fats. Some of the especially delicious ones — cheese, butter, cream, meat — contain conjugated linoleic acid. This superstar nutrient, which is not produced by the body, actually destroys cancer cells; it also encourages the loss of body fat and muscle gain. It inhibits melanoma, as well as colorectal, lung, and breast tumors. It has also been shown to reduce fat deposits in arteries by about 30 percent.

But what about butter? Here, too, there's lots of good news. Butter is also a rich source of vitamins A, D, and E, as well as a number of trace minerals. It contains something called the X factor, a catalyst that helps absorb minerals, as well as lauric acid — which isn't found in other animal fats, and is the one saturated fat the body doesn't make itself. Butter's lecithin helps metabolize cholesterol and other fats.

And here's a real bonus: Butter has short- and medium-chain fatty acids, which are less likely than long-chain ones to cause fat storage because they burn right away. They also lower serum cholesterol and inhibit cholesterol deposits in the blood vessels.

Besides conjugated linoleic acid, of which milk fat is the richest source, cow's milk contains other cancer inhibitors and potent anticarcinogens from their feed, such as beta-carotene and gossypol. Those facts aside, a lot of researchers remain quite anti-milk. (For that side of the argument, see the Web site notmilk.com.)

Meat is the richest food source of B_{12} (other foods of animal origin have some B_{12}), an essential nutrient; without it you can die of pernicious anemia. Meat also provides sulfur-containing amino acids, which produce the raw material for free-radical scavengers, good guys who race through the body attacking dangerous oxidized elements.

There are still some lingering questions about dairy foods and meat. For instance, Dr. Ron Rosedale of the Colorado Center for Metabolic Medicine feels that meat is just a form of second-generation carbs. Your stored body fat is in fact saturated fat; if you're consuming a lot of saturated fat, that incoming fat will be burned for energy first — i.e., there's no reason to burn your body fat if you have plenty of saturated fat in your diet. There's some evidence that saturated fat changes the cell membrane so that it's less receptive to insulin. And several of the saturated fatty acids seem to stimulate the liver to produce more LDL cholesterol (the dangerous kind), but that's only true for some people and not to a very large degree. There's also a suspicion that for some people saturated fats increase insulin resistance — the last thing we want to do.

Not at all controversial are the omega-3 oils, part of the essential-fatty-acid group. In fact, an insufficiency of essential fatty acids is the major culprit in cardiovascular disease, according to Dr. Edward N. Siguel, author of *Essential Fatty Acids in Health and Disease*. The omega-6s (found in safflower, sunflower, and corn oils) are also essential, but you want to keep the balance skewed very much in favor of the

Getting Your Omega-3s

Omega-3s reduce the risk of cancer, heart disease, inflammatory diseases, and depression. They keep your blood thin, regulate blood sugar and glucose metabolism, reduce blood pressure, enhance immune function, and act as natural calcium channel blockers to maintain a steady heart rate. They help the body burn fat, and the body burns them quickly too, so they don't get stored. Dieting depletes omega-3s in the body, so you need even more of them if you're losing weight.

Omega-3s are found in the coldwater fatty fish, including sardines, salmon, anchovies, cod, sea bass, and herring. Sardines and anchovies are also high in RNA and DNA, the essential building blocks for new cells, and important anti-aging elements. In addition, they contain DMAE, a precursor to acetylcholine — a neurotransmitter that increases alertness and concentration — so they're also good brain food.

For the sardine-phobic, the Doctors Eades recommend a health-food-store product called Carlson's Cod Liver Oil, which is practically tasteless. In theory, you could substitute fish-oil capsules, but these tend to go rancid very quickly, and once they've turned, they're actually dangerous to consume.

One of the richest sources of omega-3s is flax oil. Johanna Budwig, Germany's leading biochemist and an expert on essential fatty acids, may have single-handedly launched the craze for flaxseed oil. She was certainly the first to note its health benefits: anti-tumor activity, increased metabolism, improved immune function, reduced cholesterol, reduced blood pressure, inhibition of cancer cell growth. Flaxseed oil also helps the cells, especially muscle cells, respond better to insulin, so they burn calories more efficiently. (Dr. David G. Williams, author of the *Alternatives* newsletter, says adding 3 tablespoons of flaxseed oil a day will produce weight loss all by itself.)

Dr. Budwig notes that for flax oil to work best, it should be bound to a protein, so that it's water soluble and free-flowing. In this form, the energy it provides is fully and immediately mobilized when needed. Her protein of choice is low-fat cottage cheese. Here's the formula:

2 tablespoons flax oil
¼ cup low-fat cottage cheese

Not a bad snack idea, considering all its putative benefits.

Those who think flax oil tastes like an old sewing machine can swallow flax oil capsules, then eat the cottage cheese.

Flax oil isn't much more stable than fish oil and needs to be carefully refrigerated. So do the capsules. Bite into one every day to make sure they haven't gone rancid.

A little more appealing is actual flaxseed, which you can grind in a blender or food processor.

All of the above have a slight drawback: They may cause gas and diarrhea.

Much easier to take — and new on the market; it was previously used only in research labs because it's cheaper and more stable than the other products — is perilla oil, from a plant that's also known as the beefsteak plant. Perilla, which has been studied extensively in Japan and elsewhere, interferes with the action of two clotting substances that leads to heart attacks and strokes without increasing the risk of brain hemorrhage — which has been a concern with excessive consumption of fish oils. Perilla oil is available in softgel capsules from Health-n-Energy at 800-571-2999.

The best plant source of omega-3s is purslane, a weed with a small, spoon-shaped, succulent leaf, that may be in your garden — or at the farmers market. Because the cultivated variety doesn't have the mega omega-3, ask for the wild purslane.

Purslane is terrific in salads, and cooked with other greens. Aside from being delicious, it also has virtually no carbs, so it's definitely worth searching out.

Other sources include buffalo and venison (omega-3s are found in grass-fed animals but not grain-fed ones), green leafy vegetables, and unrefined walnut and canola oils.

3s, since cancer tumor cells love the 6s, and too many of them can actually cancel out the benefits of the 3s.

If you want to cut back on omega-6 oils, which oils should you use for cooking? Cold-pressed olive oil, preferably unfiltered, is great for almost everything, including sautéing, since it has a high smoke point. Peanut oil has the same good nutritional profile as olive oil. If you want a less strongly flavored oil than either of these, choose cold-pressed canola oil (regular canola oil is highly processed and may have lost some of its valuable omega-3s). Nut oils are great to use as a dressing for vegetables or salads, but avoid anything marked "salad oil" or "vegetable oil" — these will have been highly processed, and are probably full of damaged fats. Soy oil contains dangerous trans fats.

Try to have at least three servings a week of the coldwater fish. Wild fish have the most omega-3s. Farmed fish are fed on carbs, so their level is much lower. As long as you're getting enough of the essential fatty acids, don't worry about fat at all — it may be hard to believe, but it's actually good for you.

Peanuts

The peanut police are out in force and recently they've begun taking away even our airline peanuts on the grounds that someone might inadvertently eat some and have a fatal allergic attack. Peanut allergies are, of course, a serious matter (though rare), and you should never sneak peanuts or peanut butter into any dish without telling your guests. But aside from aflatoxin, a mold that can appear in peanuts that

<blockquote>

Looking for the Best

If you can afford it, I strongly recommend you search out free-range meats, organic if possible (see Sources). These meats are lean and tasty, and they have the best fat profile.

Organic dairy products are only a minor luxury, and they protect you from BHT and other unwanted additions to the real thing. Besides, they taste much better, as do organic eggs.

</blockquote>

aren't handled carefully (and that will virtually disappear soon, thanks to a new benign fungus enemy introduced by the peanut industry; meanwhile, Walnut Acres sells guaranteed aflatoxin-free peanuts: 800-433-3998), and the evil hydrogenated fats that are mixed into commercial high-sugar peanut butters, this little non-nut (it's a legume, remember) is a very good food.

Goobers have more protein than any other bean or nut — 24 percent — and they have seven times more resveratrol than grapes (the heart-protective factor that appears in red wine — which has eight times more of it than grapes). Fifteen peanuts (1 ounce) gives you 10 percent of your daily folic acid requirement (another heart protector). Peanuts are a great source of vitamin E, and a good source of magnesium, copper, selenium, potassium, and zinc — minerals that aren't so easy to come by in the typical diet. Peanut oil is just as good as olive oil and unrefined canola oil in the healthy Mediterranean Diet profile, according to a Penn State study.

And here's something interesting to think about: Dr. Frank Sacks of Harvard says that peanuts, like pasta, are energy dense — these foods may not be as well absorbed as other carbohydrates, so they elicit a lower insulin response. And people who eat peanuts spontaneously reduce their calorie consumption, they're that satisfying. If you're trying to lose weight, eating a lot of peanuts is counterproductive, of course. But a few, like the amount in the nearly obsolete airline packet, are a really good idea — and a lot of fun.

- 1 ounce of peanuts (about 15) is a little less than 4g carb.
- 2 tablespoons of chunky peanut butter is between 4 and 6g carb, depending on the brand.
- If you're a glycemic index believer (see page 9), you'll be glad to know that ½ cup of peanuts is very low on the scale, only 14.
- Dry-roasted peanuts have about 15 percent more carbs than oil-roasted peanuts, oddly enough, but they don't contain any trans fats.

Alcohol

Although some low-carb gurus are dead set against alcohol on the grounds that it raises blood sugar levels (which is unproven), others tout its health benefits — though always urging moderation. The American Cancer Society reported a study over a nine-year period that indicated those who drank one to two glasses of alcohol a day reduced their risk of early death by 20 percent, including a lower risk for cardiovascular disease. A German study reported in *Time* magazine noted that one to two drinks daily can kill off *H. pylori,* the bacteria thought to cause stomach ulcers. Wine protects against macular degeneration, reduces your chance of getting kidney stones by more than 50 percent, protects against ischemic stroke, and won't, according to a Colorado State University study, make you fat in the process — perhaps because it increases insulin sensitivity. Alcohol of all kinds seems to be beneficial, but the most striking study results are those for red wine.

Red wine may reduce the risk of untimely death up to 50 percent, some researchers theorize. Wine raises HDL (the good cholesterol), inhibits the formation of blood clots, prevents atherosclerosis, and helps dissolve clots that have formed. It also increases estrogen levels in women, which may account for its lowering the risk of osteoporosis. Of special interest to low-carbers, it has beneficial effects on glucose and insulin levels.

If you've heard reports about women who drink being at higher risk for breast cancer, the latest studies disprove that, at least at the one-drink-a-day level. Women who *never* drink have a higher risk of breast cancer, according to the Harvard Nurses Study.

The salutary effects of red wine are transient — they last only 24 to 48 hours — so you need to be consistent about drinking it. There's also a slight rebound effect: If you don't drink regularly, the body seems to compensate by increasing the platelet stickiness (which sets the stage for blood clots) between drinks. During weight loss, platelet stickiness increases in any case, so it's important to have your wine if you're dieting.

All these good things happen with the consumption of one to two glasses a day with meals. But what if you drink more? A French study noted that men who drank two to five glasses of red wine a day had a 24 to 31 percent reduction in their overall death rate 15 years later. However, by increasing your consumption of red wine to more than two glasses a day you also run the risk of increasing your triglyceride levels, which is the last thing you want to do.

A glass of red wine will cost you about 3g carb — a great health bargain, and a huge pleasure, as well.

Teetotalers can achieve the same benefits, carb-free, by taking 100 to 300mg of grapeseed extract daily. A good source of resveratrol, wine's protective substance, is Resveratrol Plus (800-728-2288).

Your Kidneys

Ever since 1972, when Dr. Atkins started selling huge numbers of his *Diet Revolution,* the health establishment has been on the offensive — and their most serious charge against Atkins and all other low-carb proponents is that the diet damages the kidneys.

In fact, it is true that if you have serious kidney problems (which would definitely show up on a routine blood check), low-carb wouldn't be a good regime for you. But if your kidneys are normal, low-carb diets can actually *increase* kidney function. As Drs. Michael and Mary Dan Eades, authors of *Protein Power,* wrote in the introduction to my *Low-Carb Cookbook,* the kidney damage myth is easily disproved. Dr. Miriam Blum, a leading expert in the field, discovered no differences at all in kidney function between a group of high-protein eaters and a group of long-term vegetarians.

It's important, however, to keep up your water consumption — you could, at least in theory, cause your kidneys some problems if you ate a high-protein diet and failed to drink at least eight 8-ounce glasses of water a day. But you'd want to do that in any case, to maximize your weight loss and keep your body fully hydrated (see page 59).

Ketosis

The very word *ketosis* alarms many traditional doctors, who remember from med school days that ketoacidosis is a dangerous state. But ketoacidosis is another thing altogether, and it is in fact dangerous for Type I diabetics (which ketosis is not). This error has been repeated again and again in the popular press, and it's the main charge against Dr. Atkins: that by putting people in a state of ketosis he is endangering their lives.

To understand ketosis, you need to know that the body has two different fuel-delivery systems, sort of like gasoline and diesel. One of them is glucose, the sugar in the blood that keeps all the cells in your body alive. Glucose comes from the food you eat, obviously; everything you eat except fiber can be burned and turned into glucose, even protein (though at a much slower rate than carbohydrates). Your liver stores some extra glucose in the form of glycogen — like a spare tank of gas, glycogen will keep the engine turning over for another 12 hours, long enough to get you through a mini-fast.

The other fuel-delivery system involves ketones, which Dr. Atkins describes as "the little carbon fragments that are the fuels created by the burning of fat stores." If you don't have enough glucose from your diet or from your liver stores, then your body has to use your own fat to keep the engine going — so it burns the fat to produce ketones. In fact, some studies done at Harvard demonstrated that all the major organs — including the brain, which had been previously thought to be fueled only by glucose — actually preferred ketones as a fuel.

For those of us who need to lose weight, being in ketosis — that is, using ketones, made from our own fat, for fuel — is an ideal situation. We burn off that extra fat much faster than we would if we weren't in ketosis and had a relatively high amount of circulating insulin. For some people, ketosis begins when we consume under 40 grams of carbohydrate a day — others, especially the obese, achieve ketosis only when the carb level is below 20 grams or even closer to zero.

Once you've cut the carbs drastically, it will take a couple of days to get into ketosis — it takes that long to make the enzyme switch. Once you're in ketosis (which you can test with Ketostix, the little strips that measure the level of ketones in your urine), you'll be eliminating ketones not only in your urine but also through your skin and your breath (which can be a problem — see page 33). The more ketones you lose this way, the more ketones you'll need to harvest from your fat stores, and the more fat you'll burn.

It takes about three weeks for the brain to adjust to using ketones. To assist this process, be sure you're consuming enough sodium, potassium, and magnesium, as noted below.

When you're just starting into ketosis, you'll lose a lot of water, along with some potassium. This may make you feel giddy and tired; to avoid this problem, drink some beef broth and use some Morton Lite salt (which has extra potassium) on your food. You can also add L-carnitine (see page 47) to help cut cravings and maximize weight loss. But again, the crucial step is to drink water, lots of water, not only to protect your kidneys but to maximize your weight loss.

If you're having trouble getting into ketosis, it may be caffeine that's the problem. Dr. Atkins doesn't allow coffee on his induction plan for this reason. Try dropping it.

Is it essential to be in ketosis to make low-carbing work? Not at all, but it's a good idea to begin that way, since you'll jump-start both your weight loss and your general health benefits by turning things around dramatically.

Ketosis is the cornerstone of the carb-cycling program, in which you spend 1½ days carbing-up, then 5½ days in ketosis, on a very low-carb diet, with bouts of strenuous exercise to set things off by burning your stored glycogen. This is a very intense, complicated method of low-carbing and not for the casual dieter.

While you're in ketosis you may have high uric acid levels (associated with gout) at the start, if you're prone to them. (Most women aren't.) Once your triglycerides come down, both high uric acid levels and gout — if you have it — will probably disappear, as it did in my case. If not, raise your level of carb intake slightly — if you keep it to 5 percent of your total diet, you should still be able to stay in ketosis and avoid the gout.

Will even a tiny bit of carbohydrate throw you out of ketosis? As many a low-carber has discovered, that seldom occurs, as long as your ketosis is well established and you don't undermine it very often. A single piece of cake, or even a single meal, will probably have no effect whatsoever. The problem is, of course, that the carbs retain their old addictive power, which has only been enhanced by their long absence, so it may be really hard to stop at just one indulgence. It's then that the trouble begins — when you decide to have a bad carb day and not just a bad carb meal. Try a little indulgence every now and then and see what happens. As with everything else, this strategy may or may not work for you, but if it does, it can be a godsend to keep you on your low-carb path.

Most people feel really good in a state of ketosis, but some people feel foggy or anxious and fluttery. If you have these feelings and they persist more than three weeks on a low-carb diet, you'll need to add carbs, up to about 60 grams a day. You'll still lose weight and correct your health problems; it will just take a little longer.

DANA, 40

For four years now, Dana's been eating low-carb — about 50 grams a day by her count — and has dropped about 47 pounds. She'd been following the recommended low-fat, high-complex-carb diet we've all been told to eat and found it only made her fatter; it also left her with killer mood swings, and very low energy. Her four sessions of advanced-level step aerobics a week didn't lose her an ounce, and she was frustrated. At a used-book sale she picked up an old copy of a Gaylord Hauser book in which he stated flatly that obesity was a carbohydrate-intolerance disease. That reminded her of the Atkins diet, and she decided to give it a try. Two days into it she felt much better; two and a half weeks down the low-carb road, she'd lost ten pounds. The borderline high blood pressure she'd experienced on the low-fat diet completely normalized, and she was ecstatic that she'd found the answer.

From the Atkins diet, she progressed to the Zone ("hungry all the time"), the Carbohydrate Addict's Diet ("hungry a lot, felt drugged after eating my high-carb meal, plateaued rapidly"), and eventually settled on a mix of Atkins and Protein Power. She tried altering that with a few low-glycemic carbs, but they made her gain weight and she ended up craving more carbs, so she gave it up. Dana never passed through the extremely low-carb induction stage virtually all low-carb diets recommend, but it didn't seem to matter. Today she still eats about 50 grams of carbohydrate a day and drinks two glasses of wine every evening. When she got her bloodwork done recently, the nurses were begging to know the secret of her amazing numbers: total cholesterol 190, HDL 69, triglycerides 50. Dana was only too happy to share the secret: "Three eggs a day and all the red meat I can scarf!"

For breakfast, it's three eggs, usually fried, and a pot of tea. (Dana drinks half-caffeinated tea the rest of the day, iced in the summer.)

Lunch tends to be tuna salad, made with a couple of celery ribs, a quarter of a red onion, half a green pepper, a can of water-packed tuna, and 2 or 3 tablespoons of mayonnaise. Sometimes this goes in a tomato shell, sometimes it's accompanied by a few low-carb crackers.

Snacks tend to be nuts, seeds, leftover meat, or low-carb crackers with butter and salt. Every now and then a pork rind craving hits, but four is about her limit now.

Although she eats sugar less than ten times a year, she does have occasional planned indulgences, sugar buffered with protein to minimize the insulin-raising damage. It leaves her feeling terrible, and one bad day can account for as much as six new pounds the next day.

Actually it's the feeling great that keeps Dana low-carb. She has completely lost her addiction to food, the emotional attachment that kept her in thrall. As she says, "You'd need a crowbar and a gun to get me to go back to eating a high-carb diet again."

Dragon Breath

For some people, but not all, the ketones given off by the lungs when you're in a state of ketosis produce a really nasty bad breath. This is caused by acetone, the same ingredient that gives cheap nail polish remover its unpleasant smell. You can imagine what getting a kiss from someone who'd just gargled with nail polish remover would be like. . . .

You can brush your teeth often and use standard mouthwashes and chew sugarless gum and breath mints, but they won't really do the trick. Much more effective is Yow!, a sugarless tablet that bubbles up in your mouth to destroy bacteria, plaque, and bad odors — and whitens your teeth in the process. Yow! is sold at Target stores and in some supermarkets. (You can also order it direct from the manufacturer at 800-YOW-LABS.) This is such a great product that you should try it even if you don't have ketone breath.

For extreme cases, try TheraBreath (800-997-7999).

If all else fails, try upping your carbs by tiny increments, so that you're just on the edge of ketosis — you'll still lose weight at a good clip and you shouldn't have the breath problem.

PART TWO

Secret Weapons

Although the low-carb diet is one of the easiest diets to follow ever devised, it's a way of eating that's quite contrary to our own food culture — by which I mean everything from what's served at restaurants to what's on supermarket shelves to what's been brought to our family tables for decades. Dealing with the food that's all around us can be the hardest thing about this diet — and in a way, this entire book is about that effort.

There's lots of help out there, however, and I wish I had known about some of these products and strategies when I first began low-carbing. Here are the ones I find particularly useful.

Developing a Diet Style

As you'll notice from the Real-Life Stories that appear throughout this book, everyone does the diet a bit differently. And almost no one does it the way he or she started out doing it. Most of us began with a single book, *Dr. Atkins' Diet Revolution* or *Protein Power* or *The Carbohydrate Addict's Diet*. Low-carb worked, so we decided to explore the horizons a bit. Maybe we really wanted coffee or really hated ketosis, so we dropped those parts of Atkins and moved on. Possibly we joined an Internet low-carb support group or tech group and learned some interesting possibilities to add to the regime. Different supplements, different exercise options, whatever — they all went into the mix.

In the end, the only diet plan that will really work for you, it almost goes without saying, is one that actually helps you lose weight and corrects your health problems. We're all biochemically unique, for one thing, so there's no one-diet-fits-all approach in any case. You're the only person who knows how you feel on the diet, how satisfied you are with what you're eating and drinking, and how your health is affected.

Most of us look and feel so good on this diet, have such great energy and calm focus and even occasional euphoria, that we tend to be motivated to stay on it. The only real problem is how to be happy when you're not eating your favorite foods, the very foods your culture touts constantly and even your tax dollars are spent to insist you eat.

The best way to handle this dilemma is to face it head-on. Try making a list of your favorite foods, an A list and a B list. Probably the A list will be full of carbs, but possibly not. Break it down further into food groups: Which fruits do you love most, which vegetables? Try to work out a way to have those elements you love best at least occasionally, so you'll feel undeprived and satisfied. If you must have bananas, have a tiny finger one at breakfast, or half a banana with some cottage cheese, say. Check the Cravings list (page 70) to see how you can substitute for some of the things you really can't have routinely. For the things you're crazy about that you can't have, plan to indulge in them as treats — for your birthday, for Christmas — and just block them as effectively as you can (pages 51–52). There's no question that if you simply resolve you'll *never* eat these foods again, you'll go off the diet altogether in fairly short order.

There's a fine line between establishing a routine, which is very helpful — for example, you know what the breakfast choices are, and they're all more or less available to you when you need them — and falling into a rut, which is easy to do. If you eat a protein bar for breakfast, and tuna salad with celery sticks for lunch, and a hard-cooked egg for a snack, and meat with salad and green vegetables for dinner every single day, you'll take no pleasure in eating and eventually you'll ditch not only these foods but the diet itself.

In fact, we need a fair amount of variety in our diet just to be sure we're getting enough nutrients. That usually means cooking our own food, and having an arsenal of recipes available with the carbs already counted so we're not scrambling for the carb counter at every meal.

I'm fairly bad at breaking the routine myself; I have to work at not falling into automatic pilot and cooking and eating the same foods all the time. One way to handle this is to eat fairly automatically during the week and promise yourself to cook something new on the weekends: Have pancakes for breakfast, get an expensive exotic melon, make up a pitcher of margaritas — anything to break the monotony. Go to the farmers market and see what interesting new vegetables are on the stands. Go to a cheese store and get something you've never tasted before. Pay special attention to what's in season where you live: Not only will this food be fresher, it will also taste much better, and its arrival will give you something to look forward to from month to month. Spring is wonderful for everyone, but for us it means asparagus and rhubarb, two of the great joys of low-carb eating.

Eventually you'll work out a style of snacks or no snacks, diet drinks or none, a serious exercise routine or a casual one. You'll know exactly how far you can push the carb envelope without completely blowing it or what it will cost you if you do. You'll have your protein allowance nailed, so you could plan a meal in your sleep and be exactly on target. You'll evolve your supplement-taking in the way we all have, by reading and listening and seeing what works.

And of course, your diet style will continue to change and evolve, as the mysteries of human nutrition and health are unraveled and as your own needs change. Though by habit we all refer to this eating plan as a "diet," you shouldn't really think of it as one, because the term implies a short-term fix you'll soon abandon. For those of us who need to eat that way, low-carb is for life, and we need to be both flexible and dedicated to make sure it continues to work for us.

Keeping a Food Diary

This little strategy sounds very boring, but in fact it's a very useful exercise. It's important to know not only what you're actually eating, but what you *want* to eat, so that you can bring those two elements closer together. Even more boring is measuring quantities, but again, it's a very good idea to do so. For instance, put the splash of milk you usually add to your morning coffee into the cup first, then measure it. You may think it's only a couple of teaspoons, but it may turn out to be more like ¼ cup, which is a significant amount of carbs. If you have more than one cup of coffee a day, plus some tea with milk, you can be adding a lot of unsuspected carbs that can sink your diet.

The basic idea is to write down every mouthful and to note when you ate it and under what circumstances. Grabbing lunch on the run is different from boredom eating or binge eating, and you need some clues about when and why you're eating what. Don't think too much about it at the time — just jot it all down. At the end of the week, or when you weigh yourself, figure out what you actually ate and how it all worked out. Keeping a wish list — what you yearned to be eating, or what you passed up — will also be instructive. You'll start to see a pattern, and then you can intervene and devise a better solution.

It's particularly important to keep a food diary when ordinary life is temporarily suspended — holidays, vacations — because it's very easy to simply zone out and forget all about what goes into your mouth. Be forearmed.

Blood Checks

One of the great joys of being on a low-carb diet is going to your skeptical doctor and having him or her test your blood periodically — which he'll definitely want to do if he's convinced you're ruining your health with this regime. Then there's the complete delight of the results: drastically lowered triglycerides, raised HDL, often lowered LDL, lower glucose, lower uric acid. Your blood pressure is probably down as well.

Wait until you've been on the diet about three months before you test, since it will take that long for the full effects to be seen in the blood. Once every six months thereafter will confirm your good health.

At some point you'll probably also want to have your hormone levels checked, since they're crucial to metabolism and your health. A low-carb regime makes all your hormones work much better in general, but if you have a deficiency, it won't correct it. (If you do correct it, you'll have much better results from the diet.) If your doctor isn't willing to order this test, you can do it yourself, using a saliva test. If you find a serious deficit, and your doctor isn't helpful, contact the Broda Barnes Foundation (www.brodabarnes.org) for a knowledgeable physician in your area.

Some Curiosities . . .

- If you move to a high-altitude location, you lose 10 percent of your body weight in the first year after you arrive. The reason may be that it takes extra physical effort, especially for women, to do things like climb stairs, carry groceries, and walk distances in thinner air.

- Corn grown in temperate climates has more carbs than hot-weather crops — so if you're going to indulge, ignore that early-season flown-in corn and wait for the real thing in the heat of summer.

- Maybe being fat is catching? There's some evidence, according to the University of Wisconsin Medical School, that obesity may have a viral cause. A human adenovirus known as AD-36, an upper respiratory virus, causes obesity when injected into chickens and mice. And when humans were tested for it, 15 percent of the obese subjects had the antibodies to the virus, whereas none of the normal-weight subjects showed a trace of it. The bird virus SMAM-1 causes unusual intra-abdominal fat in chickens. Of 52 obese people checked, 19 percent had antibodies to that virus and were larger than the obese subjects who tested negative.

- Caramelized sugar (sugar that's been heated to the point of liquefying and then slightly burned) has fewer calories and carbs than table sugar because some of them have been burned off. It's hard to say how much less, but less is less.

- One gram of carbohydrate will raise blood sugar only 5mg in most people — a negligible amount that you don't need to keep track of, unless you gang up your single carbs. A carb gram is what a packet of Equal or a squeeze of lemon costs.

- Scientists at Glasgow University note that the highest levels of flavonols (the potent antioxidants found in food that are much more potent anti-free-radical compounds than vitamin E or C) vary enormously among different kinds of vegetables. Red and yellow onions are crammed with flavonols, while white onions have hardly any. Cherry tomatoes are much richer in flavonols than beefsteak tomatoes, and red-tinged lettuce (such as Lollo Rosso) is much higher than green lettuce (the red color is from the same flavonol that gives red wine its health benefits.) And even among the red wines, cabernet sauvignon has the highest flavonol count, while the Chilean reds contain the widest variety of flavonols.

- Some pilots make a point of not drinking aspartame-sweetened diet sodas when they're flying. At high altitudes the methanol in aspartame (10 percent) can lead to dizziness, loss of vision, sudden memory loss, and even epilepsy.

CHARLES, OVER 50

Of course, some low-carbers have a rougher time than others giving up starches and sweets — but Charlie has a special problem: he's a professional baker. He's passionate about bread, and he eats some every day, for breakfast. He's lucky in that he doesn't crave sweets (unlike his wife, who manages to get by with a little piece of bittersweet chocolate every day).

One reason he may be able to get away with eating bread — and we're talking about real, high-quality bread here, not ersatz low-carb bread — is that he's a long-term low-carber. He started off on the Atkins diet in the seventies and has more or less kept to the program ever since, which may have made his insulin receptors much more sensitive. He's also very active physically, playing tennis at least three times a week and working out daily in his home gym.

Over the years he gained a few pounds, however, and when *Protein Power* came out, he went on the diet strictly and lost about 20 pounds. He also noticed that his energy level increased dramatically, and he so much liked the way he feels that he's done it ever since, with a few alterations.

Every morning begins with a glass of tomato juice, into which he stirs a big tablespoon of oat bran and the juice of a lemon. Breakfast is usually an egg with ham or sausage or bacon plus toast and coffee. Lunch might be a mixed green salad with tomatoes and chicken and a glass of wine. For dinner he tries hard to keep the carbs very low, with just protein and a salad or some sautéed greens and a glass of wine.

If sweets aren't a problem for him, potatoes are — he has a real craving for them and succumbs frequently. Pasta is much easier to give up, and he indulges only about every three weeks. Several times a year he and his wife will have pancakes for breakfast.

Charlie figures his maintenance carb level is about 60 to 80 grams a day; if he starts to gain weight, he just goes back on the strict program until it levels out. He's never really discussed his diet, which he considers extremely healthy, with his doctor, but so far so good. His one anxiety is that he's eating too much saturated fat, with so much animal protein in his diet; he'd like to eat more fish, but high-quality fish is hard to find in his part of the country.

Asked if he plans to eat this way the rest of his life, Charlie points out that he has in fact eaten this way for most of his life and is very happy with the results. The fact that he's managed to make a professional life in what some of us consider the enemy camp — the seductive world of bread — and live a low-carb personal life as well is quite extraordinary. And it also proves just how flexible this way of eating can be.

When in Doubt, Test-It-Yourself

It's often helpful when you're on a low-carb plan to behave as if you were actually a diabetic — which you may eventually become, if you don't correct your diet successfully.

There's no reason you can't use the tools of the diabetic to discover how a particular food affects your own blood sugar.

For example, you can take Dr. Richard Bernstein's suggestion and test food you're unsure of, such as restaurant fare, using the urine-testing Clinistix or Diastix strips designed for diabetics to see what the actual sugar content is. The strips, available at pharmacies, come

Chomp, Chomp

As the first astronauts quickly learned, you don't actually feel you've eaten unless you've spent some time chewing. This phenomenon holds true for all mammals — ask any pig who's been raised on liquid feed and has to eat all the time to get any satisfaction.

You can take advantage of this fact and chew sugarless gum to increase your oral satisfaction, especially when you feel like eating a little something between meals. This actually counts as exercise, too: According to a new study from the Mayo Clinic, chewing half a pack of sugarless gum for half an hour raises your metabolic rate 19 percent and burns off a measly 11 calories.

wrapped in foil and cost less than $10 for a package of 50. Take a bite of the food, chew it, and let it mix with your saliva to release the glucose. Spit a bit of the food onto the testing strip and see what the sugar registers. This handy little technique works for everything but lactose (milk sugars) and fructose (fruit sugars). For fruit sugars, you'd need a refractometer, which will set you back about $175 (800-473-0577).

Carry a few testing sticks with you and use them to decide whether or not you should eat something when you have no idea of its carb content.

A glucometer (for Dr. Bernstein's current recommendation on brands, call 914-698-7500 — they change from time to time, but Elite has been the choice for years now) will give you a fairly accurate blood sugar reading and can be found at any large pharmacy for under $100. You have to prick your finger to get the blood to test, but if you're squeamish you'll find that you get over that part fairly quickly. Eat a food, such as pasta, on an empty stomach and without accompaniments, using only a minimal-carb sauce such as oil and garlic. Test your blood before you eat the pasta, then again after 15 minutes (to see how rapidly the blood sugar rises), and again after 2 hours. Anything beyond a surge of about 20 points is pushing the envelope for insulin problems, and rapid escalations are especially bad, since they trigger a big insulin response. The results, however, will vary from day to day, depending on things like your stress level and other factors.

The Amazing L-Carnitine

If you've always thought there was some missing piece in the diet puzzle, something that keeps you from losing weight even though you're doing everything exactly by the book, you're probably right. Assuming it's not a low-thyroid condition, it could very well be L-carnitine, a nutrient you may never have heard of before, though it has profound effects on your body and your life itself.

Every cell in your body has a little L-carnitine, a natural nutrient the body manufactures from sources such as red meat. (If you're a vegetarian, it's likely you're deficient in this essential nutrient.) What if you're deficient in this substance? You're probably fat, and you might also be tired all the time. That's because without L-carnitine, the cells, or, more accurately, the mitrochondria that do all the work of the cells, can't burn fat efficiently. If you don't have enough L-carnitine, no matter how strictly you diet you'll have a very hard time losing weight because the furnace just won't operate correctly.

L-carnitine brings the fatty acids to the mitochondria to be burned off — but it can be stopped in its tracks by too much insulin, our old nemesis. So needless to say, L-carnitine works best for weight loss when you follow a low-carb diet and keep the insulin levels low. If there's too much insulin circulating, the fatty acids will be taken elsewhere to use later — and you know what that means: to the fat cells to be stored.

But fat-burning isn't L-carnitine's only job. It also protects your heart, stimulates your brain, and boosts your immune system. It actually lowers cholesterol and triglyceride levels, relieves PMS, chronic fatigue, and Parkinson's symptoms — *and* encourages peak performance in general. Finally, it contributes greatly to longevity, and it has anti-aging properties.

But there's more. . . . Carnitine affects the way you feel; it gives you a sense of well-being, improves circulation, and diminishes food cravings. The bottom line is that carnitine gives your cells the ability to produce the energy they need, which they can use any way they want, whether it's building new tissue or making your body work better or last longer.

Why isn't everyone in America taking this supplement? Because the research has only recently been put together in a readable way by Robert Crayhon, M.S., in *The Carnitine Miracle. Self* magazine has called Crayhon one of the top ten nutritionists in the country. He himself is a recovering vegetarian — who feels strongly that vegetarians must supplement with carnitine.

What might lead you to be deficient in carnitine? Some likely causes are: if you don't eat a Stone Age diet, if you're no longer a young pup (you need more carnitine as you age, when you in fact begin to make less), or if you have too much stress in your life. Our bodies produce a small amount of carnitine from red meat, especially lamb (which very few Americans eat), and from other animal products such as dairy foods, and we ingest a very small amount from tempeh and avocados (not major menu items, either). We might get as much as 50 mg a day in our normal diet, says Crayhon (though in the low-fat era that's extremely optimistic), while in the Stone Age we probably took in 500 to 2000 mg a day, which is in fact what we need for optimal health. For weight loss, we need even more: at least 1000 and up to 4000 mg daily. "Obesity," Crayhon says, "is nearly always a functional carnitine deficiency."

But even the optimum amount won't work very efficiently unless it is accompanied by the very healthy omega-3 oils (see page 23). And here's one of the most important points Crayhon makes: When you diet, the omega-3 oils, the very ones you need most, are the first to go, and need replacing. If you don't have enough of them, you easily regain the weight you've lost so painstakingly. And it will be even harder to lose the weight the next time you diet, because you now have a serious omega-3 deficit, so your insulin won't work as well and your metabolism will be slower. Sound familiar? So here's another missing piece of the puzzle, one that certainly explains my own diet history — and sent me racing for the flaxseed oil and carnitine.

Atkins dieters, please note: As Crayhon points out, if you're in ketosis you need extra carnitine to convert protein to blood sugar, which will negate the headaches and fatigue that so often accompany ketosis.

Diabetics, please note: You have lower carnitine levels to begin with, and excrete much more carnitine in urine. Carnitine is crucial for managing diabetes, according to Crayhon.

Now to the nitty-gritty: There's no simple test you can take to find out if you're carnitine-deficient, but because carnitine has zero toxicity, a much smarter approach is simply to take supplements, starting with 500mg a day and increasing it by an additional 500mg until you feel extremely good and highly energized — but do not take more than 4000mg a day, Crayhon says. Take it in two doses, before breakfast and lunch, with flaxseed oil or another omega-3 source (1½ teaspoons per dose). At the natural foods store, you'll discover there are two kinds of carnitine: L-carnitine (the natural form) and acetyl-L-carnitine, which is much more expensive. For maximum effect on your brain's health, take the acetyl kind, which stimulates the release of acetylcholine, a neurotransmitter essential for learning and memory. Otherwise, choose L-carnitine tartrate, the most effective form (which still isn't cheap). Diabolically, supplement manufacturers don't identify the tartrate form (Crayhon advises tasting the capsules; if they taste tart, they're the right kind, but that means buying a whole bottle to check). Or opt for the Twinlab 500mg tablets, which are tartrate; their other carnitine products (except the 250mg capsules), including CarniFuel, a liquid form, are not. Crayhon sells his own carnitine tartrate mixed with some of the expensive acetyl form in a 4-to-1 ratio. They can be ordered from Designs for Health at 203-371-4383.

Crayhon has many, many more ideas about weight loss and optimal health — among other things, he advocates taking CoQ10* (with

---

* This co-enzyme (i.e., enzyme helper) is a potent fat-soluble antioxidant produced by the body, at least in youth. As we age, levels decline. CoQ10 has many functions, but most important is its role in energy production. It's also important for the heart and in the prevention of breast cancer.

oil) and magnesium malate to make carnitine work even better. His low-carb diet starts out quite moderately and only gradually increases to a very low carb level — which is appealing for, say, people very attached to the low-fat diet. But all serious low-carb dieters should read his book — it's sheer enlightenment, and very exciting work. This is one of those books that can change your life.

Block That Sugar

Vanadyl sulfate is a not-particularly-expensive trace mineral used by diabetics to help control blood sugar, improve glucose metabolism, lower high blood pressure, and control hyperglycemia. It does these things by acting like insulin to help the cells absorb sugar more easily — so that in theory, at least, it can reduce the need for insulin. Both Dr. Atkins and the Eadeses use it in their practice.

There's also a theory that if you take some vanadyl sulfate — roughly 20mg — about half an hour before indulging in a sweet treat, you won't require a huge outpouring of insulin (with its potential for fat storage) to deal with the sugars you've consumed. Some researchers think there's also a morning-after possibility with vanadyl; if you forget to take it before you eat something sweet, try taking it afterward.

Dr. Atkins cautions that you shouldn't exceed 30mg of vanadyl daily, since there are some contraindications for very large doses. If you take too much, say some experts, there's a danger of renal toxicity. To avoid this, even diabetics need to alternate their dosage, one month on vanadyl, one month off. A contrary opinion comes from Dr. Julian Whitaker, who says the toxicity study came from a single researcher whose results have never been duplicated. Whitaker has given up to 150mg per day to thousands of diabetic patients with no problems.

Does this little trick work? No research has been done one way or the other, but I always have vanadyl with me, even though I don't actually take it very often. Its mere presence is reassuring.

Block That Starch

One of the great low-carb fantasies is that someone will develop a magical substance that takes the starch right out of food so that we can guiltlessly eat bread, pasta, potatoes, doughnuts, rice — the whole nine yards. In fact, someone actually claims to have done so. John Marshall, Ph.D., developed Phase'oLean, a bean-based product that blocks alpha-amylase, the enzyme responsible for turning starch into sugar. The uncoverted large starch molecules then pass right on through the digestive tract, absorbing water as they go — so you need to drink extra water if you try this product. Any nutrients in the food are absorbed.

The manufacturer recommends you take a tablet exactly 15 to 20 minutes before you eat starch — too early and it won't be blocked. For a starchy snack, you can use just half a tablet. Each tablet blocks more than 100 grams of starch (about 400 calories), and you can take another one halfway through your meal to deal with another 400 calories of starch if you're really carb-indulging.

Does this product work? The starch blockers of the seventies definitely didn't work, because they were formulated incorrectly. Supposedly those problems have been corrected. Phase'oLean got me through a month in Italy eating plenty of pasta and bread with only a four-pound weight gain — all water, basically, which disappeared virtually overnight when I returned. I'm not brave enough to eat starch all the time to see if Phase'oLean can deal with it. And I wouldn't be tempted in any case because it's so expensive, about $40 a bottle. No studies have been conducted to prove its effects.

Phase'oLean is available in 90-tablet bottles from Life Plus at 800-572-8446. Life Plus also sells a book by John Marshall, *Have Your Bread and Eat It.*

Block That Fat

Although fat doesn't seem to be a problem for low-carb dieters in the long term, it certainly can be in the short term — that is, immediately

51

after you eat a very rich meal. Your postprandial blood will be filled with triglycerides — which can increase your risk of heart attack, according to the *New England Journal of Medicine*. The fat will also have a strongly negative effect on your blood vessel walls, an effect that takes place in just a couple of hours.

Gary Plotnick of the University of Maryland Medical School discovered that if you take some antioxidants — 1000mg of vitamin C along with 800 units of vitamin E an hour before you indulge — no triglycerides will form. This natural fat-blocking duo is just what you need for the holidays or when you're headed for the cheese tasting. But remember, they don't, alas, take the calories away, too.

Exercise

Despite everything you've heard, exercise — unless it's very intense — doesn't make you lose fat and won't make you live longer. For the obese, as a 1999 study reported, moderate exercise had no real effect on weight loss. Exercise is also hard and makes you tired and sweaty, so why would you want to do it? Here are a few good reasons . . .

- For 24 hours after a workout, you're more sensitive to your own insulin, meaning you'll need to make less of this fat-storing hormone.
- You'll look and feel better, livelier, younger, stronger.
- Your levels of dangerous blood fats will drop and the good protective blood fat, HDL, will increase (by about 20 percent).
- Your metabolism will be revved up, just for a short period, so you burn a few more calories.
- Your cardiovascular system will benefit.
- Exercise is very important for diabetics, for blood sugar control.
- It's just about the only thing, besides eating low-carb, that will increase the levels of glucagon, the fat-burning hormone.
- You'll be less stressed and will sleep better.
- There's a small increase in mental acuity and creativity.
- More than 95 percent of successful dieters exercise regularly, according to the National Weight Control Registry.

- You'll have better sex.
- Your levels of homocysteine, which may promote heart disease, will drop.
- When you're in your eighties, according to Dr. Kenneth Cooper, if you haven't been exercising, you'll probably be in a nursing home; if you're active, you'll stay active.

So do you have to join a gym, set one up in your house, run day and night, hire a personal trainer, jump rope, power-walk through sleet and snow? If you enjoy those activities, fine, but there's an absolutely great exercise that anyone, including the feeble wreck you may be, can do, given a not terribly expensive piece of equipment. It's called a rebounder, and it's a sort of mini-trampoline that's a huge improvement over the old version.

The rebounder is low-impact, safe, and fun, and it gives you both an aerobic (the sweaty kind) and a resistance (the weight-lifting muscle-building kind) workout. It improves your health at the cellular level because it uses gravity to do its work, affecting every cell in your body — it even increases circulation in your eyes, which may improve your vision in the process. It boosts the effectiveness of your thyroid gland, it does serious bone and muscle building, it reduces blood pressure, and it facilitates lymphatic drainage (which removes the toxins from your body). Studies at NASA and UCLA have discovered it also greatly improves mood and sense of well-being. All this for a little bouncing while you watch TV or otherwise amuse yourself.

If you're frail or sick or extremely ungainly, you can still use a rebounder — just order the stabilizing bar, which is about $50 and gives you something to hang on to while you bounce.

The best brand of rebounder is the Needak SoftBounce, and it's available for about $200 from 800-362-0168. It's small and extremely portable. So now you have no more excuses. (Unless you have glaucoma; if you do, just walk on the rebounder, since heavy bouncing could be dangerous for your eyes.)

If you'd like to sculpt your body a bit and boost your energy, try the aerobic breathing used in the Body Flex system developed by Greer Childers. The theory is that by increasing your oxygen intake, you're also increasing your metabolic rate and fat burn. In just 15 minutes a day, you can dramatically change your body — in the first week, I lost an inch off my waist — while doing almost nothing, just some serious breathing and holding various yoga-like poses for a few seconds. Sometimes you feel like a complete idiot as you make the Ugly Face, for instance, and it also seems strange that you actually feel you've had a bit of a workout once you've gone through the undemanding paces.

A set of Body Flex tapes costs about $30: call 800-374-8215.

Remember, use it or lose it. If you don't exercise, you'll gradually lose your muscles as well as your heart and lung function, a bit each year.

LARRY, 50

Larry was fairly astonished to learn, after he collapsed one day, that he had serious heart problems. His blood lipids were "terrible," one of his two coronary arteries was 95 percent blocked, and he needed an angioplasty. During the course of the procedure, the other artery, the only blood supply to his heart, was accidentally torn, resulting in terrible pain and emergency bypass surgery.

When doctors get sick, they usually obey medical orders. As a highly respected pediatric surgeon, Larry consulted all available cardiology experts and followed their advice to the letter. He started out with the standard low-fat program, dropping down gradually when it didn't work to 2 percent fat, an insanely low number that would please only Dr. Dean Ornish. But he was actually getting worse on the low-fat regime, which he stuck to for about a year. His HDL (good) cholesterol levels were plummeting like a rock, and there was no change in the other, dangerous blood fats. He also felt lousy; he had headaches and felt hungry all the time.

Larry got fairly desperate — he was doing everything by the book and there was no improvement. Finally he called Mike and Mary Dan Eades at their clinic to see if it would possibly be safe for a heart patient to go on Protein Power. They reassured him, and Larry has now been eating low-carb for about three years. His blood levels are now much improved, he has excellent energy, and there's no question he'll eat this way for the rest of his life. He feels he's on a more even keel now, and that his low-carb diet is a much less contrived eating plan than the low-fat regime.

It took a while to get used to the low-carb lifestyle — to understand how to shop for groceries, for instance. Now he and his wife just head straight for the meat and fish counters, then stop at the produce aisle, rarely venturing beyond these two areas. About six months passed before they became entirely comfortable with the regime, but now they're happy with it and it's second nature.

As with all low-carb dieters, Larry's big question is where to spend the carbs. He and his wife choose vegetables and a few fruits, keeping to the low-glycemic foods. They each average less than 100 grams of carbohydrate a day. Larry finds that the lower he keeps the carbs, the better the results, not only in terms of how he feels but his blood levels as well. He advises low-carb friends to be guided by their bloodwork; if the results are good, continue eating what you're eating. If they're not, change your diet by lowering the carbs and check the results.

One thing Larry is passionate about is avoiding trans fats, keeping them to a minimum while eating about 125 grams of protein a day. Because he's an active exerciser, doing an hour of aerobics and half an hour of resistance work six days a week, he needs a lot of protein. He eats snacks throughout the day — usually beef jerky, sliced turkey, or some nuts — and almost always has the same breakfast: ¼ cup oat bran flakes, 30g soy protein, 2 tablespoons flax meal, a little stevia (a natural herb sweetener; see page 107), and enough milk to wash it down.

Larry takes a lot of supplements, too many to list here, but they fall into the basic categories of antioxidants, essential fatty acids, methyl donors, and insulin sensitizers.

Although he still craves bread and cherry pie, he's so happy about the way he feels eating low-carb, not to mention his newfound health, that there's no question he'll stay on his plan.

Carbs for Breakfast

On the theory — and it's just a theory, but it seems to work for a lot of people — that your insulin receptors are more sensitive after their overnight fast, you can indulge a bit in carbs for your morning meal.

This might mean a glass of juice for some people, or fruit, or toast — whatever appeals.

How high can you afford to go? If you keep the carb grams under 20, assuming you're trying to maintain your weight or improve a health problem, you should be fine.

The morning is also a great time to indulge in what you've been craving. In the summer, I have corn on the cob on weekends, with some bacon or ham, and I've never had a weight-gain problem from that, even when I eat two ears. If you're dying for a cookie or a slice of watermelon or a waffle, or even ice cream, have it for breakfast. A bagel may send you over the edge, but half a bagel is fine, as is half a banana (but not together).

Just remember to eat some protein with your carbs, so you don't set off a cycle of carb craving and insulin overload. If a breakfast indulgence does send you into major carb craving, skip it, because you'll struggle endlessly to stay in control, and it's not worth the few minutes of pleasure.

Lighten Up Your Liver

In French novels, the characters are always carrying on about the dire state of their liver. Americans don't pay much attention to this organ, which is a shame, since it has a huge role to play in our well-being. Among the liver's jobs are:

- filtering toxins from the blood, at a rate of up to 2 quarts of blood a minute
- regulating carbohydrate and protein metabolism
- regulating hormones
- processing blood sugar and storing it as glycogen
- emulsifying fat and getting rid of it

These functions are all crucial to the process of weight loss and to the maintenance of our general health. If the liver isn't functioning at its peak, there are no blood tests available to tell us so, until the liver is so damaged that it's seriously diseased. A person (like me) whose gall-bladder has been removed definitely needs to take special care of the liver, because it no longer has the help of little squirts of bile coming from the gallbladder to help digest fats.

An overburdened liver gives out signals that are vague and potentially attributable to several other causes. The eyes aren't clear and bright, the skin may be dry and itchy, there's general fatigue, there may be circles under the eyes, the tongue may be coated, the libido may be down, and there may be autoimmune disorders, high blood pressure, and weight gain. Around the eyes there may be little fatty granules of yellow skin. Sugar cravings, constipation, depression, unstable blood sugars, bad morning breath, and excessive body heat may also occur. The liver enzymes may be slightly elevated in these cases, but not beyond the range of normal. So how can you tell if you need to be concerned?

If the symptom list sounds familiar, you might want to try a little liver cleansing. You can still find liver tonics — an old-fashioned remedy that seems to be coming back into fashion — but you can also treat your liver to a specially designed diet, one proposed by Dr. Sandra Cabot, an Australian endocrinologist who's the author of *The Liver Cleansing Diet*. For low-carbers, the regime is a bit of a challenge, since it prohibits meat and dairy products for two months, and allows chicken and eggs for only four weeks of that time. The book is a little frustrating because it doesn't always explain some of its advice. You may not know why you're being urged to eat a lot of raw carrots and beets ("very good for your liver"), and the diet isn't so much set out in a series of principles as encoded in some recipes to be eaten at every meal. The meals also require the commitment of a substantial amount of prep time. Still, you can adapt the basic idea easily: as little fat as possible, no alcohol, as much raw food as possible, and lots and lots of water. Dr. Cabot believes artificial sweeteners are very bad for the liver, so they're out, as is caffeine. But for some the results may be well worth it, if you can just hang in there. Dr. Cabot also has a Web site, liver-doctor.com, where you can take her body type test (odds are you're a lymphatic type, which used to be called endomorph) and find out where to buy her liver tonic.

You might want to try something easier first: Milk thistle, an herbal remedy, can be hugely beneficial for the liver, and is the major ingredient in nearly all the commercially produced liver tonics. It's a potent antioxidant that actually stimulates new cell growth in the liver as well as detoxifying it. In hundreds of studies, milk thistle is one of the few herbal remedies that's been shown to be consistently effective. Those who try this approach typically take 150mg of milk thistle (standardized to 80 percent silymarin) three times a day for two months. After that, one pill a day should do it, with periodic returns to the cleansing routine.

If you're stuck on a long plateau, as I've sometimes been for months, the problem could be your liver. If the liver isn't functioning at its peak, the reasoning goes, it can't filter out all the toxins properly, and so it binds fat to the toxins in an effort to protect the body from them. The fat cells enlarge to be more effective, and the liver ceases doing its job of getting rid of fat — no matter what you're eating, you won't lose fat unless your liver is working properly. And when the liver is finally cleaned of its excess fat and toxins, they're sent directly into the bloodstream — which is why you need to drink a huge amount of water if you're cleaning your liver.

My favorite liver-cleansing supplement is BHB Plus, which doesn't require dietary changes and not only cleans the liver, but helps you lose weight, increase your energy, and rebuild your exhausted adrenal glands. This formula was devised by Texas biochemist Jim Dews, who's at work on a cancer project with the National Institutes of Health. It also has many other miraculous benefits, according to articles about it, ranging from producing good dreams to eliminating migraines. The main ingredient is amino-B-hydroxybutyric acid (250mg); it also contains tyramine, a hormone precursor, and threonine, as well as methyl butrate — the chemical given to cows to produce leaner meat. The extra tyramine helps your endocrine system to make whatever hormones it needs — including thyroid. A fatty liver gets plugged with excessive fatty deposits and cannot produce enough bile, says Dews — and it's bile that breaks down saturated fat into individual fatty acids that can be absorbed. This process directly leads into hormone production, and of course hormones control every aspect of everything alive. Then you have a vicious circle of *more* fat depositing in the liver, lower hormone function, and so on. BHB Plus has no known side effects and is inexpensive. To find out more, call 940-325-0208; to order, call 940-325-9286.

The Water Cure

We all know that we're supposed to be drinking huge amounts of water, but we're rarely told why — or how, for that matter. I used to feel bloated when I drank enough water and I'd worry about being stranded somewhere without a bathroom. But with the help of Dr. Donald Robertson of Phoenix, a well-known obesity expert, I've solved the problem.

Why should you drink water? Because it cleanses the liver and kidneys, it may keep you from developing Alzheimer's (patients have a remarkable history of not drinking enough water), and it will definitely help you lose weight — not to mention helping flush away any ketones and toxins you produce in the course of weight loss.

Our bodies are over 72 percent water, and the brain is thought to be 85 percent water. Dehydration, which is extremely common, affects the brain first; the signs include irritability, moodiness, headaches, back pain, and fatigue. If you're feeling cranky, maybe you're just thirsty. Symptoms of serious dehydration include dizziness, muscle cramping, nausea, diarrhea, and confusion. Chronic dehydration can cause kidney damage and kidney stones.

According to obesity expert Dr. Donald Robertson of Phoenix, if you're not drinking 2 quarts a day, you're definitely storing your old water, which makes you weigh more — it's just one of those mysterious paradoxes. Once you get your water in balance, you reach the "breakthrough point," a concept pioneered by Dr. Peter Lindner, a California obesity expert. In breakthrough, your body stops retaining fluid, your endocrine system function improves, more fat is used for fuel because the liver is free to metabolize it, *and* you stop feeling hungry. You also regain your natural thirst, so you actually want to drink enough water. However, if you fall back and stop drinking enough, you have to start the whole process all over again.

But how do you drink this much water without losing your mind? Start the minute you get up, with two 8-ounce glasses, and have another glass before breakfast. All this water should have run through your system within 90 minutes, or before you leave the house, assuming you get up in time. Do the same thing at noon — three glasses — consumed within 30 minutes. Between five and six P.M. have another two glasses. If you drink your water too late, your automatic overnight antidiuretic mechanism will kick in, and you'll keep that water locked in for a very long time.

Is eight glasses enough? Obviously you need more water if it's hot or if you're exercising vigorously. You also need an extra glass for every 25 pounds overweight you are. And cold water works best, says Dr. Robertson.

If you're stuck on a diet plateau and you haven't been drinking enough water, you'll be amazed at what happens when you do. A great imported bottled water is Gerolsteiner Sprudel — really tasty and satisfying, and full of good minerals. Gerolsteiner has twice as much magnesium as Pellegrino and four times as much potassium, with a third more calcium. Delicious as it is, it's also low in sodium.

Caution: If you have glaucoma, you should *not* drink a lot of water in a short period of time. Two glasses in 15 minutes is too much. You can still drink the suggested amounts of water, but spread it out through the day, or you may raise the pressure in your eyes to a dangerous level for an hour at a time.

PART THREE

Troubleshooting

Blowing It

At some point, everyone will surrender and indulge in a high-carb meal, and many of us do it frequently. If you don't have serious health problems to worry about, you may simply fall into an I-don't-care mood, or may drink too much and temporarily lose your willpower; or life may just seem too short, and you want to have a good time and eat something that tastes great.

Here's what happens to you physically when you blow it: You immediately retain water to deal with the carbohydrate load, lots and lots of water. That's because carbohydrates prompt the kidneys to hold on to extra water and salt. You feel bloated, tired, sluggish, depressed, with a profound sense of malaise. You move in a kind of mental fog, forgetting things and failing to focus on whatever you're doing.

It has to be said: Carbs not only make you fat, they make you fart. After banishing them from your diet for a while, you don't really have the proper enzymes to digest them — that would take a few days of carbs to establish — and in the meantime you produce huge amounts of gas.

It's very easy to keep eating carbs once you've started, partly just because you feel so miserable, partly because more carbs boost your brain's serotonin level so you do, if only momentarily, feel better. If you eat high carbs for two days, however, more fat will go into your blood than if you ate nothing but fat — because your liver is now hard at work making dangerous triglycerides.

That's why, if you're going to go over the edge at all, it's especially important to stop at a single high-carb meal. You'll do far less damage and you can still easily regain your equilibrium because you don't yet have the right enzymes to get into full-carb metabolism.

And don't forget, if you *do* completely tumble and eat high carbs for days or weeks, the fat you regain will be pure fat, whereas your earlier weight loss included some muscle tissue. So if you regain all your lost weight, you'll actually be fatter than when you started.

Don't waste any time feeling guilty or getting angry with yourself — these lapses are all part of the game and to be expected. Just jump right back on the strictest low-carb plan, drink huge amounts of water, and don't give it another thought. If you confine your lapse to a single meal, chances are it won't affect your weight or your health, assuming you were already in good control of your blood sugar. If you do indulge beyond a single meal, you'll pile on some water weight, but that should come off quickly. A few days' worth of carbs, however, and you're in trouble, not only because of the carbs but also because your insulin sensitivity will be affected and you'll need more insulin to do the job — thus setting yourself up to gain even more weight.

If you know a big splurge is a possibility, it's best to be prepared for it and hold the fort.

Planned Indulgences

It can happen anytime. You may be on vacation, or it's Christmas, or you're going on your honeymoon, or you've just decided to stop low-carbing for a while. You can do so intelligently, with a minimum of damage, if you plan ahead.

First, you'll need your arsenal of secret weapons. Even if you're eating carbs, taking carnitine an hour before you indulge will help. Remember to take a starch blocker or a fat blocker before you eat, too. You can always try the method recommended by Barry Sears: Eat some ice cream along with some sliced turkey on the theory that the protein offsets the carbs. (If you're diabetic, this wouldn't be a good idea; see the warning about high glycerin protein bars on pages 327–328). Some dieters swear this procedure works.

Eat your extravaganza meal as early in the day as you can and exercise afterward — a long walk, several runs at the stairs, and more vigorous exercise if you can. Exercise really will burn off some of the carbs.

Keep drinking lots of water. You'll need extra water to accommodate the carbs in any case — you'll wake up thirsty in the middle of the night if you don't.

Jump right back on the program as soon as you can, and don't look back. Above all, if you've planned to go off your regime, enjoy every wonderful minute of it. And if the indulgence wasn't worth it, better still — you'll think twice next time.

Emergency! Fast Pound Drop

Sometimes you just have to lose 10 pounds fast — for your class reunion, a wedding, whatever. Here's how to give it your best shot.

First of all, pull out all the stops with the supplements: liver cleansing, L-carnitine, omega-3s. Drink even more water than usual — a gallon a day wouldn't be too much — and exercise even more than usual. Eat enough protein but not too much, and try to keep it to fish, eggs, and protein shakes. Cut back drastically on the dairy products or eliminate them altogether. Keep fruit to an absolute minimum. Drop the alcohol. Be careful about nuts, and emphasize green vegetables and salad. Check to be sure your calories are somewhere between 1,200 and 1,500, depending on your size.

Don't follow this regimen for more than two weeks at a time; you don't want to send your body into starvation mode, which will slow down your metabolism and leave you with a permanent limited calorie budget.

Vitamins and Other Supplements

If you read a lot of books on the subject and spend too much time at the natural foods store, you can end up taking literally dozens of tablets and capsules a day. Some of these you undoubtedly need, some may be helpful, and some may be just useless. How do you know? One problem is that most of the people who know the most about supplements are not doctors, so they don't have a medically trained understanding of the body's biochemistry and they don't actually prescribe for patients and carefully monitor the results with lab tests. And needless to say, they usually don't work with people on low-carb diets.

Two exceptions to this situation are Dr. Robert Atkins and Dr. Mary Dan Eades, both of whom have written books on the subject. Supplementation is a very individual prescription, so ideally your doctor would be one who is knowledgeable about both low-carb nutrition and supplements who can guide you into the best program for your own needs. If you don't have such a doctor, however, you should definitely check out *Dr. Atkins' Vita-Nutrient Solution* and the Eadeses' *Protein Power Lifeplan* for the best advice on the subject from doctors who've worked with thousands and thousands of low-carb patients.

Beyond the sophisticated prescription, however (which may include carnitine, alpha lipoic acid, and CoQ^{10}, among other things), here's a bare-bones list of supplements you should consider taking. Remember that you may be slightly low in B vitamins if you're on a low-carb diet, since they appear mainly in grain products, so a B multivitamin, including 400mcg folate, is a good idea.

- Magnesium. We're nearly all deficient in this crucial mineral (and *all* diabetics are deficient), which has almost disappeared from our water supply and our soils. The Eadeses (in *The Protein Power Lifeplan*) call magnesium a miracle nutrient, and they're hardly overstating the case. It strengthens the heart, normalizes high blood pressure, has positive effects on mood disorders (such as anxiety and depression), and does a dozen other essential good works. It's also a natural laxative and sleeping aid.

Magnesium's partner, calcium (ideally in a one-to-one ratio), has escalated wildly in our diet — and left to its own devices, calcium can form deposits on artery walls and do other damage; it doesn't just automatically deposit in your bones. To control calcium, doctors often prescribe calcium channel blockers, but magnesium, as the Eadeses point out, is a natural calcium channel blocker.

Standard dosage is 300mg to 600mg of chelated magnesium (malate, citrate, or aspartate) before bed.

- Vitamin E. The American Heart Association has for years now been recommending vitamin E, but not everyone has received the message. Not only does this workhorse vitamin act to prevent heart disease, it's also a potent free-radical attacker, clot-buster, and anti-aging soldier — you won't get as many wrinkles if you take vitamin E. For our purposes, it's really important because it increases insulin sensitivity (the more sensitive your cells are to insulin, the less you need to produce) even if you don't change your diet. It's almost impossible to get adequate vitamin E through food alone.

  Standard dosage is 400mg of vitamin E (in a tocotrienol mix, not just alpha-tocopherol) with fat — it's a fat-soluble vitamin.

- Folate. Also known as folic acid, this B vitamin works against high levels of homocysteine, thought to be a major player in heart disease. Read more about this essential nutrient in *The Heart Revolution,* by Kilmer and Martha McCully. The McCullys also recommend a low-carb diet to prevent heart disease. Good food sources of folate include bananas and beans, so you can see why you might be deficient if you're on a low-carb diet.

  Everyone should be getting 400mcg of folate a day — the amount that's usually in multivitamins. If your homocysteine levels are high (above 10), you need much more, but there's no toxicity associated with even very high doses of folate.

What If You Don't Like to Cook?

This attitude could end up sabotaging your success at low-carbing. There are two solutions here: make cooking much more of a pleasure, share the work with friends or other members of your household; or become a minimalist cook who basically assembles food from takeout sources, leftovers, and the easiest possible recipes (of which there are quite a few in this book).

You can turn the time you spend in the kitchen into a pleasant interlude. Consider it a break from the daily whirlwind. Play your favorite music, keep fresh flowers in the kitchen, and think about something while you're cooking that you don't have time to think about the rest of the day. Time alone can be at a premium for some of us, and cooking time can be used to enjoy our own company. Be sensitive to the sensual parts of cooking: the vivid colors and shapes of fresh produce, the delicious aromas coming from the garlic sautéing in oil, the little hisses and snaps food makes as it cooks.

Children like to help in the kitchen and can actually take on little jobs such as tailing beans or drying salad greens. Getting kids involved in making their meals is a good way to prepare them for not inheriting your own attitude about cooking.

For the minimalist cook, there's lots of help available, some of it in the form of appliances such as the food processor (instant coleslaw and zucchini shreds for sautéing), grills (George Foreman's tabletop grill from Salton is a winner), a heavy-duty blender.

The two main components of low-carbing are, of course, protein and vegetables. You *must* keep protein on hand — cans of tuna and salmon and sardines are excellent, as are eggs (especially hard-cooked eggs, which anyone can cook in her sleep). Have a takeout roast chicken hot one night, then make chicken salad sandwiches on low-carb bread from the leftovers. Any scraps can go into soup.

If you can manage to roast a turkey breast, you'll have an excellent protein supply for days. Add a little ham, cheese, scallions, avocado, hard-cooked egg, and romaine lettuce, dress it, and you've got chef's salad. Deli roast beef and ham offer similar options, as does takeout poached or grilled salmon. (Buy twice the amount you need for one meal and make a salad with the leftovers.)

You can broil or roast almost any protein and almost any vegetable. Even with only a minimalist pantry on hand — olive oil, vinegar, cumin, paprika, oregano, thyme, chilies (if you like heat), garlic, hot pepper sauce, Worcestershire sauce, soy sauce, mustard, mayonnaise — you have the ingredients to transform a simple dish into something memorable.

A good knife, some intelligent shopping, and an awareness that you're actually creating something when you make a meal can empower you to cook successfully and actually start to enjoy it.

The Snack Problem

Snacks are probably the most burning question on the minds of the majority of low-carbers. The approved ones can often get boring, but what's the alternative? While you don't always feel the need for them, it's great to have them on hand when you do. Here are some things that have passed my lips in the middle of the afternoon:

- the old Welsh miners' lunch: cheese wrapped in a cabbage leaf
- peanut butter or almond butter on a celery rib
- nuts, but not more than ¼ cup — roasted, toasted, raw, or fried
- leftover meat, poultry, or fish with mustard or Dijonnaise
- grated cheese, broiled or skillet-fried — eat with a fork
- prosciutto and melon
- deviled egg or hard-cooked egg sprinkled with seasonings
- egg or tuna salad on Fiber-Rich cracker or romaine leaf
- string cheese
- jerky
- half a low-carb protein bar
- shrimp with seasoned mayonnaise or guacamole
- leftover grilled shiitakes filled with grated cheese and broiled
- Wasa cracker with cream cheese, toasted sesame seeds, and paprika
- Just the Cheese wafers (see Sources)

- Energy Burst Protein Snack Mix (see Sources)
- baked seasoned tofu
- cottage cheese with drizzle of sugar-free maple syrup or berries
- soy nuts
- Seasoned Pumpkin Seeds (see page 120)
- Corn Crisps (see page 134)

Sweet Treats

When I attended a very intense liquid-diet program at a major New York hospital, my fellow dieters' eating habits amazed me. A number of them were volume eaters, people who didn't care at all what they ate as long as there was plenty of it, buckets and buckets. A few others were like me, taste eaters, who wanted everything to taste good and could possibly restrain themselves from eating more than enough if in fact the food was sufficiently delicious. The one thing we all had in common, however, is that we craved treats. For some people, treats were something to be enjoyed many times a day, which is probably why they wound up in this program in the first place.

Treats aren't a very good idea, of course, because by their nature they tend to leave you wanting more. If it's a question of enabling you to stay on the diet, however, a little indulgence every now and then is a smart strategy. Here are a few that won't break the bank. If you find they trigger cravings, however, skip them.

- chocolate-covered coffee beans
- Life Savers Sugar-Free Flavor Pops (2g carb)
- square of bittersweet chocolate (see page 300)
- Chocolate Coconut Bites (see page 313)
- macadamia nuts
- Peanut M&Ms
- almonds or pecans fried in butter
- Swiss Miss Fat-Free Cocoa
- Irish coffee
- Sugar-Free Eskimo Pie

Eating Out

Unlike many diets, the low-carb regimen is actually easy to follow when you're eating in a restaurant, assuming you're not at a pizzeria. (And if you are, eat just the topping.) Persuade your dining companions to keep the bread basket to themselves on their side of the table, politely refuse all rolls and muffins put on your plate (or just break a piece of bread and leave it alone), and order the simplest possible food: grilled, roasted, or broiled meat, fish, or poultry; a salad (hold the croutons or pick them out); and maybe some raspberries for dessert. Have a glass of wine and a bite of a sympathetic companion's dessert, just so you'll know what it tastes like.

Restaurants where you may have problems include vegetarian or "healthy" restaurants (which usually have high-carb, low-fat menus), and those featuring Indian, Thai, Chinese, and other low-protein cuisines. But again, there are solutions. In Indian restaurants you can usually order tandoori dishes, which will be prepared with skinless chicken or meat or seafood. Ignore the rice, the bread, and the lentils; a cucumber raita should be fine, and the spinach paneer is borderline fine. If there are salads, order them, but try to be sure beforehand that they don't include sugar as well as bits of potato or bread. Don't order the lassi drinks, especially mango lassi, which is very sweet. Have tea instead. Probably everyone else at your table will be reveling in the breads — have one bite if you need to, but otherwise ignore them. Indian desserts are incredibly sweet, and you probably won't be offered fruit — but if you are, melon would be a good choice.

Thai restaurants are a nightmare from the low-carb point of view. Everything is both sweet and starchy, even the pure protein, such as the Chinese sausage, which is quite sweet. Your best bet is to order a whole fish; if it comes with a sweet sauce, just scrape it off. The wonderful shrimp crackers that are sometimes brought to the table in big pastel puffs are of course carby, but one won't kill you. Keep away from the noodles, and ask if any salads can be made without sugar in the dressing.

A much better choice, if there is one nearby, is a South American restaurant, especially the churrasco places that have begun to open in this country. The Argentines in particular understand how to serve meat: In one of these restaurants you'll be presented with tray after tray of grilled meats and some seafood, with a few salads and vegetables on the side. This is perfect for our purposes; you just take what you want from each course.

Mexican restaurants offer a number of good low-carb options along with a huge number of fatal temptations. They usually serve a ceviche, some grilled fish or meat, as well as some excellent vegetable possibilities. If it's a Southwest restaurant, fajitas are a sensible choice. Guacamole is perfect (but no chips), and most salads will be fine, as is salsa. Enchiladas are hopeless, but tacos will work as long as you don't actually eat the taco shell.

Middle Eastern or Greek restaurants are good choices because they always feature something more or less fresh and simple. Usually it's lamb, roasted or grilled, or fish. A big fresh salad with lots of low-carb vegetables is also standard fare. You can have a little hummus or baba ganoush, but not on bread. Ask for sliced cucumbers instead. Check out the tabbouleh — if it's properly made, it will include a lot of parsley and almost no grain, in which case dive in. These restaurants almost always offer kebabs — have only a little of the onion. Desserts in these restaurants are generally hopeless, so just skip them. Mint tea can be wonderful, but since it's often murderously sweet, ask to have it made with no sugar.

Chinese food also can be good for low-carb diners, as long as you avoid the rice, noodles, and things like oily scallion pancakes. Sauces are often full of sugar and starch. Stir-frys usually have a little sweet element, but it probably won't be enough to make a big difference in your insulin level. Skip the fried dishes, which are often breaded and sweetened as well. Watch out for bean paste, barbecued meats, and red-cooked anything. No wonton or sweet and sour soup, but egg drop will be fine, as will hot and sour. Some Chinese restaurants offer slices of orange for dessert, which is very refreshing — have a couple and just read your fortune, don't eat its wrapper. An almond cookie will set you back 20 carb grams.

In a Japanese restaurant, start with miso soup and go on to sushi or sashimi, if that's an option, skipping the rice. You might think seaweed salad would be safe, but it's actually quite sweet. Have some *edamame* (steamed soybeans salted in the pod) with your drinks. (But don't drink sake, which is sweet.) Spinach with sesame seeds is a good choice for a vegetable. *Negimaki* — little bits of beef with scallion — are great with the spinach.

If you have access to a Korean restaurant, you're lucky — this is great low-carb food (as long as you skip the rice and noodles, of course), with lots of vegetables and unencumbered meat. Sometimes kimchi, the very spicy cabbage-based relish, is actually sweet, but more often it's not — and it's supposed to be very good for you.

At an Italian or French restaurant, just use common sense: pass up the carbs and choose from among the many excellent possibilities.

If you're at a restaurant where the food seems iffy in the carb division, you can first try telling your waiter that you're a diabetic and you absolutely can't have any sugar or starch. Of course, he probably won't be able to tell which foods contain hidden starches, so this strategy won't get you too far. A better alternative is the trick that diabetes guru Dr. Richard Bernstein uses: Carry with you some Clinistix or Diastix. Ask the waiter for a taste of whatever you're considering ordering, unless it's cooked to order — in which case you can order it the way you want it, anyway. Take a bite of the food, chew it around a little to release the glucose, put a bit of the food on the strip, and see how much sugar it contains — don't eat it if it doesn't pass the test.

Come On Over for Dinner . . .

These words have struck fear in the hearts of many a low-carb dieter, who is likely to find himself facing a meal of pizza, lasagna, tacos, or a backyard picnic featuring fried chicken and baked beans, or the old standby pasta and bread and salad. If it's a good friend who's inviting you, of course, you can casually ask what's on the menu and offer to bring what you need to stay on your diet. Otherwise, under the guise of bringing something you can simply inquire what's on the menu and contribute a single dish you can eat that will work with what's being served — even if your host declines your help, go ahead and bring a low-carb dish.

If You're Craving . . .

- **Pizza:** Try covering pressed tofu with sauce (Rao's brand pasta sauce is only 4g carb for ½ cup), a little oregano, and grated mozzarella — broil until the cheese melts. Or make an oven frittata (page 340), top it with sauce and cheese, and broil it until the cheese melts. Grilled eggplant is another good base for this trick.
- **Bread:** My favorite is Alvarado Street Bakery's California Protein Bread at 8g carb per slice. Or try Sara Bakery's little pita breads at 3g. (See pages 101–102.)
- **Potatoes:** Try the potato skins on page 255.
- **Potato chips:** Deep-fry potato skins (see page 255), or make zucchini strings (page 269).
- **Ice cream:** Put some full-fat ricotta (you can make your own, page 345) in a bowl and add a little cream. Whip with an immersion blender or a whisk. Serve chilled with berries or Wet Walnut Sauce (page 309).
- **Chocolate:** Have a chocolate protein shake or a piece of a low-carb protein bar. Or pop a few chocolate-covered espresso beans, about 1g carb each.
- **Pasta:** Microwave some spaghetti squash (page 261), 4g carb for ½ cup, and toss with pasta sauce or pesto or just butter and Parmesan. Or make wide zucchini noodles with a vegetable peeler, salt them and let them drain 15 minutes, then dry them and sauté in olive oil with garlic or pasta sauce. Top with some grated Parmesan and you're set.

Should you, perhaps, bring your own dinner? No, unless you want to be the main subject of conversation and feel like a complete idiot, having to explain and defend what you're eating. I once made the mistake of rolling out a very fancy can of tuna at a dinner party given by a superlative cook for a group of major players in my field — and I'll never do so again.

Should you tell your hosts in advance that you have a special diet? That would be impolite, although it's also impolite of the hosts not to ask you whether that's the case. These days, though, a host who inquires can hear about five different diets that don't intersect — there's bound to be a vegetarian and at least one low-fat eater, whose menu requirements are usually the opposite of yours. In case you need to pluck up your courage about all this, remember that if you were a diabetic you would indeed be very restricted in what you ate, and your hosts should certainly know about that.

You can always bring a low-carb dessert — there's never too much dessert at a party, and usually you don't have to worry about upstaging the host if you explain your situation. However, I've seen people ignore the major high-carb dessert being offered and demand some of the low-carb cheesecake or the low-carb homemade ice cream, even when they hear it's sugarless. One bite and they love it.

What about a true emergency — a crucial client, say, who would be distressed to learn that you don't eat what everyone else eats, or dinner at the boss's house when the family specialty, Potato Bliss, is the centerpiece? Sometimes you just have to resign yourself to the inevitable and eat a *little,* not a lot. But again, you can always bring a contribution to the dinner. And of course, you wouldn't go entirely unprepared. You'd have eaten a hard-cooked egg (so you won't be hungry) and taken a starch blocker (page 51) and some vanadyl sulfate (page 50) before you even walked in the door.

Even if you completely lose control and eat everything in sight, remember, the crucial thing is to jump right back on the program. If you were doing well before, your slip may not even register on the scale.

Holidays Without Tears

The holidays are undoubtedly the toughest time of the year for low-carbers. There's a huge emotional pull as we anticipate our family's traditional foods, and expectations run high. We may even be expected to actually produce these foods. (Find someone else to do it if you think you'll lose control and eat half the cookie dough while you're baking.) Some relative will be heartbroken when you decline her special fruit-cake or fudge, which had always been your favorite. It may seem like giving in is the easiest course of action, but take it from me: It isn't. More than once I've succumbed, thinking I'd just lop off those few extra holiday pounds in no time. Wrong. Months later, they were still mine.

One problem is that the holidays seem to go on forever. Office parties start in late November, followed by a steady round of festivities for most of us, right up to Christmas. Then there's the night before, the breakfast on the day, the celebratory Christmas dinner, the special meals for visiting relatives, and food gifts of candy and cakes and cookies. It doesn't really end until after New Year's Day. If you don't have a plan, you can easily get swept away by the tide of treats.

Plan number one is to anticipate how much you will drink. Be sure to set a limit and stick to it. If you drink to excess, you won't care about your diet and you'll surrender to an excess of food. Before a party eat a hard-cooked egg and drink a couple of glasses of water.

If you're planning to seriously overindulge, be prepared: Use alternative-medicine guru Dr. Julian Whitaker's formula: 500mg N-acetylcysteine, 1000mg vitamin C, 50 mg vitamin B_1, and 150mg standardized milk thistle extract. Drink as much water as you can before you go to bed, and more when you get up in the morning. And avoid acetaminophen, which can damage your liver in combination with alcohol.

You also need to plan what you're going to eat, so you won't be overwhelmed by the panoply of carbs at the buffet table. The only way you can be sure this will happen is if you bring a food contribution yourself, something you can eat. This could be a great cheese, smoked salmon, a big container of spiced nuts, a savory cheesecake — whatever's appropriate.

If you receive a high-carb food gift, as you undoubtedly will, give it to a local shelter or soup kitchen.

If you're the host of a holiday meal, there's obviously no problem; you can just add some higher-carb dishes, or ask some of your guests to supply them. If you're the guest, follow the advice in the preceding section, remembering to limit the indulgences you allow yourself. There's something incredibly depressing about starting a new year many pounds heavier than you were just several weeks earlier. And very few things you do in your adult life can make you feel so foolish.

On the Road

You're away on business, or you're on vacation, or you're visiting your grandparents, or for some other reason, you've abandoned your entire routine, and you've lost control of what you're eating. Under these circumstances it can be very tempting to just give up. And if you're on vacation, you probably *do* want to give up a little, if you can afford it carb-wise.

Many of these occasions begin with a plane trip, which is usually a recipe for disaster. If it's breakfast, you might luck into an omelet, but chances are your airline will be obeying the government's healthy-eating dictates, which means low-fat, high-carb, as well as lots of synthetic food like nondairy creamers. A low-carb protein bar is the answer here; you should always have at least one with you whenever you leave the house. You might be lucky enough to find something like a hot dog (no bun) if you're stuck at an airport for a long siege, but what's available is usually total carb.

If it's later in the day, you might get some peanuts (some American flights and Delta) or some mixed nuts (United), but you're more likely to be offered "healthy" pretzels. Lunch can be a hot sandwich (peel the cheese and meat out from the bread), but dinner is a carb extravaganza. Much better to bring your own: nuts, tuna salad, coleslaw, raw vegetables, sliced turkey, whatever appeals. You can order a special seafood plate (at least 24 hours ahead of your flight), but be sure it doesn't contain surimi, the fake seafood, which includes sugar. It's especially important on planes to drink extra water, since you'll become dehydrated if you just drink the same amount you usually do.

If you're driving, keep large bottles of water in the car, as well as protein bars and other sustenance such as hard-cooked eggs, jerky, or nuts. On the highway, it may be especially hard to avoid junk food, so you should always bring along enough healthy food and water to see you through the next meal.

Virtually any establishment can provide you with what you need: meat, fish, poultry, cheese, or eggs, and a big salad or a salad and vegetables. Pitfalls include coleslaw, which often contains a lot of sugar. Don't be afraid to ask for a taste of something before you order, since the server may not know what's actually in the food, and sometimes it's a sugary condiment, not sugar itself that's the problem. No one will be upset if you trot out your trusty low-carb crackers. (ClickClack, the food container company, makes a great 1-pound plastic airtight container that just exactly fits these crackers — order from the Baker's Catalogue, King Arthur's Flour, 800-827-6836). For a beverage, iced tea is a good option, if it has no sugar; otherwise, stick to the mineral water you've brought.

Traveling abroad can be a little dicier, especially for breakfast. Here, the more exotic locales are often somewhat easier. In Egypt, for instance, you have a whole bevy of salads to choose from, as well as yogurt and cheese and eggs. France is a tough one — a croissant wouldn't kill you, since it has so much butter to slow down the rate of starch absorption, but you'd need to balance it with protein, which will not be forthcoming. Best to just have a protein bar in your hotel room and enjoy the coffee later. Italy is another place you'll need a large stash of protein bars.

Part of the whole point of visiting a place like Italy, though, is to enjoy the food. Are you really going to go there and not eat any pasta? On an extended trip to Italy recently, which was actually centered around food, I had a pleasant surprise: I gained only four pounds — water weight, which left almost immediately after my return home — and I ate and drank extremely well. I had pasta several times, but only after I'd taken Phase'oLean, the starch blocker. I rarely ate bread, but I enjoyed gelato a number of times, usually after a very long and vigorous walk. And I was lucky enough to be invited to some private homes for dinner, where I simply ate the meal, avoiding the bread and trying hard not to eat too much dessert. It's important to counteract a meal like that with some vigorous exercise afterward — if nothing else is possible, walk up and down stairs ten times. And don't head out without an arsenal of protein bars, starch blockers, vanadyl sulfate, vitamins C and E. When you decide to indulge, the damage should be minimal. The point, I think, is to enjoy yourself sensibly without blowing the whole diet.

If you do blow a day, again, pick yourself up the next morning and be strict. Otherwise you'll come home miserable, literally sick that you undid all your good work and now have to start all over again. It's never worth it in retrospect, only in the moment.

In the Woods

Heading into the wilderness with a backpack or in a canoe and trying to eat low-carb is a real challenge. The standard camping foods — beans, grains, gorp, dried fruit — obviously won't cut it.

For the first day out, you can bring along some more perishable foods, such as hard-cooked eggs and fresh cheeses. After that, you can rely on some more durable items — pepperoni sticks, aged cheese, tuna, sardines, jerky — for the long haul. Somewhere in the middle are seasoned tofu, yogurt, and avocados. (Let green ones ripen on your trip.) Cabbage and bell peppers will keep four days.

Obviously you'll be bringing protein bars (Balance Outdoor bars won't melt) and protein shake mix you can just mix with water. Seventy percent cacao chocolate can be a big treat on a trip like this.

Fiber may be your biggest problem, so be sure to include some Fiber-Rich crackers — good to spread with nut butters. And bring along whole nuts and pumpkin seeds as well.

The Energy Burst Protein Snack Mix is both light and tasty (see Sources).

Here are some more ideas from Alan Silverstein, a frequent con-tributor to the low-carb tech group (lowcarb@maelstrom.stjohns.edu):

79

TVP (textured vegetable protein)
soy nuts
dried tofu (Snow Dried Tofu)
sun-dried tomatoes
kiwi fruit (fragile)
jicama
broccoli
cauliflower
broccoli sprouts
olive oil, in plastic
spices, garlic
dehydrated eggs
butter
halvah
string cheese

The View from the Plateau

For almost all dieters, there comes a point (if not several) at which you reach a plateau. A major one occurs after about six months of dieting. No matter what you do, you can't lose a pound. Most plateaus last at least two weeks and not much beyond six weeks, but that's hardly a comfort to the person who's enduring one — and continuing to follow a diet scrupulously.

Various substances have been implicated as plateau-initiators, including citric acid (which besides being in citrus fruits is in almost everything canned, including diet soda). There is a little evidence to suggest that might be true, true enough to try eliminating for a while foods that contain it. Another popular culprit is the artificial sweetener aspartame; again, try dropping it and see if the pounds drop as well.

Another school of thought holds that hidden food allergies can trigger plateaus. And of course, if you're eating a monotonous diet, as so many of us are, you're more likely to set off a food allergy by consuming large quantities of a single food. The theory is that if your body treats a food as a toxic substance (that is, develops an allergy to it), the fat cells will bind to it in an effort to act as a buffer and isolate the toxin. When this happens, the fat cells naturally enlarge. You then develop a chronic overactivity of the immune system, which especially attacks the thyroid, slowing metabolism.

You can check yourself for food allergies by taking the ALCAT test — call 800-881-2685 for information. Or you can just stop eating specific foods, one by one (dairy foods and wheat are good places to start), and see what your reaction is. If food allergies are the problem, when you target the correct food the body desensitizes and may release the stored toxins as well as the fat. So be sure to drink a huge amount of water if you're trying out this theory. Once you've corrected the problem and the fat is coming off again, it will most likely be pure fat, and not the usual mix of fat and muscle — the thighs, especially, will release fat, for unknown reasons.

Saturated fats can be hard to burn; your body prefers to store them, according to Dr. Ron Rosedale. When you're losing weight, you're burning your own (saturated) fat and the last thing you want to do is compete with that released fat by ingesting even more saturated fat — which also may cause insulin resistance. So it may be a good idea to cut back on the animal fats and see if it makes a difference.

You can also try just simply readjusting your diet to see if you can't start the fat loss again. Change your balance of nutrients: add more fat, or more carb. Try Dr. Atkins's all-fat diet or an all-fruit diet for a few days. Whatever you do, though, don't drop your calorie intake even further — you may end up with a permanently lowered metabolism, which is the last thing you want.

Some dieters have had good results by switching to the Paleo diet: Eat nothing your ancient ancestors didn't eat, which means only basic protein plus leaves, nuts, and berries — no dairy products, no caffeine, and no alcohol.

My own plateau cure is the liver-cleansing routine (pages 56–59). I take BHB Plus and do a modified, higher-protein version of Dr. Cabot's diet, with an emphasis on omega-3 fats (nuts, avocado, seeds, oily fish) and raw foods. For me, dairy products seem to be a major problem — you might try dropping those if nothing else seems to work.

Help! I'm About to Go Off My Diet . . .

It isn't just temptation that gets us derailed. Very often it's the ordinary ups and downs of daily life that arrive like little devils to take us away. Everything from boredom, frustration, anxiety, stress, garden-variety depression, or just the feeling that you can't stand it another minute may send you to the carbs. If you've been a lifelong carb addict, there may also be what I call the Popeye Effect: If things aren't going right, just eat some carbs and you'll feel strong and happy very shortly. For a while; soon enough your blood sugar will be way down and you'll either need more carbs or you'll feel really rotten. Much better to follow Popeye's example and eat some spinach.

But what do you do when you're in that mood? The first thing I do is take a long, tall drink of water. Then I chew a few pieces of sugarless gum and wait 15 minutes to see if it passes. If not, it's another glass of water and a rinse of mouthwash — or I brush my teeth if that's possible. If I'm still stuck after all that, I think it through: What do I *really* want? Do I want the immediate gratification of eating the carbs, or do I want the long-term goal I've already sacrificed so much for? In the end, taming these demons always comes down to choosing the long-term goal — you have to want that more than you want the taste of something wonderful right that minute. Usually I can engage the adult in my head and pass up the carbs, but not always. If I really want the carbs, I go ahead and eat them and let myself enjoy them — then jump right back on the straight and narrow.

The Thyroid Blues

Once I discovered my own low-thyroid status and started supplementing with natural thyroid, I thought my slow metabolism problems were solved. But twice now, I've discovered that my thyroid was once again low — most recently, I'd been strenuously dieting after several binges on trips to interesting places and couldn't seem to lose a single pound. After a couple of weeks I became alarmed, but it wasn't until a friend suggested the thyroid possibility that I realized I'd once again dropped below the line.

The symptoms of low thyroid are so vague and so diverse that they sneak up on you, and often seem like normal bodily reactions. Dry skin could just be winter coming on; cold feet could just be a personal quirk your bed partner teases you about; muscle and joint stiffness could just be encroaching age; constipation could just be a result of eating too little fiber; hair loss could be from dieting itself; depression seems to be at least an occasional visitor at everyone's house. And of course almost everyone has trouble losing weight . . .

So let's say you suspect low thyroid is the culprit behind all these symptoms and you get it checked. Your doctor says your blood test is within the normal range. But there may still be a problem, for the normal range is so broad that it's almost meaningless. And because hormones are produced throughout a 24-hour cycle at different levels, a single blood sample will tell you only what's circulating at that particular moment, not your average thyroid level. If your blood sample comes back with a low-normal reading, you may need to be supplemented with thyroid.

Ask your physician to give you a TSH (thyroid-stimulating hormone) test, which is new and much more accurate. And if it turns out you need thyroid, consider a natural brand such as Armour, which already has some of the T4 thyroid converted to T3, the usable form. If your doctor is unconvinced, get him or her a copy of the October 6, 1989, *Journal of the American Medical Association,* which has an article by Dr. Alan Gaby on the subject.

You can also order this article from the Broda Barnes Foundation, at 203-261-2101. They can also send you a list of doctors in your area who will understand the biochemistry involved. The Barnes Foundation offers a complete hormone screening (via a 24-hour urine test) at a very reasonable cost. In my experience, doctors respond very favorably to seeing the lab numbers and the recommendations from the Barnes physicians.

Meantime, you can test your thyroid level yourself by testing your body temperature. For four consecutive days (women should do this on the first four days of their period), before you get out of bed or do anything at all, place a non-digital thermometer in your armpit for 10 minutes. Take an average of the four days' reading. Anything under 97.8 suggests low thyroid. And if your thyroid's low, you may have a nightmare of a time losing weight. Once you have the condition corrected, you'll not only lose weight more efficiently, you'll feel infinitely better — and you'll improve your general health in a fairly dramatic way.

If your thyroid is low, you may have elevated homocysteine levels, a heart attack precursor. If so, correcting the thyroid problem will undoubtedly correct the homocysteine problem, without resorting to folic acid supplementation.

The estimates are that up to 12 percent of Americans have mild hypothyroidism, but among older women the estimate is 20 percent. Dr. Broda Barnes, the thyroid expert, estimated that up to 40 percent of the general population is actually affected. Even if you're taking thyroid, estimates are that 40 percent of patients still have abnormal levels, either too high or too low. If you're hypothyroid, the liver won't do its jobs properly — and it won't release its stored sugar.

Eating more protein requires more thyroid, as does being in a state of ketosis, so low-carbing may make some demands on your thyroid supply.

Once you're taking thyroid, you may find on later tests that the TSH level is low, which might indicate too much thyroid. That's because you're being supplemented, but most doctors will become alarmed at this signal, and advise you to lower your thyroid dose to avoid hyperthyroidism and osteoporosis. (If you actually had hyperthyroidism, an overactive thyroid, you'd be acutely uncomfortable, with hand tremors, racing pulse, and — the good news — rapid weight loss.) According to Pat Puglio of the Barnes Foundation, that's an incorrect prescription; the tests that perpetuated this idea were done on women with cancer who were taking synthetic thyroid, not the Armour natural thyroid. Because they had cancer, they had adrenal problems, which means they couldn't use their thyroid effectively and actually had *low* thyroid, not too much. If you follow the lower-dose theory, you'll end up with all your old hypothyroid symptoms, says

Puglio. And because natural thyroid *builds* bone, you're not in danger of getting osteoporosis in any case. Obviously enough, if your thyroid level was too high, all the blood levels — T4, T3, free thyroid — would also be high. If they're not, don't worry.

But there's more than one point of view on this subject. Dr. Ron Rosedale, of the Colorado Center for Metabolic Medicine, thinks there's nothing wrong with a slightly low temperature. Your cells can only turn over a certain number of times in your lifetime, and if you raise the idling speed of the engine by increasing the amount of thyroid you take, he argues, you simply add wear and tear and shorten your lifespan. You also increase your blood sugar levels and decrease your insulin sensitivity. It's much better, he believes, to make everything work more efficiently by means of a very low-carb diet, omega-3 oils, and supplements, with thyroid used only in extreme cases.

Once again, you need to be a fairly sophisticated medical consumer to sort out the thyroid problem, if it applies to you. The best solution may be to take thyroid if you're symptomatic and then try to improve your thyroid function through diet and supplements such as BHB Plus (see page 58).

Note: If you're low thyroid, you shouldn't take oral estrogen, which binds T4 so it can't convert to usable T3 — which makes you *more* hypothyroid.

That Blocked Feeling

At some point, it happens to most of us: We're eating a lot of protein and not enough fiber and forgetting to drink enough water. The results are somewhere between uncomfortable and agonizing.

Obviously you need to get back to eating enough fiber — the Eadeses recommend 24 grams a day — and drinking enough water, at least 2 quarts a day. But the crucial thing is to take magnesium, which you ought to be doing in any case for your general health. If you're getting 600mg of magnesium malate or aspartate, drinking the water, and chomping down on the fiber (broccoli, cabbage, raspberries), you probably won't have a problem with constipation.

Weird Bruises

Some people who lose a lot of weight get strange bruising, especially in areas where they've lost substantial amounts, such as the thighs. The theory is that the old blood supply that fed these giant fat cells now doesn't have much real work to do, but because the capillaries are still delivering the blood to the site, it pools and shows up as bruising. One solution is to take 4 grams (4000mg) of vitamin C each day; you may be able to get by with less, but talk to your doctor if you have this condition.

PART FOUR

Special Situations

Vegetarianism

Although it's not impossible to be a low-carb vegetarian, it's certainly a challenge — especially if you're a vegan (someone who avoids eggs and dairy products as well as animal flesh). It's much easier if you allow yourself fish, but of course, only you can decide whether that's acceptable.

I have to say frankly that I don't think vegetarianism is a healthy choice. Neither does superstar nutritionist Robert Crayhon, who was a dedicated vegetarian for health reasons (or so he thought) for 11 years. If it's a moral or religious choice, however, and you're committed to a vegetarian lifestyle, you need to be quite careful about what you eat.

Vegetarians have a higher cancer rate (but possibly not if they watch their carbohydrates; see page 21), and female vegetarians have a higher rate of death from coronary heart disease than meat-eaters (*American Journal of Clinical Nutrition*, 1970).

These statistics may have a lot to do with deficiencies in the vegetarian diet you'll need to compensate for, such as:

- no carnitine
- low lysine

- low taurine
- low omega-3 fats
- excess omega-6 fats (which increase risk of heart disease and inflammatory conditions)
- low B$_{12}$ (which can cause neurological problems as well as artery disease)

If you're not eating fish, you'll naturally gravitate toward soy (see page 104) as your major protein, along with dairy products. Although it has a number of health benefits, soy also has some drawbacks as a major protein source, according to Robert Crayhon.

- It is low in methionine, an amino acid essential for tissue growth and overall health.
- It has been shown to cause Type I diabetes in animals.
- Soy milk, like grains, contains phytates that block mineral absorption.
- Soy-based formulas have caused zinc deficiency in infants.
- Soy lowers levels of HDL (good) cholesterol along with LDL (the bad form).

There are ways around all these problems, of course, but you'll need to be a creative cook and a careful eater and supplementer to find them.

Being vegetarian doesn't mean you're off the hook for protein requirements; you need just as much protein as everyone else does. If you're not eating dairy products, check out the algae spirulina as another protein source.

Dana Carpender's *How I Gave Up My Low-Fat Diet* has a useful list of low-carb products available at the natural foods store and other places. These include soy cheese and other acquired tastes. Among the soy milks, the only ones to date that don't have added sugar are Westsoy unsweetened and White Wave Silk. High-protein vegetarian burgers include Natural Touch Garden Burgers and Morning Star Farms vegetarian sausage patties. The Hellers' Carbohydrate Addict's Gram Counter includes a vegetarian section.

I have no doubt that there will one day be a vegetarian low-carb cookbook, but until that essential item comes along, you'll have to wing it. Vegetarian recipes in this book are indicated in the index by italics, and of course, there are a number of good soy cookbooks on the market. The all-time best vegetarian cookbook, by my lights, is Deborah Madison's *Vegetarian Cooking for Everyone,* and a number of her recipes will work for low-carbers. *This Can't Be Tofu!,* her soy cookbook, has many low-carb recipes.

Diabetes

Before the advent of low-fat diets, diabetes was treated with a relatively low-carbohydrate diet to stabilize blood sugar. Then the thinking changed, and diabetics, both Type I (juvenile) and Type II (adult onset), were encouraged to eat some sugar and especially more starch — which of course turns into sugar in the body. In the low-fat era, diabetes has become almost epidemic. Perhaps most alarming, childhood diabetes has increased by 20 percent in the last decade.

One man, Dr. Richard Bernstein, has more or less single-handedly reversed the trend and steered diabetics — he himself is a Type I (juvenile onset) diabetic — in the direction of low carbs, very often using diet alone to normalize blood sugar.

My son Ben became a Type I diabetic at 29 — probably the result of a viral infection — and spent more than a year on a diet as close to zero carbs as possible. Although he was producing very little insulin on his own, he was able to avoid taking insulin shots and managed his diabetes entirely through diet and supplements, under the guidance of Dr. Ron Rosedale. The hope was that by giving his pancreas a long vacation, it would recover enough to make more insulin. Although Dr. Rosedale has a young patient who's done exactly that, Ben wasn't quite so lucky. Now he takes a very small amount of insulin and still keeps his carbs very low. So far, his general health is excellent, and there's been no further deterioration in his condition.

Other diabetics swear by a low-carb diet based on the Glycemic Index — though Dr. Bernstein remains completely opposed to the idea, on the grounds that all carbs are contraindicated for diabetics, whether they raise blood sugar quickly or over a longer period of time.

In a fascinating study of 157 Type II diabetics presented at the 1999 annual meeting of the Endocrine Society, a low-carb, high-fat diet (50 percent fat, of which a whopping 90 percent was saturated) produced an average 40-pound weight loss in a year. All of the patients had been on the American Diabetes Association recommended diet for a year before starting the low-carb diet, which they also followed for a year. On the low-carb diet, most (90 pcercent) of them achieved ADA target levels for HDL (the good cholesterol, which increased), LDL, and triglycerides (both of which decreased). As Dr. James Hays, an endocrinologist and Director of the Limestone Medical Center in Wilmington, Delaware, noted: "If you have a diet that results in weight loss, lower cholesterol, and a better lipid profile, eventually everybody will be eating that way. It's going to come whether we like it or not." It should also be noted that these patients were not in ketosis.

If you're diabetic, or have diabetes in your family, it's very important to read *Dr. Bernstein's Diabetes Solution.* Even if you're not diabetic, this is an excellent book on low-carb dieting — and you may save yourself a case of adult-onset diabetes by following his guidelines before you need them.

JUNE, 76

For 33 years now, June has been a Type I diabetic, trying to control her diabetes through diet and a small amount of insulin. For the last four years, she's been using Dr. Richard Bernstein's plan (see page 91), and she now has normal blood sugars, at last. June uses 6 of her daily 30 grams of carbohydrate for breakfast, 12 each for lunch and dinner. She's evolved her own version of the Bernstein diet, adding a few low-carb fruits and some carbs from soy flour. She doesn't worry about protein or fat, just eats what she wants outside the carbohydrate restriction. Sometimes she thinks she should be worrying about saturated fat, but her very high HDL — 109 — reassures her about that.

She's rigorous about exercise, not only walking but using the exercycle, weights, and stretching. Her lineup of supplements: vitamin C, E, zinc, calcium, and gingerroot.

Although she finds some things about this regime hard — having to plan ahead constantly, keeping protein on hand, cooking from scratch, and having to eat carefully at friends' houses — in general she's happy with how she feels and especially with her normal blood sugars. She's free from cravings now except for bread, which she sometimes eats in the form of crusts at restaurants, taking a little extra insulin to cope with the extra carbs.

Because she's so pleased with her health status, she almost never strays from the diet. And what does her doctor think? She doesn't have a professional to advise her about diabetes; she's been her own doctor and the results are so impressive many a professional would be envious.

And what does she actually eat? Breakfast is the big variety meal: it could be "cereal" in the form of Bran-a-Crisp crackers crumbled with some nuts and moistened with a half-cream, half-water mixture, or cold cuts and Wasa crackers, smoked salmon and cream cheese, fried eggs and soy bread toast, or her own homemade soy-bran muffins.

Lunch might be a hot dog on a low-carb whole wheat tortilla (see page 102) plus a lettuce salad. Dinner one night began with an asparagus salad followed by a pseudo-pizza (Italian sausage, cheese, and mushrooms on a low-carb tortilla) with ½ cup of strawberries perked up with a bit of Hawaiian papaya and a sprinkle of rum. For snacks, June chooses nuts, Almondina cookies, crispbread and peanut butter, low-carb fruit and cheese, or — big treat — low-carb ice cream.

This way of eating is so satisfying and so successfully controls her diabetes that of course June plans to eat low-carb the rest of her life — cheating isn't even a possibility.

Pregnancy and Nursing

This is a little-explored area of the low-carb world, though there's no question that pregnancy sets off huge hormonal changes that affect insulin levels in many women — and, as Rachael and Richard Heller (*The Carbohydrate Addict's Diet*) have noted, for many a lifelong weight problem results. Although the Hellers don't specifically discuss using a low-carb diet during pregnancy, Dr. Atkins thinks it's fine as long as you stay above 40 grams of carb daily. The *Sugar Busters* doctors recommend their diet for pregnant women. And a lower-carb diet may prevent some pregnancy complications, such as excessive weight gain, high blood pressure, and late-term diabetes.

Whether you should or shouldn't stay low-carb during pregnancy — and how low you should go if you do — depends on a number of factors, including your weight, the state of your health, your family history, and the guidance of your doctor. If you can't find a doctor who endorses your wish to stay low-carb or relatively low-carb, you won't have the expertise and support you need to guide you through the process and make any changes as necessary.

No one's suggesting, however, that it's a great idea to eat a lot of sugar and starch while you're pregnant. New research shows that the kind of nutrition a baby receives in utero can predispose him or her to weight problems later in life as well as some serious health complications, such as diabetes (see *Newsweek,* September 27, 1999.) And that includes insulin resistance and a tendency toward weight gain. To short circuit those problems, you should avoid eating refined carbohydrates early in pregnancy and eat more protein in the last trimester.

If you decide to increase your carb allowance, eat whole foods — not only to get the maximum nutrient benefits, but to curtail the problems. It may help to contact some of the many moms on the Internet who have had successful low-carb pregnancies.

Nursing is another matter. It takes an enormous amount of energy to produce human milk, so you get to eat a lot, which is just one of the joys of nursing. Again, it's not a good idea to be in ketosis, and you want to raise your protein, your carb level, and your good-fats level (omega-3s) to be sure you're getting enough calories and nutrients. Take advantage of the huge calorie budget you need and enjoy some carbs for a change.

In anecdotal reports, low-carb diets have been effective for postpartum depression.

PART FIVE

In the Kitchen

The Pantry

Obviously, the more flavor options you have, the better your food will taste — and the less bored you'll be. Here are some things I keep on hand, some of them staples and some of them just frequent visitors.

- Consorzio Fat-Free Mango Dressing and Marinade. This used to be called Mango Vignette, but it's still the same delicious product at the same 1g carb per teaspoon. I use it several times a week.
- The Ojai Cook's Lemonnaise. This is one of the few low-fat products allowed in my kitchen, but it's so delicious and citrusy that it's almost a sauce on its own. Available in gourmet stores.
- Delouis Fils mayonnaise and garlic mayonnaise. These are like homemade; real, fresh mayonnaises from France that keep for about a month in the refrigerator.
- Frontera salsas. A powerful punch for only 1g carb per teaspoon. Try mixing these into mayonnaise for a dip or just smearing them on almost anything, especially items destined for the grill. Tangy Toasted Arbol is smoky as well as tangy — great with eggs, fish, on

a taco. Roasted Sweet Chipotle is a robust table sauce from Veracruz — wonderful with fish. For information, call 800-509-4441.

- California Press nut oils and nut flours (call 707-944-0343). These extra-virgin nut oils (try pistachio!) make great sauces for vegetables as well as livening up salad dressings. The nut flours can be used half and half with regular flour to uncarb a cake a bit. They're also great for breading fish or chicken to fry.

- Loriva oils. Widely distributed in natural foods stores and many supermarkets, these high-quality oils add a lot to almost all courses of a meal. Try the roasted peanut, sesame, walnut, pumpkin, macadamia nut, and even the garlic oil and canola oil. For more information and recipes, visit their Web site: www.loriva.com.

- Ginger juice. Royal Pacific brand is in many gourmet stores and has negligible carbs. It's great for stir-frys, salads, and drinks.

- Porcini broth cubes from Star Brodo. Look for them in Italian markets and gourmet stores. These are great in stews and soups and make a pleasant pick-me-up cup of broth on a cold afternoon.

- Spanish oak-smoked paprika. I'm crazy about this intensely fragrant stuff, which comes in both hot and sweet varieties. Try it with greens, with eggs, in a rub for meat or chicken. Look for it at gourmet stores or order a tin from Formaggio Kitchen (888-212-3224).

- American Spoon Foods jams and spreads. These fresh fruit jams and cocktail spreads have no preservatives, just fresh ingredients. Some of them are remarkably low-carb: Apple butter is just 4g carb for a whole tablespoon. Eggplant-and-cumin spread is less than 2g carb, and olive-and-red-pepper is just 1. For more information, call 800-222-5886.

- Pumpkorn. A good snack, when I'm too lazy to make my own Seasoned Pumpkin Seeds (see page 120) — or I'm on the road and need a few nibbles for plane trips or days when I'm not sure when I'll be eating again. Available at natural food stores. Just 2g carb for a 1/3 cup serving.

- Pork rinds. This staple of the low-carb diet comes in a new microwavable form that's quite tasty.

- Ducktrap Farm smoked trout. This is a great product, and it keeps well in the refrigerator for weeks. Order from 800-828-3825.
- Coco Pazzo pasta sauce. The label says only 2g carb in a ½ cup serving (but we know there's some math problem here, since there are 3g sugar in the same amount, an impossibility).
- Garlic spray. For just a whiff of garlic, this spray bottle from Garlic Valley Farms is useful. To find it, call 800-424-7990.
- Low-carb breads and crackers. See pages 101–104.

It's Dangerous Out There . . . Wrestling with Labels

You might think the government, in its infinite wisdom, would have re-solved with its labeling laws all our questions about what's actually in our food. But alas, that's not true. To begin with, not everything is la-beled; if you go to the natural foods store, for instance, you might find Tropical Source chocolate chips made with tofu. You might buy them, thinking the tofu will mean they're lower-carb. In fact, you have to call the company to discover that they're actually quite a bit *higher* in sugar than the (to me) infinitely tastier pure chocolate brands.

At the same natural foods store, you might find Horizon organic sour cream, which seems like a more or less generic item. You know that a cup of sour cream has 9.8g carbs. But Horizon has added ingre-dients like cornstarch, guar gum, locust bean gum, and carrageenan — and a cup of this innocent-looking sour cream actually clocks in at 16 carb grams, not 9.8.

Even whole foods can be deceiving. Del Monte's supersweet Gold pineapple has 17 carb grams for two 3-inch slices — several grams more than regular pineapple, but it's not listed anywhere.

As a dedicated low-carber, you may be used to more or less un-consciously subtracting the fiber grams from the total carb grams — which is correct, since the fiber grams are counted as carbs but are not metabolized. But a manufacturer may do that *and* list the fiber grams as well. For example, Dr. Vogel's Swiss Mixed Grain bread, a Southern California product, seemed almost carb-free, less than 2g carb per slice. But the manufacturer listed the fiber grams and also subtracted them from the total carb grams (contrary to FDA labeling laws), so that consumers were actually getting about 6 carb grams per slice, triple the amount listed on the label.

If a product has *added* fiber, that fiber can't be subtracted from the overall count; it's just whole foods this rule affects.

Many protein bars containing glycerin are notorious offenders in this category (see pages 326–328). To go into sugar shock, just eat one of these bars on an empty stomach. You'll know right away that something's wrong.

So what can you do to protect yourself? You still have to read the labels carefully, and if in doubt, call the manufacturer and ask pointed questions. One big clue is the sugars listed: If the sugar grams are higher than the carb grams, you know that's impossible. If the sugar grams are high at all, pass the product by.

Pay particular attention to the serving size listed on the label. I got all excited once at an airport when I encountered a soft ice cream with an extremely low carb count — which turned out to be for 1 ounce; an actual serving was more like 16 ounces, and the total carbs were way beyond Häagen-Dazs's.

Another problem with tiny-quantity labeling is that many foods are low-enough carb so that they come out zero in very small quantity (i.e., less than 1 gram) — but that doesn't mean a larger quantity is also zero. Artificial sweeteners are good examples. A teaspoon of NutraSweet is less than 1 carb gram, which is negligible, but if you're using several tablespoons in a dessert, it can add up. A tablespoon of cream is just 0.4 gram of carb, almost nothing, but a cup is over 6 grams.

There are great carb bargains out there that really deliver terrific taste, but they're few and far between — a good rule of thumb is, If it seems too good to be true, it probably is.

The Bread Problem

As I know all too well, the biggest single problem for low-carb dieters is finding some sort of bread that works. I have very high standards for bread, maybe a lot higher than they should be, but for me almost none of the "diet" breads make it onto the table. I find them dry, tasteless, lacking in character, unsatisfying, and not at all worth the carbs they cost. Charlie VanOver, a breadmaster whose breadmaking cookbook has won every culinary award there is to win, always eats some real bread every day — but everything else he consumes is extremely low-carb, and he's an athlete who works himself hard to enjoy his bread. He points out that he wouldn't go looking for ersatz wine, so why try to put together a low-carb bread?

But for those of us who aren't athletes or who for health reasons can't handle the carbs of real bread, there are still some good choices. Here are mine, in order of preference. Note that all low-carb breads taste better toasted, especially if they've been buttered first. Check labels carefully, including the weight — a slice that weighs 34 grams will be more satisfying than one that weighs 30 grams but has the same amount of carbs.

- Alvarado Street Bakery's California Style Protein Bread. This flourless, nutty-tasting bread weighs in at just 8g carb per slice, and it's quite delicious. It is my breakfast toast, my raft for a grilled cheese sandwich, my bread crumb source. It's made from sprouted organic grains, soybeans, and lentils, and has no preservatives. Because it's flourless, it freezes beautifully for six months and it keeps well in the refrigerator. Alvarado also makes a tasty Soy Crunch bread, which is 9g carb a slice. A single slice of these breads makes 11 tablespoons of bread crumbs (just whiz it in the food processor).

  The breads are widely available in natural foods stores all over the country, as well as many supermarkets; they're even distributed in Canada. Alvarado, which is run by a collective, doesn't mail order, but they'll direct you to the distributor for your state if you call them at 707-585-3293. Or check their Web site: www.alvaradostreetbakery.com.

101

- Sara Bakery pita. This little bakery in Richardson, Texas, makes a delicious, very thin pita bread that weighs in at a little over 3g carb. As of January 2000, Sara was retesting its pita — call for an update. Sara mail-orders; call 972-437-1122.
- Natural Ovens of Manitowoc. This Wisconsin super-bakery, owned by Paul and Barbara Stitt, turns out a huge number of products — their big interests are natural grains, low-fat (unfortunately), and omega-3 oil (yes!). But a number of their breads are relatively low-carb. You have to pick and choose your way through them to avoid the fructose and carbs, but the bread is quite good. Many of the breads — Right Wheat, Hunger Filler — come in at 8g carb and weigh 34g a slice. Stay Trim, cruelly, is also 8g carb but weighs a mere 31g. Glorious Cinnamon and Raisin Bread is 12g carb, and not, for me at least, worth the carbs. This is probably the only bakery in America that gives you an omega-3 oil count on the nutrition label.

  Manitowoc ships all over the country — orders received by noon on Thursday in Wisconsin are shipped on Monday. You can also tour their factory and see their huge tunnel oven. If you order or stop by, encourage the Stitts to work on a very low-carb bread. Sooner or later, someone will develop a delicious one, and that person will make a fortune.
- Dr. Vogel's Soy and Flax Bread. This new product is just 8g carb a slice. Available by mail order (a five-loaf minimum) from North's Bakery in Los Angeles, 818-761-2892.
- La Tortilla Factory whole wheat fat-free low-carb/high-fiber tortillas. At less than 3g carb each plus almost 10g fiber, these are really lifesavers in the low-carb kitchen. The tortillas have been reformulated as of 2000 with a new soy flour from Arrowhead Mills and no added sugar. The secret is to throw them directly on the burner and flip them quickly — don't try frying them (they get leathery) and don't slowly warm them in a skillet. You can use them as toast, as a sandwich wrapper (just fold like a taco), as a pizza base (if you have a good imagination), and of course for quesadillas or anything else you'd use a tortilla for.

  New are flavored tortillas, such as taco and cilantro, and a burrito, for 7g carb. La Tortilla distributes widely in the West and also mail-orders: 800-446-1516. You get 10 packages of 10 big tortillas in an order, but they freeze well, so you won't mind receiving so many. Be sure to order the low-carb tortillas; La Tortilla makes several other varieties that are anything but low-carb.

- Bunny Bread. This bread is made all over the country by various bakeries with slightly different formulas. The version produced in Ohio is very low-carb and tasty, at less than 4g carb a slice. If you see Bunny Bread in your area, check the label — you might be lucky.

- RyVita sesame crackers are particularly delicious and have just a fraction more carb than Wasas (see below).

- Wasa Fiber Rye Crispbread. These are more crackers than bread, but I'm happy enough to have a large, tasty slab of grain, call it what you will, on which to spread a little butter or cheese, or smoked salmon, or egg salad, or a smear of cream cheese with chives. Look for the sesame seed variety, which are especially tasty and about 5g carb.

- Fiber-Rich/Bran-a-Crisp crackers. This product has two different names and quite different packaging (Fiber-Rich can be found in supermarkets, its cousin in natural foods stores), but they're the same. This is, to be honest, a bit more like fodder than food and actually has about 3g carb per cracker, though the label suggests they're 0g. The *Diabetes Reader* (which has ceased publication) recommended breaking up these crackers into a cereal bowl and dousing the crumbs with cream. Try this with a sliced finger banana (about 5g carb) and a shake of cinnamon.

- Blue Diamond Nut Thins. These supermarket crackers are just a little over 1g carb each — but they're small. Still, they're tasty and crunchy and if you can stop yourself from eating a whole bunch of them, they're very useful. They come in almond and hazelnut flavors. Be sure to check the expiration date.

- Oyster crackers. Okay, they're not bread, but they're crunchy, and you can get a lot of mileage out of them at about 5 crackers for 1g carb (check labels).

- Finn Crisp: These elegant, ethereally crisp wafers are made of just

LIVING LOW-CARB

rye flour and caraway seeds. A skinny wafer is 3g carb — less of a carb bargain than the giant Wasas, but very satisfying. Great with slivers of cheese or a layer of smoked salmon, nut butters, egg salad. Your guests will love them.

- Other diet breads: "Diet" still means "low-fat" almost everywhere in America, so be careful that your diet bread isn't loaded with sugars or starches. You *must* read the labels. La Louisiana Bakery, for instance, is in *Sugar Busters* country, and they make "sugar-free" bread products — but their croutons actually have more carbs than the much tastier Chatham Village ones.

The Many Faces of Soy

If you are vegan, of course, it's essential to eat a lot of soy; it has some benefits for the rest of us as well plus some drawbacks. Soy contains all nine essential amino acids, and although it has some carbs, it also has substantial protein and fiber. Soy has a fair amount of fat, but it's a vegetable fat (good), though its ratio of beneficial omega-3 oils to omega-6 is quite a bit less than ideal, according to Dr. Ron Rosedale. But that can be dealt with by eating fish, as we should be anyway. If you're a strict vegetarian, of course, this option won't work for you.

Tofu is probably the form of soy we're all most familiar with, and it has a lot of virtues. It's cheap, easy to prepare, easy to keep on hand (the Mori-Nu boxes are especially good), and it's a good source of instant dinner. Soy expert Lorna Sass likes the extra-firm tofu best, and points out that it contains less water, and therefore has more protein. The amount of calcium in tofu varies — check the labels. The Chinese style of tofu is pressed, while the Japanese is more custardy and silky.

To prepare tofu, you have to press the water out. Wrap it in a kitchen towel, press against a cutting board tilted into the sink, squeezing out as much water as you can, and dry it thoroughly. Cut it lengthwise and then lift each piece gently with the knife. Tofu takes almost any seasoning beautifully, but especially chopped scallions, grated ginger, soy sauce, toasted sesame oil, peanut oil, and hot pepper oil — and it definitely needs seasoning, since it's very bland by itself. Try it cold with an icy light beer on a hot day.

Baked tofu from the natural foods store (White Wave is a good brand) makes a good snack — one piece is just 2g carb. Just toss it into the microwave to heat it.

Tofu can replace sour cream, soft cheeses, and eggs; it can be the base for soups, dips, spreads, shakes, and dressings.

Soy milk is a bit more of an acquired taste, especially in coffee — though children seem to like it immediately, especially vanilla soy. Be sure you get organic soy milk, and unsweetened if you can find it (Westsoy is a good brand). Many brands have added sugars, sometimes in the form of barley extract. Baking with soy milk is a bit tricky; it doesn't always behave like milk. It can suddenly curdle, for instance, especially in the presence of acid. You can add it to soup for a creamy quality, stirring it in just before serving to avoid curdling. You can even make yogurt out of soy milk: Just get acidophilus and bulgaricus cultures at the natural foods store, warm the soy milk, stir in the cultures, and follow the directions that come with them for making milk yogurt. Once it's opened, soy milk lasts about 10 days — but it will keep months unopened on the shelf.

Tempeh is fermented soy, and because it's fermented, it's easily digestible, which isn't always true of soy products. It's also definitely an acquired taste.

Miso is a fermented soybean paste that makes instant soup and good salad dressing. It has an interesting complex flavor — the lighter the color, the more delicate the taste. The dark style is almost beefy in its complexity. American Miso Company makes a good miso that is widely available.

Soy sauce comes in endless varieties. Soy expert Lorna Sass prefers the Japanese, because she finds the Chinese too salty. But avoid supermarket brands, which sometimes have no soy in them at all. The best soy sauce is the fine condiment kind, which has the richest flavor — Eden is a good brand.

Edamame are salted green soybeans, usually found frozen in Asian markets. Cook them in boiling water or steam them for five minutes and drain. Serve at room temperature with drinks — just open the pods and pull out the tasty little beans.

And finally, a rave for Eden's canned black soybeans (see page 236). These are instant, tasty, and low-carb, with fairly substantial protein. You can sometimes find these dried as well, and they're the kind you want for a long-simmered soup — they take about 1½ hours to cook.

To find out about the health benefits of soy, read *The Simple Soybean and Your Health* by Mark Messina. On the Internet, check out www.soyfoods.com.

Confusingly enough, there are also some negative things about soy that suggest it shouldn't be your major protein source. As Dr. William Campbell Douglass notes in his newsletter *Second Opinion,* the protein in commercial soy powders has been highly processed and thereby denatured enough that farmers need to supplement soy pellets for animal feed with lysine — something humans neglect to do. The phytoestrogens in soy are potent; they can have drastic effects on human hormones, everything from bringing on menstrual periods in postmenopausal women to depressing thyroid function, which may lead to weight gain. Soy oil is highly processed and contains dangerous trans fats. The phytates in soy block mineral absorption; the protease inhibitors they contain can cause pancreas enlargement and interfere with protein digestion. Finally, if you're eating a lot of soy you'll need more B vitamins, especially B_{12} — and if you're a vegan, you're already at risk for not having enough B_{12}, which can raise dangerous homocysteine levels. All this is not to say you should avoid soy altogether — just eat it judiciously.

The Looking-Glass World of Fake Sugar

Americans just love sugar; the latest statistics reveal that we eat over 150 pounds of it per person in a year. We're pretty keen on fake sugar, too, with average individual consumption of 24 pounds a year — and since most fake sugars don't weigh much, that quantity is even greater than it sounds.

I'm no exception. In my cupboard at the moment are sucralose (Splenda, from Canada), Equal (aspartame), DiabetiSweet (a mix of three fake sugars), KiSweet (made out of kiwi), one made from low-glycemic agave cactus, Sunette, stevia, and a fructo-oligosaccharide (a fruity bean concoction) combined with stevia. I don't particularly like any of them, but there are times when you just have to have something sweet to keep on going. Here's some general information to help you figure out which products you might want to use.

A general rule of thumb: The powdered sweeteners have sugars in them, amazingly enough. These sugars are usually dextrose and mal-todextrin, thought to be even more glycemic than sugar — so watch out for anything that ends in -ose. Sweet 'n Low, Equal, The Sweet One, and Sugar Twin all have about 96 percent sugar. The small packets are carefully calibrated so that there's less than 1g carb in each one — but just a fraction less. One gram of carb won't raise your blood sugar much, but if you're using much more — to make a dessert, for example, or if you're stirring several packets into your coffee cup — you're getting 3 to 4 grams of carb, which is significant. One cup of Splenda costs 24 grams. Instead of using a little packet of Equal, you're much better off getting the tablet form and crushing it, which will leave you with no blood sugar reaction since there are no added sugars.

Many people believe that the real enemy among the sweeteners is aspartame — several Web sites are devoted to attacking it (among them holisticmed.com). It's been linked to everything from headaches, multiple sclerosis, loss of brain function, epilepsy, chronic fatigue syndrome, Parkinson's, Alzheimer's, brain tumors, lymphoma, and lupus to diabetes itself. Some people may be sensitive to aspartame, which most commonly causes headaches. Still, a 1998 study done at MIT found that even large daily doses had no effect at all on the brain. There's no question that aspartame doesn't raise blood sugar — a question that still remains for some of the "bitter sweeteners" (the ones with a bitter aftertaste), which include saccharine, cyclamate, stevia, and acesulfame-K (Sunette). I'm still unsure why anyone would choose a bitter sweetener, but they do seem to increase insulin a bit.

An alternative to aspartame, one that doesn't have the added sugars and is stable at all temperatures — a problem with many of synthetics — is DiabetiSweet, a mixture of three different sweeteners (aspartame, isomalt, and sunette). Isomalt is another.

Some expensive sweeteners that supposedly don't raise blood sugar levels precipitately are KiSweet, Sweet Balance (both developed by Dr. Ann DeWees Allen), and various fructo-oligosaccharides, some combined with stevia. Dr. Allen says her sweeteners are also thermogenic, that is, they encourage fat-burning, unlike dextrose and maltodextrin, which encourage fat storage.

The sweeteners that are supposed to save us from all this angst over fake sugars are stevia, a natural plant sugar (as is glucose, so that's not so important a point), and sucralose (aka Splenda). Stevia tastes fine to some people, but not to me — I find its bitter aftertaste unpleasant; personally, I'd rather have no sweetener at all. And although it's been used for decades in other countries without complaint, there are some animal studies that suggest that stevia at high levels can interfere with energy metabolism. Sucralose is real sugar that's been chlorinated and had its molecules rearranged so that the body doesn't recognize it and simply passes it through. On the plus side, it has almost no aftertaste, it works measure to measure with sugar, and more than 100 studies in over 25 countries give it a green light. The manufacturer claims it has zero effect on blood sugar, which is probably true when it is used in food products; however, in the form we consumers will be using it, the fluffy sugarlike powder, it's been cut just like Equal with the high glycemic sugars. And in pre-testing at the FDA, sucralose was found to have shrunk thymus glands and enlarged livers and kidneys.

Next are the sugar alcohols, most of which are used only in food products. Manufacturers claim that these are not metabolized as carbohydrates in the body, so they're "free." Two of them, sorbitol and mannitol, can cause diarrhea if consumed in excess — in chocolates, for example. Glycerin, technically a polyol, often appears on labels as a non-carbohydrate but in fact it is one, according to the FDA, and is metabolized, up to 75 percent (see the warning about glycerin on pages 327–328). It's also used as antifreeze in RV vehicles. Better is xylitol, which you won't find at the supermarket or even the drugstore — but you can order it (917-441-1038). Xylitol, made from birch tree sap, is classified as a sugar alcohol although it's neither a sugar nor an alcohol, confusingly enough. Among its virtues: It's antibacterial, yeast (such as candida) can't feed off it, and it's at most 40 percent absorbed, and very slowly, so it doesn't spike blood sugar. Xylitol has a cool, minty quality — it's very fresh-tasting, but it's a distinct flavor that doesn't go with everything.

Given the absence of a perfect fake sugar, should you just use a little real sugar every now and then and not worry about it? Sometimes I do that, when I'm cooking and a little sugar will make a huge difference. But more often I remember sugar's devastating effect on blood sugar (and the insulin surge it delivers). And if that's not dissuading enough, I remember the NASA study that showed sugar consumption was the single most important predictor of heart disease in women — in men, it was crucial, too, but not as important as animal fat. So it seems to me we should make the best of a bad bargain and choose a sweetener that tastes relatively good and does relatively little damage. Fake sugar has, of course, a huge market, and many more sweeteners are on the way; maybe one of them will be just what we want.

The Right Stuff

Some kitchen tools and gadgets make cooking a lot easier — they're not essential, but they're fun to have if there's room for them in your kitchen and in your budget.

- Indoor grill. This gizmo seems too good to be true, but it's actually very convenient for instantly cooking meat, fish, and chicken, as well as grilling cheese sandwiches (on low-carb bread, of course). George Foreman's Lean Mean Fat-Reducing Machine, made by Salton, is widely distributed, and comes in two sizes, impossibly small and reasonably okay. Buy the larger size, for about $60. The grill gets incredibly hot — which is why it cooks in moments, leaving appetizing grill marks on the food — so be careful!
- Ice cream maker. If you invest in a good model, you always know what to make for dessert when company's coming. You can use all

sugar (the cream has enough fat so that it helps buffer the insulin-raising effect of the sugar to some degree), half-sugar and half-sweetener, or all fake sugar. A cheap Donvier will be fine if you're using sugar or gelatin, the Italian Williams-Sonoma electric at a little over $400 would be even better, and the Dream Machine, a little under $1,000 at Zabar's (800-697-6301) will knock your socks off. Aside from its stunning price, the Dream Machine takes up a fair amount of space — but you'll never be sorry you bought it, and it can handle even artificial-sugar ice creams without any problem (no more gelatin in the ice cream). The same manufacturer makes the Lello, a slightly smaller machine at about half the price; it's available at Sur La Table (800-243-0852).

Any Way You Slice It

Since vegetables are at the heart of any low-carb regime, it helps tremendously to have more options for how to serve them. One of the most interesting ways to expand their possibilities is to explore the various ways of slicing them. Amazingly, how they're sliced makes a big difference in how they taste. And happily enough, the low-carb vegetables are the easiest to work with on these slicers.

Some of the tools listed below are real luxuries, and most things they can do you can do yourself, given some superlative knife skills and a lot of spare time. Still, these devices are an inspiration to cook something more unusual, so if you can afford them and the space they take up in the kitchen, try them.

- Feemster's Famous Slicer. This old-time gadget has been sold by a company in Ohio for many decades, and it still works very, very well. For slicing cucumbers or peeled broccoli stems or slicing cabbage for coleslaw, it can't be beat, though it doesn't make very thin slices. (Seed and salt the cucumbers first and let them stand for a while to get as much moisture out as possible before rinsing, draining, and drying on kitchen towels.) The Feemster is available from Sur La Table (800-243-0852) for well under $10.

- Japanese mandolines, aka Benriner cutters. These come in small and large versions; the big one is good for making julienne slices and shaving vegetables.

  Be very careful; these slicers are extremely sharp. Any vegetable with a top — radishes, turnips, kohlrabi — should be held by this convenient handle, and you should also wrap your slicing hand in a kitchen towel for extra protection. Benriners are available in Asian markets and from Williams-Sonoma (800-541-2233). The larger one is about $50.

- Spiral slicer. Once again the Japanese come through with what looks like a woodworking tool but is actually a device for turning zucchini, daikon, turnips, and other hard vegetables into ribbons of various widths that are perfect for salads or vegetable pasta. Available from Sur La Table (800-243-0852) for about $50. The Joyce Chen version costs about $40.

- Matfer mandoline. The Cadillac of slicers, this recently updated mandoline is the best on the market. It makes paper-thin slices, vegetable noodles, waffle cuts, crinkle cuts, perfect julienne slices, and almost anything else you can imagine. Shaved peeled asparagus, for instance, makes a great raw salad with a fresh taste. Giant zucchini turn into fettuccine in a flash, and a shaved salad is made in moments.

  The Matfer is extremely well designed; the guard works perfectly without compromising your sense of control; the blades slot in so they're changed in no time; there's a clockwise knob to dial for thinner or thicker slices. The Matfer comes with its own encouraging video and is available from Williams-Sonoma for about $160.

  With all mandolines, you should slide the vegetable over the blade in an easy, fluid motion, using even pressure to ensure uniform slices.

  A great resource is Gene Opton's *Mandoline Cookbook* from the Williams-Sonoma Cookware series. It's full of tips as well as a number of very good low-carb recipes.

Zesters

- Microplane rasp. This kitchen tool didn't even exist — except in carpenters' toolboxes — until 1998, but now I can't imagine cooking without it. It's a long metal wand with tiny perforations that grates the zest — the perfumed colored rind — right off citrus fruits in moments, leaving the bitter white pith behind. The Microplane does the same thing to chocolate and cheese. Even over-the-hill Parmesan that's too hard to grate on any other grater produces clouds of snowy cheese bits when it's grated on the rasp. (But the best-of-all cheese grater is a slightly different rasp, one with a handle.) These graters go in the dishwasher.

   The grater device can be had for about $15 from Sur La Table (800-243-0852) and many other cookware stores. Or go directly to the manufacturer, Grace Manufacturing (800-555-2767).

- Ovos zester. Yet another zester, the French Ovos, does something quite different: It cuts ribbons of citrus zest. (Try sautéing strips of orange zest quickly in nut oil, such as roasted peanut oil, and using them for a tasty garnish.) Turn it the other way and it zips open an orange, so you can remove just a few sections without peeling the whole thing — a big treat for just a few carbs. The Ovos zester is available from Dean & DeLuca (800-221-7714).

PART SIX

Recipes

A Note on the Recipes

All of these recipes are low-carbohydrate (with the exception of several moderately higher dessert recipes), but the carbohydrate counts may not be the same as counts in standard reference books. In the analysis for recipes in this book, the fiber count has been subtracted from the total carbohydrate count, since the fiber component is not metabolically active and does not raise blood sugar levels or trigger any insulin response.

Nutrition analysis was provided by NutriCalc (see Sources).

Vegetarian dishes are given in italics in the index.

Appetizers

Cairo Almonds

In her book *Spices, Salt and Aromatics in the English Kitchen,* the great British food writer Elizabeth David tells of learning to make these almonds when she lived in Cairo. Her tutor was a Sudanese cook named Suleiman, and he was clearly a minimalist. This is one of those great, absurdly simple recipes that I make over and over again — the almonds are just stunningly good, and as David says, you can't leave them alone.

The trick here is to make them the day you serve them, not more than about 5 hours ahead. David prefers sweet almond oil for the pan, but butter or olive oil works perfectly. The nuts are delicate and elegant, and they squeak when you bite into them.

SERVES 6

1 teaspoon butter or olive oil
8 ounces blanched almonds, about 1½ cups
3 tablespoons coarse sea salt or kosher salt
Cayenne pepper

Preheat the oven to 225°F. Grease a baking sheet with the butter and pour the almonds onto it, spreading them out in a single layer.

Toast the almonds 45 minutes, or until they're a pale toasty color, stirring occasionally. Spread the salt over a sheet of wax paper and dump the almonds on top. With a spoon or a spatula, flip the almonds around in the salt. Make a package of the salted almonds: Gather them together in a sausage shape along the length of the paper and fold the sides of the paper together, butcher-wrap style. Twist the ends together and store the packet of nuts out of sight, so you won't be tempted.

Several hours later, when you're ready to serve them, put them in a sieve and shake off the excess salt. Dust the nuts with a tiny sprinkle of cayenne pepper — or more if you like — and put them in a bowl to serve. Eat them all up; they don't keep well.

PER SERVING:
Carbohydrate: 2.9g plus 5g fiber   Protein: 8g   Fat: 20g

117

Spanish Almonds

These nuts are served at tapas bars in Spain and are quite addictive. They're also fast, an almost instant snack or accompaniment for drinks to make anytime, since you probably have all the ingredients on hand.

SERVES 4
Extra-virgin olive oil
1 cup blanched almonds
Kosher salt

Pour enough oil to cover the bottom into a skillet just large enough to hold the nuts in a single layer. Heat the oil over medium-high heat, and when it starts to ripple, add the nuts, flipping them with a spatula so they don't burn. They'll begin to color, then make little popping sounds. When they start to smell delicious, they're done.

Scoop the nuts immediately onto paper towels to drain, then sprinkle with salt. Shake them inside the paper towels to distribute the salt and blot the oil. Serve warm.

PER SERVING:
Carbohydrate: 2g plus 5g fiber   Protein: 7.5g   Fat: 22g

Snow Almonds

This Turkish way of preparing almonds is most of all a curiosity — they're very subtle, tender and sweet, like virgin almonds. They're also very useful to serve to people who eat only raw nuts. On a hot day, they're particularly appealing.

SERVES 8

NOTE: **Start four days ahead**

I cup raw almonds, with skins

Put the almonds in a jar with a screw-top lid and fill it with cold water to cover the nuts. Refrigerate overnight. The next day, drain off the water and add fresh cold water. Refrigerate overnight and repeat the process for a third day.

The fourth day, serving day, drain the almonds and peel the skin off. Serve them cold, on top of cracked ice.

PER SERVING:
Carbohydrate: 1.4g plus 2g fiber   Protein: 3.6g   Fat: 9g

Seasoned Pumpkin Seeds

If you're a fan of Pumpkorn, the tasty seasoned pumpkin seeds, you'll be surprised at how easily you can make your own version.

MAKES 2 CUPS (6 SERVINGS)

2 cups hulled pumpkin seeds
1 tablespoon olive oil
2 tablespoons soy sauce
2 teaspoons chili powder
¼ teaspoon garlic powder
¼ teaspoon salt

Preheat the oven to 350°F. In a bowl, mix the seeds with the olive oil and soy sauce, stirring well. Sprinkle on the chili powder, garlic powder, and salt; stir again.

Roast the seasoned seeds on a baking sheet about 10 minutes or a little longer, stirring a couple of times. The seeds are done when they smell toasty and are golden brown.

PER SERVING:
Carbohydrate: 6.7g plus 2g fiber   Protein: 12g   Fat: 23.5g

Red Pepper Dip for Shrimp or Raw Vegetables

You can make this dip with drained water-packed red peppers from a jar (Mancini is a good brand), but home-roasted ones will have more flavor. Once the dip is made, let it season several hours to develop its full flavors. Serve it in a hollowed-out red or yellow pepper.

MAKES 1½ CUPS (24 TABLESPOONS)

3 red bell peppers, roasted, peeled, and seeded (see page 122)
6 oil-packed sun-dried tomatoes, drained
1 tablespoon pureed chipotle chili in adobo (see page 221)
1 garlic clove, chopped
2 tablespoons extra-virgin olive oil
Salt
1 hollowed-out red or yellow bell pepper for serving (optional)

Puree all ingredients except the salt and hollowed-out pepper in a food processor, scraping down the sides of the workbowl as necessary. Taste for salt and add if necessary. Let the dip season in the refrigerator several hours or overnight. Place in hollowed-out pepper, if using, and serve at room temperature with shrimp or crudités.

PER 1-TABLESPOON SERVING:
Carbohydrate: 0.8g plus 0.3g fiber   Protein: 0.1g   Fat: 1.3g

Roasting and Peeling Peppers

This is one of those fiddly kitchen chores that seems daunting when you even think about it — but once you've done it a few times, it becomes second nature, and roasting a bunch of peppers on sale or at harvesttime will seem routine. Then you can just reach into the freezer, pull out your peppers, and let them thaw overnight in the refrigerator, ready to make all sorts of interesting dishes.

Bell Peppers: Place a large piece of foil on the broiler pan and turn on the broiler. Arrange the peppers — it's easier to do several of them at a time and store them to use later — on the foil-covered pan and set them right under the broiler. After about 4 minutes, check to see how they're doing; the skin on top should be blistered, but you don't want the pepper itself to burn. Using tongs, turn the peppers so each part becomes blistered. When they're all done, either fold up the foil around them and let them steam 15 minutes or longer, or put them in a bowl with a plate on top to steam. Once they're steamed, the skin will come off easily.

When the peppers are cool, pull off as much of the skin as you can — don't worry if it doesn't all come off, it's just fiber, after all. Start peeling with your fingers and move on to a paring knife when it becomes more difficult. Next, working over a bowl to catch any juice, slit the peppers open lengthwise and remove and discard the stem, core, and seeds. Store the peppers in the refrigerator for several days or freeze them for up to 6 months. Put them in a freezer-weight zip-close bag, pour any juices over them, squeeze out as much air as you can, and zip the bag closed.

Chili peppers: Roast these peppers directly over the gas flame or under the broiler, as above. Turn them as they char so that all sides are eventually roasted. Put them in a bowl, cover with a

Tuna Dip with Red Pepper

My friend the food writer Suzanne Hamlin loves canned tuna so much she has an arsenal of recipes devoted to it. This is one of her favorites. The dip is delicious on crackers, but it is also good on radish slices, celery sticks, or cauliflower florets.

SERVES 10

2 (3½-ounce) cans light tuna packed in olive oil, well drained
4 tablespoons (½ stick) butter, softened
1 red bell pepper, roasted, peeled, seeded, and cut into fine dice
    (see page 122)
¼ cup minced fresh parsley

Mix everything together well in a bowl and set aside to season for 30 minutes or longer (refrigerate and bring back to room temperature before serving if it's going to be longer than an hour).

PER SERVING:
Carbohydrate: 0.5g plus 0.3g fiber   Protein: 6g   Fat: 6.2g

plate, and let steam 15 minutes. (Wear rubber gloves if you have sensitive skin.) Cut a slit down the side of the chilies and remove the stem, seeds, and the (very hot) ribs. Pull the chilies into strips and store in the refrigerator for 3 days or freeze for up to 6 months, packed as above.

Marinated Green Olives with Sesame, Orange, and Mint

These Moorish-style olives are a favorite at the Culinary Institute of America at Greystone in the Napa Valley, where the recipe is taught in the Ethnic Flavors course. The olives taste best when they've sat a few hours and picked up all the delicious flavors, but they're also good made on the spur of the moment.

SERVES 6

½ pound (one 10-ounce can) Spanish green olives in brine, unpitted

1 orange

1 teaspoon black peppercorns

1 tablespoon sesame seeds, lightly toasted in a skillet

½ cup olive oil

1 tablespoon chopped fresh mint

Drain the olives and place them in a bowl.

Wash the orange well and dry it. Using a zester or rasp (page 112), take off all the zest (the colored part of the peel). Add the orange zest to the olives.

Remove the white pith from the orange and discard. Divide the orange into segments and cut the segments into small chunks. Add the orange chunks to the olives.

Crack the peppercorns using a mortar and pestle. Add the sesame seeds and crush them very slightly into the peppercorns. Combine the peppercorns and sesame seeds with the oil and mint, mix well, and pour over the olives. Combine thoroughly. Serve immediately or let marinate in the refrigerator, covered, for several hours.

PER SERVING:

Carbohydrate: 2.7g plus 1.3g fiber   Protein: 1g   Fat: 23.5g

Grilled Parmesan Chunks

If you're barbecuing, this South American treat makes a good beginning to the meal to serve with drinks, especially red wine. You can use provolone if you'd prefer; in fact, in Argentina this dish is called *provoleta*. If the only Parmesan available is very dry, choose provolone.

You'll need a hinged grilling basket for cooking the cheese.

SERVES 8
1 pound Parmesan or provolone, cut into ½-inch cubes
Olive oil
Fresh oregano leaves, crushed, or dried oregano

Brush cheese cubes with olive oil and oil the grilling basket.

When the coals are gray and the fire is ready, grill the cheese about 6 inches above the coals just until it's starting to get brown and soft — don't let it melt too much.

Transfer the cheese to a platter and sprinkle with oregano. Serve immediately; let the guests spear the cheese cubes with a fork or a toothpick.

PER SERVING:
Carbohydrate: 2g   Protein: 20.3g   Fat: 18g

Daikon Two Ways

Daikon is the giant white radish most of us stare at as we wheel past it at the produce market. But don't pass it by; it's sweet, crunchy, and very low-carb: ½ cup of raw daikon contains just a fraction over 1 gram of carbs (once the fiber grams have been subtracted), so a slice is almost free. A plate of little rafts of daikon with interesting toppings is enticing.

With Lime and Cilantro
Rub ¼-inch-thick slices of peeled daikon with a cut lime, then sprinkle with salt and some minced fresh cilantro. (Carbs: negligible)

With Zesty Cream Cheese or Tofu
Spread ¼-inch-thick daikon slices with cream cheese (or firm tofu, drained and whirled in the food processor until creamy) that's been seasoned with a little lime zest, minced chives, and minced pickled ginger, to taste. Top with a chive tip or a chive flower, if you have them. (Carbs: about 1g per slice)

Marinated Caper Berries

You're probably familiar with capers, the little buds that come pre-served in brine or vinegar or just salt. They're a good carb bargain, be-cause they provide a big flavor bang for their buck, which is minimal. Caper berries, which appear on the caper bush after the buds bloom, are more recent on the market here, available in gourmet stores and some supermarkets. They look like big tadpoles and come packed in brine in glass jars.

These are also good for the carb budget, and they make a very in-triguing tidbit to serve with drinks instead of the usual olives.

SERVES 8

- 1 cup caper berries
- 2 tablespoons olive oil
- 1 teaspoon whole cumin seeds, toasted
- 2 garlic cloves, minced

Drain the caper berries well and put them in a bowl. Toss with the re-maining ingredients and set aside to season for at least 1 hour and up to 4 hours. Serve at room temperature.

PER SERVING:
Carbohydrate: 0.8g plus 0.6g fiber   Protein: 1.3g   Fat: 3.4g

Celery, Simple but Superb

This is a subtler variation on the traditional radishes with sweet butter and salt, a great low-carb snack or tidbit with drinks. There are just three elements: the inner ribs of organic celery, the best butter you can find, and pure sea salt such as Maldon salt (supermarket sea salt will work, but it has additives).

Spread each celery rib with 1 teaspoon soft butter and arrange the ribs in a sunburst pattern on a plate. Provide a little dish of sea salt so your guests can season the celery to taste.

PER CELERY RIB:

Carbohydrate: 0.8g plus 0.7g fiber   Protein: 0.3g   Fat: 3.9g

A Wild and Crazy Radish

It's watermelon radish, and no, it's not as big as a watermelon — only as big as a beet — but it has a little of the sweet crispness we love so much about the fruit. A type of daikon, this glamour-puss of radishes is a stunning magenta bleeding into white at the edges of a slice. It turns up in farmers markets in California and elsewhere.

Sliced into ¼-inch-thick rounds, it's a terrific little cracker with drinks or salads. Grated, it's a salad — just add a very little olive oil, some fresh lime juice, salt and pepper, and perhaps a little minced cilantro if you like. Carbs are close to zero.

Watermelon radish hasn't turned up in mainstream seed catalogs yet, but that's only a matter of time. Grab it when you see it — or order from Indian Rock Produce (see Sources). This is the sweetest, loveliest radish yet.

Red Peppers with Prosciutto and Smoked Mozzarella

These peppers, with their melted cheese and prosciutto stuffing, are almost addictive — I find I crave them several times a year. There isn't quite enough protein here for a whole meal, so if you want to offer them as a light main course, serve with a salad that has a little extra, or a dessert that has protein — a custard, for instance.

SERVES 2

4 paper-thin slices of prosciutto

2 large red bell peppers, roasted, peeled, cut in half lengthwise, and seeded (see page 122)

4 thin slices smoked mozzarella or Italian fontina cheese

1 teaspoon dried oregano

Preheat the broiler.

Fold each slice of prosciutto and fit it into a pepper half. Add a slice of cheese and sprinkle oregano over each pepper.

Arrange the filled peppers on a baking sheet and run under the broiler until the cheese is melted, just a few minutes.

PER SERVING:

Carbohydrate: 9.4g plus 3.6g fiber   Protein: 24.6g   Fat: 11g

Cheesy Stuffed Mushrooms

This is a variation of a famous old recipe of James Beard's from 1940. It's still a delicious idea, and a cinch to make and serve, since it's not actually cooked.

SERVES 6

¼ pound Roquefort cheese, at room temperature

½ cup (1 stick) butter, softened

½ teaspoon dry mustard, preferably Colman's

12 medium mushroom caps, as perfect as possible, wiped clean

¼ cup toasted chopped walnuts

In a small bowl, cream the cheese, butter, and mustard with a fork until smooth.

Fill the mushroom caps with the cheese mixture and sprinkle with the toasted walnuts.

PER SERVING:

Carbohydrate: 1.6g plus 0.6g fiber   Protein: 6.7g   Fat: 24.1g

Italian Stuffed Mushrooms

These tasty morsels were being served one Sunday afternoon in the test kitchen at my local supermarket, and they're very good — just right for a fall treat before the last of the basil disappears. The original version of this recipe comes from chef Carlo Armellino in the Veneto region of Italy and calls for wild mushrooms.

SERVES 4

16 cremini mushrooms, wiped clean
1 tablespoon extra-virgin olive oil
1 garlic clove, minced
¼ pound ham, finely chopped
⅓ cup chopped fresh parsley
Salt and pepper
¼ pound taleggio cheese, grated
¼ cup minced fresh basil
1 rounded tablespoon grated Parmesan cheese

Preheat the oven to 375°F. Mince the mushroom stems and set aside. Place the caps in a microwave-safe dish and cover with plastic wrap. Microwave 2 to 3 minutes (you may have to do this in batches), until the mushroom caps are just beginning to soften. Lay the steamed caps stem side down in a shallow baking dish large enough to hold them in a single layer.

Heat the oil in a large skillet over medium heat. Add the mushroom stems, the garlic, the ham, and the parsley. Stir together and cook about 5 minutes, or until the mushrooms and the garlic are soft. Season to taste with salt and pepper.

Remove the skillet from the heat and stir in the taleggio and the basil. Fill the mushroom caps with the stuffing and sprinkle the Parmesan over the tops. Bake about 15 minutes, or until the mushrooms are browned and bubbly.

PER SERVING:
Carbohydrate: 2.7g plus 1.1g fiber   Protein: 15.4g   Fat: 15.2g

Egg Pancakes

These are like crepes, airy little nothings to fold around some crème fraîche paired with creamed spinach or smoked salmon or caviar — almost anything will work.

SERVES 4

4 large eggs
¼ cup water
Salt and pepper
Snipped fresh chives (optional)
Canola oil for the pan
Crème fraîche
Filling of your choice: see above

Whisk the eggs and water together well, then add the salt and pepper to taste and the chives.

Heat a crepe pan over high heat until it's very hot. Add a film of canola oil and pour in one-quarter of the batter. Cook the pancake on one side only until cooked through, about 1 minute, then remove it to a warm platter and start with the next one.

Stack the pancakes to keep them warm. To serve, put a spoonful of crème fraîche on one half of each pancake, add a filling, and fold over the other half to make a half-moon.

PER SERVING:

Carbohydrate: 0.1g plus 0.1g fiber   Protein: 6.6g   Fat: 13.3g

Pumpkin Seed Cheese Crisps

These crunchy little crisps are just a little spicy — and can be a lot more if you'd prefer them that way. They'll keep several days stored in an airtight tin.

MAKES ABOUT 24 CRISPS
½ cup hulled pumpkin seeds
½ cup grated Parmesan cheese
1 cup grated Cheddar cheese
1 rounded teaspoon chili powder, such as Gebhardt's
Freshly ground black pepper
½ rounded teaspoon ground cumin
1 large egg, beaten

Preheat the oven to 400°F. Have ready a baking sheet lined with parchment paper.

Grind the pumpkin seeds in the workbowl of a food processor until you have coarse crumbs. In a bowl, mix the ground seeds with the cheese and spices. Add the egg and mix well.

Drop tablespoons of the mixture onto the prepared baking sheet, flattening down the mounds with the back of the spoon. Bake 7 to 10 minutes or until golden brown. Remove from the oven and slide the crisps, still on the parchment paper, off the baking sheet to cool. After a few minutes, slide the crisps off the paper onto a baking rack to finish cooling.

PER SERVING (1 CRISP):
Carbohydrate: 0.2g plus 1.5g fiber   Protein: 3.8g   Fat: 3.6g

Corn Crisps

These little crackers work with drinks, with salads or soups, or just to snack on. If you're seriously missing corn — and who among us low-carb dieters isn't — this is a good way to enjoy it.

MAKES ABOUT 3 DOZEN CRACKERS

I cup stone-ground cornmeal
¾ cup boiling water
4 large egg whites, beaten stiff
Salt and pepper
I teaspoon ground cumin
Butter for the pan

Mix the cornmeal and boiling water and set aside to cool. When it's cold, beat in the egg whites, salt to taste, pepper, and cumin. You may need to add a little more water to make a thick paste.

Preheat the oven to 300°F. Generously butter a baking sheet and drop the batter onto it by the soupspoonful.

Bake 30 minutes, or until lightly browned. Serve immediately; these don't keep very well.

PER 1-CRACKER SERVING:
Carbohydrate: 2.3g plus 0.2g fiber   Protein: 4g   Fat: 1.4g

Socca

Salade niçoise isn't the only great dish to come out of Nice, the raffish seaside city in southern France; this delectable flatbread is another knockout. In Nice it's cooked in huge flat copper pans in a wood-fired oven and served with chilled rosé wine. Use a pizza pan, a large oven-proof skillet, or the widest round pan you have — 10 inches in diameter would be the minimum.

SERVES 8

1 cup water, at room temperature
⅔ cup chickpea flour, from the natural foods store
4 tablespoons olive oil plus more to drizzle over the socca
½ teaspoon salt
1 teaspoon fresh rosemary needles, optional
Salt and pepper to taste

Mix the water, the flour, 3 tablespoons of the olive oil, and the salt in a bowl; set aside for 1 hour.

Preheat the oven to 500°F. Oil the pan (see above) with the remaining tablespoon of olive oil and pour in the batter. Bake the socca until it sets, about 6 minutes.

Turn on the broiler. Drizzle more oil over the top of the socca and sprinkle with the rosemary. Broil until crisp and golden brown, about 5 minutes. Sprinkle with salt and pepper, cut into 8 wedges, and serve hot — socca doesn't keep.

PER SERVING:
Carbohydrate: 4g   Protein: 1.4g   Fat: 7.2g

Shrimp in Mushroom Fondue

This elegant little appetizer is served on a warm plate with a toothpick for each shrimp — or serve the entire dish in a copper skillet, should you be so lucky as to have one. The shrimp are coated with the tasty and unusual sauce. If you have sauce left over, as you probably will, re-heat it with a little cream and serve it over broiled halibut or sea bass fillet.

The cheese can be almost anything lurking in your refrigerator — Cheddar, Gruyère, fontina, mozzarella, Swiss. . .

SERVES 6

18 to 24 large shrimp, peeled and deveined
2 tablespoons butter
2 garlic cloves, smashed and minced
I cup finely chopped cremini mushrooms or half a large
   stemmed portobello, finely chopped
Salt
Cayenne pepper
¼ cup dry sherry
¼ cup heavy cream
I cup grated cheese — Cheddar, fontina, Gruyère, or a mix
Minced fresh parsley for garnish

Steam the cleaned shrimp in the microwave with a small amount of wa-ter in a covered dish 3 to 5 minutes, or until just pink and springy to the touch. The shrimp can be cooked as much as 2 days ahead and re-frigerated.

In a medium-size skillet, melt the butter over medium-high heat. Add the garlic and the mushrooms and stir to coat. Add salt and cayenne to taste. (Be generous with the cayenne.) When the mush-rooms are well browned, add the sherry and sizzle off the alcohol for about 1 minute. Add the cream and let it come to the boil. Reduce heat to low and add the cheese, stirring constantly until smooth.

Toss in the cooked shrimp and stir to reheat. Spoon the mushroom fondue over the shrimp, piling it up on top. The cheese will have begun to congeal but don't worry, this won't affect the results. Each shrimp should have as much sauce on top as it will hold.

Pierce each shrimp with a toothpick and place them on a warm serving plate. Garnish with the parsley, and don't forget the napkins.

PER SERVING:

Carbohydrate: 1.2g plus 0.4g fiber   Protein: 10g   Fat: 14.5g

Tuna Tartare

There are only two crucial points here: one is to buy the best tuna you can find (sushi quality is the very best), and the other is to serve this dish icy cold. Otherwise, this is simplicity itself: clean and exhilarating food for a hot day.

Serves 4

1 pound tuna steak, minced
Wasabi (Japanese horseradish) to taste
4 scallions, minced, including the firm part of the green
Salt
Mizuna leaves or butter lettuce leaves for serving

Mix the first 3 ingredients together well, starting with ½ teaspoon of wasabi and adding more to taste. Add salt if desired and mix well again.

Cover the bowl with plastic wrap and refrigerate several hours or chill in the freezer 30 minutes. Serve immediately on greens.

Per serving:

Carbohydrate: 1.3g plus 0.7g fiber   Protein: 27g   Fat: 5.6g

Zucchini Posing as Fettuccine with Lemon Cream

This recipe of Nantucket cook Susan Simon's is elegant enough for a dinner party, and rich enough that it should be served before something simple and clean, like grilled fish. An excellent pasta impostor.

Serves 6

- 1 cup heavy cream
- 6 tender young zucchini, 6 to 7 inches long
- 1 rounded tablespoon grated Parmesan cheese
- Grated zest of 1 lemon
- Juice of half a lemon
- 1 tablespoon finely chopped fresh chives
- Salt and freshly ground white pepper

Put the cream in a small, heavy-bottomed saucepan and simmer to reduce by half, about 30 to 40 minutes. While the cream is reducing, cut the zucchini into "noodles": trim the ends off the zucchini and, using a vegetable peeler, cut each one into lengthwise strips. Bring a large saucepan of water to the boil.

Add the Parmesan and lemon zest to the reduced cream and continue to simmer while the zucchini cooks. Add the zucchini strips to the boiling water, stir a few times, and cook 2 minutes. Drain well. In a large bowl, toss with the lemon juice.

Add the chives to the cream mixture and pour over the zucchini. Add salt and pepper to taste. Serve hot or at room temperature.

Per serving:

Carbohydrate: 2g plus 0.4g fiber   Protein: 1.7g   Fat: 15g

Cheers!

O nly you can decide whether you're going to drink aspartame-sweetened sodas or spend some carbs on juice or alcohol. But for what it's worth, here are some ideas for beverages to serve with snacks.

Non-Alcoholic

- Arizona diet green tea with ginseng
- Fresh limeade: juice of 1 lime, sparkling mineral water, a little sweetener if you like
- Iced green tea with ginger: Add 2 tablespoons grated ginger to 2 cups steeping green tea. Add lemon or lime juice to taste, a little sweetener, and some grated citrus zest. Chill thoroughly and strain before serving.
- Mexican lime drink: Quarter 3 scrubbed Mexican limes or key limes and remove seeds. Put the limes in the blender with 2 cups cold water and blend until smooth. Add sweetener to taste.
- Chilled Tazo teas
- Diet tonic (regular tonic has as many carbs as cola) or club soda with bitters and lime

Alcoholic

- NOT champagne, which has added sugar and can be as high as 20 grams of carb per 4-ounce glass; most champagnes have about 12 grams per glass.
- Miller Lite, the lowest of the low-carb beers. When it's hot, try this over lots of ice with lime.
- Vodka and diet tonic with raspberries: a good festive choice; serve in champagne glasses.

- Lower-carb margarita: This formula avoids the sugar syrups most bars use, and the trick of using lime zest (as they do at the Frontera Grill in Chicago) cuts down on the amount of lime juice you need. For 8 margaritas, mix 1¾ cups tequila, ¼ cup triple sec, 1 teaspoon grated lime zest, ½ cup fresh lime juice, and 1 cup water. Let this brew steep in the refrigerator 6 to 8 hours. Taste and see if you need to add any sweetener. Rub the rims of the margarita glasses with lime and dip them in coarse salt (or not, as you like). Strain the margaritas into the glasses. About 2g carb for each 3½-ounce margarita.

- It's difficult to assess the carbs in distilled spirits. If they're unsweetened (rum, for instance, is sweet) they have no effect on your blood sugar level — though in excess of course they affect your liver, not to mention your resolve not to eat too many carbs.

- A glass of wine is about 3g carb, and there are many reasons (see page 27) to choose wine as your daily drink.

The Good Green Tea

All tea appears to be health-promoting because of its polyphenol content, but green tea has significantly more of these factors because it's the least processed tea, according to *Consumers Report* (November, 1999). A Harvard Medical School study showed that people who drink just one to 2 cups a day of ordinary black tea have 44 percent less risk of heart attack than nondrinkers — for multiple cups, the percentage goes up to 55.

Like resveratrol, the protective substance in red grapes and wine, the polyphenols in tea protect against both cancer and heart disease. A 1999 Swedish study reported that tea inhibits proliferation of new blood vessels, which fuel the growth of cancer tumors. This phenomenon is called anti-angiogenesis, and it's the subject of cutting edge research. At two major cancer centers, clinical trials using tea as a potential cancer treatment are under way.

The heart-protective element may be tea's function of inhibiting blood clots.

For dieters, tea — especially green tea — is important because it functions as a natural starch blocker, interfering with the action of amylase, the saliva enzyme that digests carbs. It has a similar function farther along in the digestive tract that minimizes the subsequent absorption of carbs. Carbs are released into the bloodstream more slowly, avoiding the sharp peaks of insulin they would normally inspire.

The effects of tea extracts in pill form are unclear, so it's best to drink the real thing. Use 2 heaping teaspoons for a 12-ounce teapot. Green tea tastes unpleasant if it's made with boiling water, so fill pot halfway with cold water, then add boiling. Let the tea steep 5 minutes to release its maximum antioxidant properties.

Salads

East Indian Salad

It's not always easy to know what to serve with Indian main courses —
obviously the usual flatbreads and rice and lentils and potatoes are out
of the question. This sprightly salad is a good solution.

SERVES 4

2 medium tomatoes, diced

1 European cucumber, diced

2 tablespoons roughly chopped fresh cilantro

6 scallions, chopped, including some of the green

1 tablespoon white wine vinegar

½ teaspoon coarse sea salt

¼ teaspoon ground cumin

¼ teaspoon cayenne pepper

3 tablespoons olive oil

Put the first 4 ingredients in a serving bowl. Put the vinegar in a small
bowl and add the salt; stir to dissolve. Add the cumin and cayenne to
the vinegar and whisk in the oil. Pour the dressing over the vegetables,
toss well, and serve.

PER SERVING:

Carbohydrate: 5g plus 2g fiber   Protein: 1.5g   Fat: 10.5g

The Taste of Sour:
What It Costs

Over and over again, you'll be making a choice about which sour elements to use in salad dressings, for vegetables, to perk up flavors in general. For the most part, because you use so little of these flavorings the carbs tend to be very low as well and not worth worrying about. However, if you're on a very low-carb budget, you should banish rice wine vinegar from your pantry.

An intriguing study in the *European Journal of Clinical Nutrition* in 1998 noted that adding vinegar to starchy meals lowered blood sugar levels — which may be one reason for the old folk wisdom of drinking a tablespoon of apple cider vinegar in a glass of water first thing in the morning.

1 tablespoon white vinegar	0 carb
1 tablespoon white wine vinegar	0 carb
1 tablespoon red wine vinegar	0 carb
1 tablespoon champagne vinegar	0 carb
1 tablespoon raspberry vinegar	1g carb
1 tablespoon fresh lemon juice	1.3g carb
1 tablespoon fresh lime juice	1.4g carb
1 tablespoon apple cider vinegar	2g carb
1 tablespoon balsamic vinegar	2g carb
1 tablespoon sherry vinegar	2g carb
1 tablespoon rice wine vinegar	6g carb

Cauliflower and Green Bean Salad with Mint and Garlic

The British food writer Jane Grigson unearthed this bright idea, which comes from the Abruzzi region of Italy, in an old Italian regional cookbook. Don't make the salad more than an hour ahead of time, but it will need a good half hour for the flavors to marry.

SERVES 4

2 cups diced steamed cauliflower florets, slightly crisp
2 cups diced steamed green beans, slightly crisp
Salt and pepper
2 tablespoons minced fresh mint
2 garlic cloves, minced
2 tablespoons extra-virgin olive oil
2 teaspoons fresh lemon juice

Drain the vegetables well and place them in a shallow serving bowl. Add salt and pepper to taste. Mix together the mint and garlic and scatter over the vegetables. Mix the oil and lemon juice and drizzle over the salad. Toss and set aside for 30 minutes in a cool place to season.

PER SERVING:
Carbohydrate: 4.5g plus 3.8g fiber   Protein: 2.5g   Fat: 7.5g

Carrot and Beet Salad with Ginger

None of these three salad elements is usually a low-carb choice — but there aren't so many carbs here, and this combination is so beneficial to your liver, that it's definitely worth the slight extra carb count. If you've been very seriously low-carb for a long time, this will taste almost like dessert.

SERVES 2

I medium carrot, preferably organic, scrubbed and trimmed
I medium beet, preferably organic, scrubbed and trimmed
I teaspoon chopped pickled ginger
I tablespoon olive oil
I tablespoon apple cider vinegar
Salt and pepper to taste

Grate the carrot and beet in the food processor or using the coarse holes of a hand grater. Mix the grated vegetables with the remaining ingredients. Serve right away or let sit up to 1 hour.

PER SERVING:
Carbohydrate: 5.7g plus 2.4g fiber   Protein: 1g   Fat: 1g

Red and Green Coleslaw

There absolutely couldn't be too many coleslaw recipes, so here's another one, with a little carrot for color and sweetness and two kinds of cabbage for contrast. You can shred the cabbage in a food processor or with a grater, or hand cut it as fine as possible — which coleslaw connoisseurs think is best.

SERVES 8

4 Kirby cucumbers, unpeeled and cut into fine dice
¾ pound red cabbage, shredded or cut fine (about 2 cups)
¾ pound green cabbage, shredded or cut fine (about 2 cups)
I cup diced celery
½ cup grated carrots
I green bell pepper, cored, seeded, and cut into fine dice
4 scallions, minced, including some of the green
¼ cup chopped fresh parsley

Dressing

½ cup mayonnaise
½ cup sour cream
2 tablespoons apple cider vinegar, or more to taste
I teaspoon prepared mustard, Dijon or ballpark, or more to taste
½ teaspoon celery seeds
White pepper to taste

Mix all the vegetables together in a large bowl. Mix the dressing ingredients together in a small bowl and taste for seasoning; adjust the elements to your taste.

Mix a couple of spoonfuls of dressing into the vegetables, just enough to sparsely cover them. Toss well and set aside for 30 minutes. Drain well and mix with the remaining dressing.

Cover and let season in the refrigerator at least 1 hour. If necessary, drain again before serving.

PER SERVING:
Carbohydrate: 7.8g plus 3.7g fiber   Protein: 2.9g   Fat: 14.6g

Chopped Salad

If you don't have a mandoline or some other vegetable shaver, you can still have terrific chopped salads of infinite variety. A Greek salad is the perfect example, but there are limitless possibilities in this genre. Just start thinking about various combinations of greens, low-carb vegetables, protein, cheese, and you're on your way. Look for rolls of prosciutto and mozzarella in the supermarket or just chop them separately.

Dianne Rossen Worthington, who's known as the California Cook, serves a variety of chopped salads in the summer. One of her favorites combines

Grilled eggplant and zucchini
Steamed green beans
Tomatoes
Cucumber
Lettuce
Prosciutto and mozzarella rolls, cut into bite-size pieces
Grated Parmesan cheese
Vinaigrette

Chop all the vegetables into bite-size pieces, then combine with the prosciutto-mozzarella pieces, the Parmesan, and the vinaigrette. Season to taste with salt and pepper. What could be better, or simpler? Grill the eggplant and zucchini while you're grilling something else and make this salad the next day.

Cucumber Salad with Red Pepper and Lime

This combination is almost more of a relish than a salad. It's both a little sweet and a little tart, with the refreshing elements of lime, cucumber, and mint. It takes about 2 minutes to make — and don't bother peeling the cucumber; the skin isn't tough and it offers both fiber and color.

SERVES 4

1 red bell pepper, cored, seeded, and cut into tiny dice
1 European cucumber or 6 Kirby cucumbers, cut into tiny dice
¼ cup fresh lime juice
2 scallions, chopped fine, including the firm part of the green
1 tablespoon chopped fresh mint
Salt to taste

Combine all the ingredients in a bowl and toss well. Serve at room temperature.

PER SERVING:
Carbohydrate: 4.5g plus 1.5g fiber   Protein: 1g   Fat: 0.2g

Celery and Beet Salad with Walnuts

This simple salad is good with cold meats or as part of a buffet. You can make it into a first course by crumbling a little blue cheese over the top.

SERVES 4

2 cups chopped celery, in small dice
1 medium beet, roasted, peeled, and cut into small dice
¼ cup walnut pieces
1 tablespoon chopped fresh dill
1 tablespoon minced fresh chives
¼ cup olive oil
1 tablespoon red wine vinegar
Salt and pepper to taste
¼ cup crumbled blue cheese (optional)

Mix the celery, beets, walnuts, dill, and chives together in a serving bowl.

In a small bowl mix together the oil, vinegar, salt, and pepper with a whisk. Pour the dressing over the vegetables and toss well. If you're using the cheese, scatter it over the top of the salad before serving.

PER SERVING INCLUDING CHEESE:
Carbohydrate: 3.6g plus 2g fiber   Protein: 1.9g   Fat: 18.2g

Greek Salad with Herbs

In Cyprus the "Greek" salad is made with cabbage, as I learned from Mediterranean food expert Paula Wolfert. The important things are to have several kinds of greens that balance each other and to use lots of fresh lemon juice.

Serves 6

⅓ cup olive oil, or more to taste

2 tablespoons fresh lemon juice, or more to taste

Salt and pepper to taste

1 cup finely grated cabbage

2 cups baby arugula leaves or larger leaves, torn

2 cups chopped fresh parsley

1 cup chopped fresh cilantro

6 scallions, chopped, including some of the green

12 cherry tomatoes, halved

½ cup pitted black kalamata olives

¼ cup crumbled feta cheese

Whisk the oil, lemon juice, salt, and pepper together in the bottom of a salad bowl. Add the remaining ingredients, toss well, and serve.

Per serving:
Carbohydrate: 4.7g plus 2.3g fiber   Protein: 2.7g   Fat: 14.6g

Java-Style Cauliflower Salad

This is a de-carbed version of a Madhur Jaffrey recipe that's still very delicious. It's also versatile; you can serve it hot or at room temperature, so it can be made ahead. You can also make it with beans instead of cauliflower if you'd prefer, especially Asian long beans or wing beans. Don't be tempted to skip the tiny amount of brown sugar; it's a secret ingredient that pulls everything together.

SERVES 4

1 medium cauliflower, cut into small florets

Dressing

1 garlic clove, chopped
4 teaspoons fresh lime juice
1 teaspoon dark brown sugar
¼ teaspoon cayenne pepper
¼ teaspoon salt
1 cup grated fresh coconut (see page 312)

Half a small red bell pepper, cored, seeded, and cut into tiny dice
2 tablespoons chopped fresh cilantro

Drop the cauliflower florets into a large pot of well-salted boiling water. Boil just a few minutes, until barely tender. Drain and dry on a kitchen towel.

Mix the dressing ingredients together in a blender and pour over the hot cauliflower. Toss well and transfer to a serving bowl, scattering the red pepper and cilantro on top.

PER SERVING:
Carbohydrate: 8.9g plus 6.2g fiber   Protein: 4.2g   Fat: 11g

Sizzling Omega-3 Salad

If you're getting a little tired of eating sardines all the time for their high omega-3 fatty acids, here's a very appealing alternative. Purslane is the superstar of omega-3; 1 cup has more grams than a 4¼-ounce tin of sardines. Here it's paired with merguez, the almost addictive Middle Eastern spicy lamb sausage (remember that lamb is a superior source of L-carnitine, the great synergistic partner of omega-3 oil).

And where do you get purslane? If you have a garden, you undoubtedly have it growing as a weed; if not, you can probably find it at the farmers market, or mail-order it from Indian Rock Produce (see Sources). Merguez will be at specialty stores and some supermarkets. It's worth keeping in the freezer to make this excellent — and very healthy — salad.

SERVES 4

1 European cucumber
Salt
16 cherry tomatoes
4 cups purslane, stemmed, rinsed, and dried
6 scallions, chopped, including some of the green
⅓ cup chopped fresh cilantro
4 merguez sausages, about ¾ pound altogether
¼ cup extra-virgin olive oil
1 tablespoon plus 1 teaspoon red wine vinegar
Pepper

Cut off the ends of the cucumber and rake it with a fork lengthwise all over (or you can peel it, but you'll lose some good fiber that way). Slice it in quarters lengthwise, then cut across to make chunks about ⅓ inch thick. Salt the chunks lightly and set them aside to drain in a colander for 30 minutes.

Meanwhile, cut the cherry tomatoes in half and salt them lightly; set aside.

Mix the purslane with the scallions and cilantro in a large bowl.

Slice the sausages ½ inch thick and fry the slices (you may need a little olive oil if the sausage is very lean) in a wide skillet over medium-high heat, turning the slices from time to time. When they're crusty and cooked through, drain them on paper towels and add them to the salad bowl along with the tomatoes. Pat the cucumbers dry and add them to the bowl.

Mix the oil and vinegar with salt and pepper to taste. Toss the salad with the dressing and serve immediately.

PER SERVING:
Carbohydrate: 6.8g plus 2.7g fiber   Protein: 23.5g   Fat: 31.2g

Broccoli Sprouts

These tasty little shoots are great in salads and atop sandwiches and stir-frys. They have all the broccoli nutrients — vitamins A and C plus other antioxidants — and, in addition, a cancer-fighting compound called sulforaphane. Broccoli has this same compound, but the sprouts have fifty times more. Attention, George Bush . . . look for these at your supermarket or the natural foods store.

Zesty Thai Salad

This incredibly simple salad is good with barbecued dishes, grilled fish or chicken, or almost anything that needs a little fresh zip. It tastes best at room temperature, so remember to take it out of the fridge 20 minutes or so before you serve it.

SERVES 4

1 large cucumber, peeled and diced
1 bunch of fat red radishes, trimmed and diced
2 tablespoons snipped fresh chives
1 small fresh chili pepper, minced (optional)
2 tablespoons minced cilantro
¼ cup champagne vinegar
1 tablespoon Splenda low-calorie sweetener, or more to taste

Put the first 5 ingredients in a serving bowl. In a small saucepan, heat the vinegar until it comes to a boil. Off heat, stir in the Splenda and taste, adding more if necessary.

Toss the vegetables with the dressing, cover, and refrigerate or set aside to season for a couple of hours before serving. Serve at room temperature.

PER SERVING:
Carbohydrate: 2.7g plus 1g fiber   Protein: 0.8g   Fat: 0.2g

BLT Salad

In the height of summer, few things are as satisfying for lunch as a bacon, lettuce, and tomato sandwich. Make it with a slice of toasted protein bread for the base and top with a big soft lettuce leaf and you've got a relatively low-carb treat. For even fewer carbs, though, try this salad, which has all the great flavors plus crunchy bacon-flavored croutons.

To make this into a main course, add strips of roasted chicken and some cubed avocado.

As with any BLT, it's essential to use the best ingredients. Niman Ranch bacon (see Sources) is the one that makes my heart beat faster.

SERVES 4

8 slices bacon

4 cups salad greens — romaine or a mixture

Salt and pepper to taste

1 slice Alvarado Street Bakery California Bread (see page 101) or other low-carb bread, cubed

2 tomatoes *or* 1 pint cherry tomatoes, cut into small chunks

4 scallions, sliced, including some of the green

¼ cup olive oil

4 teaspoons fresh lemon juice

Fry the bacon until golden brown and drain well on paper towels, reserving the bacon drippings in the pan.

In a large salad bowl, arrange the greens. Sprinkle with salt and pepper and mix with your hands to distribute the seasonings.

When you're ready to serve the salad, heat the bacon drippings until hot but not smoking. Add the bread cubes and cook until crunchy and golden brown, turning frequently. Drain well on paper towels.

Mix the salad greens again and toss with the tomatoes and scallions. Crumble the bacon and add to the salad. Mix the oil and lemon juice together well and pour over the salad. Add the croutons and toss well. Serve immediately.

PER SERVING:

Carbohydrate: 6g plus 3g fiber   Protein: 9g   Fat: 40g

Smoked Trout Salad

This minimalist salad is sweet, delicate, and smoky all at the same time — a lovely spring salad. The smoked trout fillets from Ducktrap Farm (see page 99) are particularly delicious, and reasonably priced.

SERVES 2

2 smoked trout fillets

3 cups mixed spring greens

Handful of pea shoots, if available

2 scallions, chopped, including the light green

I tablespoon champagne vinegar

Salt and pepper to taste

2 tablespoons olive oil, or more to taste

2 deviled eggs with dill (optional)

Pull the skin off the trout fillets and break the fish into bite-size pieces.

Arrange the greens, pea shoots, and scallions in a bowl and top with the trout pieces.

Mix the vinegar, salt, and pepper, then add oil to taste and whisk together. Pour the dressing over the salad and toss to combine.

Serve the salad on salad plates with the deviled eggs arranged on the side.

PER SERVING INCLUDING THE EGG:

Carbohydrate: 3.5g plus 2.5g fiber   Protein: 21.7g   Fat: 23g

Tuna Salad with Beans and Broccoli

On a hot night — or just a busy one when there's no time to cook — this salad can be dinner in moments. I used to make a salad like this one with garbanzo beans, which you could also use, but your carb debt would go way up. You'll find these black soybeans are a tasty alternative.

SERVES 6

6½-ounce can tuna packed in olive oil, drained

15-ounce can Eden black soybeans, rinsed under running water

1 cup broccoli florets, steamed 5 minutes or microwaved just until tender

2 scallions, chopped, including the firm part of the green

Half a red bell pepper, cored, seeded, and diced

Handful of fresh basil, chopped

Handful of fresh parsley, chopped

2 tablespoons olive oil

2 teaspoons red wine vinegar

1 garlic clove

Salt and pepper

Mix the tuna, soybeans, broccoli, scallions, red pepper, basil, and parsley together in a serving bowl.

In a small bowl, mix the oil and vinegar. Spear the garlic clove on a fork and use the fork to whisk the oil and vinegar together until they begin to emulsify. Add salt and pepper to taste. Whisk again with the garlic clove and pour over the salad, tossing well to combine.

PER SERVING:

Carbohydrate: 5g plus 5.6g fiber   Protein: 21.8g   Fat: 13.5g

Bring on the Sardines

In addition to their omega-3 content, sardines also contain huge amounts of nucleic acids, the DNA and RNA that reproduce healthy young cells.

People either love these oily, bony little fish or they hate them. Still, if you have certain health problems, you need to learn to love them. Start by buying lightly smoked tiny sardines packed in olive oil, then drain them and give them a good squeeze of fresh lemon juice. Then progress to some of these ideas, served on greens or low-carb crackers or toast:

- Mash the drained sardines and add a little chopped red onion, a little horseradish, and enough mayonnaise to make it all stick together. About 1g carb per 4¼ ounce serving.
- Mash the drained sardines and add 1 minced scallion, including some of the firm green part, a big squeeze of fresh lemon juice, and lots of minced parsley. About 1g carb.
- Mash the drained sardines and add 1 minced scallion, ¼ minced seeded jalapeño pepper (or more to taste), a little chopped cilantro, a little cumin, and a big squeeze of fresh lime juice. A little over 1g carb.

Tuna Salad with Watercress

This is one of those throw-it-together salads that can be dinner or lunch — and quite tasty. Obviously you can add other elements, such as cherry tomatoes or radishes, if you have them on hand.

SERVES 4

5 cups watercress, heavy stems chopped

2 celery ribs, chopped, including any tender leaves

1 European cucumber, unpeeled, chopped

4 scallions, chopped, including the firm part of the green

Handful of fresh cilantro

Salt

Olive oil

Champagne vinegar

Freshly ground pepper to taste

1 avocado, chopped

2 (6½-ounce) cans chunk light tuna in olive oil, very well
    drained and chunked with a fork

Mix the watercress, celery, cucumber, scallions, and cilantro in a salad bowl. Add a sprinkle of salt to taste, and toss the greens with your hands.

Add a trickle of olive oil over the greens — start with about 2 tablespoons — and toss with the greens, adding more oil if desired. Sprinkle vinegar on top — starting with about 2 teaspoons — and grind some pepper over the greens. Toss well and taste for seasoning, oil, and vinegar. Scatter the avocado and tuna chunks over the top of the salad and toss again gently before serving.

PER SERVING:
Carbohydrate: 4.2g plus 4.8g fiber   Protein: 9g   Fat: 18.8g

Tuna Tasting

Anyone on a low-carb diet will be opening many a can of tuna fish — inexpensive high-quality protein (plus the good omega-3 oils) in an irresistibly handy package. Most traditional dieters have come to think of white tuna canned in water as the gold standard, but strange as it seems (see the *New York Times*, February 4, 1998), this tasteless tuna in fact has just as much fat, if not more, than light tuna packed in oil (provided, of course, that you drain off the oil — the longer you drain it, the more oil comes out; 20 minutes in a strainer will give you quite lean tuna). There's a whole world of tasty light tuna out there, most of it packed in olive oil, some of it wildly expensive. Here's how the cans stack up in my cupboard.

Best:

Genoa Yellowfin tuna from Italy, packed in olive oil. The little gold-and-red cans hold my favorite locally available tuna, about 30 to 40 cents more per can than the runner-up, and nearly as good as the terrific tuna you can buy in Italy and Spain. This is the tuna to use for salade niçoise.

Progresso Chunk light tuna packed in olive oil. The *New York Times* prefers this brand to Genoa, and ever since the paper touted it, the price has gone up, often beyond Genoa's.

Very good:

Bumblebee Chunk light tuna packed in olive oil. This is my everyday tuna, the one I choose for the instant lunch. It's slightly more expensive than ordinary chunk light tuna packed in generic vegetable oil, but much, much tastier.

And that's it; for me, none of the other supermarket brands are up to scratch. But obviously that's very much a matter of personal taste. Since you'll probably be eating a lot of tuna, you might as well conduct your own tuna tasting and see what you think.

There are times — when you're serving a salade niçoise, for instance — when you want a really spectacular canned tuna. The gourmet stores have a bewilderment of choices, but here are some recommendations.

- Ortiz: Good chewy texture, almost like fresh, packed in a good oil and quite light
- Albo: Heavier oil than Ortiz, saltier, more like classic tuna
- Rizzoli: This smoked tuna is either great or terrible, depending on how you feel about smoked anything
- La Giara: The winner, this brand has great flavor and texture with a fine balance of oil and salt

Not the Same Old Salad

Inevitably people on a low-carb diet have lots and lots of both tuna salad and egg salad, which can get a little monotonous. Here are some ideas that go beyond the good old classic American versions.

Egg Salads

Tip: Grate the hard-cooked eggs on the large holes of a grater for a particularly appealing look and texture.

- With herbs: chopped parsley, dill, cilantro, and scallions
- Indian: with curry powder, chopped cilantro, and scallions
- Middle Eastern: with cumin, chopped arugula, and red pepper flakes
- Russian: with sour cream mixed with mayonnaise, chives, dill, and some chopped smoked salmon

Tuna Salads

Tip: Use chunk light tuna packed in olive oil.

- Italian: with capers, chopped olive, chopped red onion, parsley, and a little lemon juice
- Asian: with a dash of rice wine vinegar, toasted sesame seeds, scallions, and chopped radish
- Middle Eastern: with cumin, chopped scallions, cilantro, and mint
- Mexican: with cumin, chopped tomato, scallions, minced chilies, and cilantro

Soups and Stews

Spring Green Soup

When asparagus comes in, along with it comes a cornucopia of other sweet earthy things, such as the new garlic with its greens attached and the first tender leaves of basil. If you can get true spring garlic at a nearby farmers market or from your own garden, by all means use a bulb of it, chopped fine, for this rich but delicate soup. If not, fat cloves of store-bought garlic will be just fine.

If you're serving this elegant soup to company, as you certainly could, pass it through a sieve or a food mill to remove the bits of fiber. For a homey meal, by all means keep the fiber.

The soup is also delicious cold, in which case you might want to garnish with a few bits of smoked salmon and sprinkle chives on top before you serve it.

SERVES 4

1 bunch asparagus, about 1½ pounds
1 tablespoon butter
4 garlic cloves, pressed, or 1 bulb spring garlic, finely chopped
   (see above)
4 cups chicken or vegetable broth
2 egg yolks
1 cup cream
Salt
2 tablespoons torn fresh basil for garnish (optional)
Freshly ground pepper

Trim the asparagus and cut the stalks into 1-inch lengths, saving the tips for a garnish.

Melt the butter in a soup pot over medium heat and add the garlic, stirring so it doesn't burn. When it's just starting to color a bit, add the chicken broth and the asparagus (except the tips). Bring the soup to the boil, then turn down the heat to low and cover the pot, leaving the lid slightly ajar. Let the soup simmer gently 20 minutes.

Meanwhile, steam the asparagus tips just until done, about 2 minutes, and set aside.

Off heat, blend the soup in the pan using an immersion blender. Or transfer it to a regular blender, covering the top with a thick kitchen towel so the soup doesn't foam up and burn your hand.

Whisk the egg yolks together in a small bowl and add the cream, whisking thoroughly. Add several spoonfuls of the hot soup one at a time, stirring to blend well. Stir the cream mixture into the soup pot and heat very gently for 2 minutes — do not let the soup come to a boil or the eggs and cream will curdle. Taste and correct for salt if necessary.

Ladle the soup into hot soup bowls, add the reserved asparagus tips, and top with the basil. Grind a little pepper on top and serve immediately.

Per serving:

Carbohydrate: 7.9g plus 3.7g fiber   Protein: 8.7g   Fat: 29.8g

Spanish Garlic Soup

This is one of those soups that are greater than the sum of their parts, which in this case are very few. It's also homey, something you'd serve on a Sunday night just to take the edge off your hunger. Instead of rustic bread, we'll be using low-carb bread, which is tasty but can't withstand extended heating in the soup.

SERVES 2

4 fat garlic cloves
2 tablespoons olive oil
I slice low-carb bread, cut into cubes
4 cups water
Salt and pepper to taste
2 large eggs, each cracked into a saucer
Chopped fresh parsley for garnish

Smash the garlic cloves and remove the skins. Heat the olive oil in a large saucepan and add the garlic and the bread cubes. Sauté them over medium-high heat, stirring constantly and being careful not to let them get beyond the golden stage. Remove the bread cubes with a slotted spoon and set aside.

Add the water to the garlic and oil along with the salt and pepper. Bring to a simmer and cook 15 minutes. Return the bread cubes to the soup and stir them in well. Lower the heat a bit and slide the eggs into the broth to poach.

When the eggs are done, remove each with a slotted spoon to a warm soup bowl and carefully ladle the broth around them. Garnish with parsley and serve immediately.

PER SERVING
Carbohydrate: 6.5g plus 1.5g fiber   Protein: 9.5g   Fat: 20.3g

Ethereal Mexican Soup

This exquisitely light soup is a perfect evening meal — and if you add the cooked chicken you have a one-dish dinner. The key is to use a good chicken broth, either homemade or a good natural foods store brand.

SERVES 4

2 chipotle chilies (smoked jalapeños, either dried or canned)
4 garlic cloves, minced
4 cups chicken broth
2 cups cooked chicken (optional)
I avocado, finely diced
½ cup chopped fresh cilantro

Simmer the chilies and garlic in the chicken broth 30 minutes. Strain the broth and return to the pot. Bring back to a simmer and add the chicken.

Ladle the soup into warmed soup bowls and sprinkle with the avocado bits and the cilantro. Serve immediately.

PER SERVING, WITHOUT CHICKEN:
Carbohydrate: 5.3g plus 2.9g fiber   Protein: 3.4g   Fat: 3.4g

Yellow Gazpacho

There's something especially appealing about a cold yellow soup — but of course you can make this gazpacho with red tomatoes and red peppers if you'd rather. This is a food processor soup, so once the vegetables are prepped, it goes like lightning.

SERVES 8

4 yellow tomatoes, peeled, cored, seeded, and chunked
2 yellow bell peppers, cored, seeded, and chunked
2 cups chicken broth
¼ cup champagne vinegar
1 teaspoon minced garlic
2 celery ribs, strings removed, chopped
4 scallions, white part only, chopped (save the greens)
½ teaspoon ground cumin
Salt and pepper to taste
½ cup olive oil
2 tablespoons minced fresh cilantro for garnish

Combine everything but the reserved scallion greens, olive oil, and cilantro in a food processor and puree until mostly smooth but still slightly chunky. Taste for seasoning and correct. Pour the soup into a bowl and whisk in the olive oil by hand.

Cover the soup and chill at least 1 hour and up to 3 hours. Whisk again before serving, and check the seasonings. Mince the firm green parts of the scallions and mix with the cilantro. Scatter some of the minced greens over each serving.

PER SERVING:

Carbohydrate: 5.2g plus 1.8g fiber   Protein: 2.2g   Fat: 21.1g

Zucchini Vichyssoise

Who says there's no vichyssoise without potatoes? This insanely simple recipe comes from Manhattan chef Rozanne Gold, who's famous for her elegant three-ingredient recipes. It's important to use the white pepper she calls for — with so few ingredients, the flavors are crucial. I like to garnish the soup with a little snipped mint.

Serves 4

¾ cup heavy cream

1 teaspoon salt

Freshly ground white pepper

½ cup finely chopped shallots

¾ pound zucchini (about 2 medium-large), trimmed and thinly sliced

Slivered mint leaves for garnish

Put everything but the mint in a medium-size saucepan and bring it almost to the boil. Lower the heat immediately and simmer 15 minutes, until the zucchini is soft.

Using an immersion blender, puree the soup until it's smooth. Or put it in a regular blender, in two batches. Transfer to a bowl or pitcher and let cool. Cover and chill several hours.

Before serving, taste for salt and white pepper and adjust seasoning. If the soup is too thick, add a little cool water and stir in well.

Serve in small bowls with mint slivers floating on top.

Per serving:
Carbohydrate: 6.2g plus 0.4g fiber   Protein: 3.7g   Fat: 16.8g

Cream of Spinach Soup

This classic is as delicious as ever, good for a homey meal or dressed up for company. The flavor is best if you make it with fresh spinach, but left-over cooked spinach will also be good, and even frozen spinach works.

Garnish the soup with a couple of poached oysters per person for an elegant starter, or just snipped chives, crumbled bacon bits, or Ri-cotta Puffs (see page 173).

SERVES 4 TO 6

4 tablespoons (½ stick) butter

4 scallions, trimmed and chopped, including the firm part of the green

2 garlic cloves, pressed or minced

4 cups chicken or vegetable broth (low-sodium canned is fine)

I pound fresh spinach *or* I cup leftover cooked spinach

½ cup heavy cream

Pinch of nutmeg

Pinch of sugar

Instant flour to thicken, if needed

Salt and pepper

For garnish: poached oysters, crumbled bacon bits, or snipped chives

Melt the butter in a soup pot and add the scallions and garlic. Cook over medium-low heat, covered, for several minutes, until the vegetables turn golden. Add the chicken broth and the spinach, bring to the boil, then lower the heat to a simmer. Cook until the spinach is done, about 10 minutes for fresh.

Blend the soup to a puree in a blender or use an immersion blender right in the pot. (You can make the soup ahead to this point.)

About 10 minutes before serving, add the cream, nutmeg, and sugar and heat through. If the soup is too thin, add a little instant flour and cook several minutes more. Check the seasoning, and add salt and pepper to taste. Serve hot, with one of the suggested garnishes.

PER SERVING:
Carbohydrate: 4.5g plus 3.7g fiber   Protein: 6.5g   Fat: 25g

Ricotta Puffs

Faith Willinger, one of the divas of Italian food, dreamed up this very appealing idea for garnishing soup. It's a twist on the French quenelles, elegant little puffs that are tricky to make.

Faith's version is completely minimalist. Just drain some ricotta (full-fat, of course; to make your own, see page 345) for an hour or so in a fine strainer. Using two spoons, make little ovals of ricotta and perch them on top of the hot soup or on the rim of the soup plate. At the table, they can be stirred into the soup or just enjoyed bite by bite.

You can mix some chopped fresh herbs into the drained ricotta or any number of other tidbits. Each little puff will set you back less than 1g carb.

Cream of Walnut Soup

This old French soup is almost inexplicably delicious and very easy to prepare. If you live in a place where they make a fuss over the new walnut crop, such as northern California, buy the fresh walnuts and rush home to make this soup.

SERVES 6

6 ounces walnut pieces, about 1½ cups
1 large garlic clove, smashed, peeled, and minced
4 cups chicken or vegetable broth (canned is fine) or less, as needed
½ cup heavy cream
Salt and pepper

Put the walnuts and the garlic in a blender or food processor with a little of the chicken broth and blend until you have a smooth paste. Slowly add the remaining broth, just until the soup is creamy — don't thin it out too much.

Pour the soup through a fine sieve into a saucepan and bring to the boil. Remove the soup from the heat, add the cream, stir in well, and add salt and pepper to taste. Serve immediately in warmed soup bowls.

PER SERVING:
Carbohydrate: 3.4g plus 1.4g fiber   Protein: 8.6g   Fat: 24.7g

Quick Mexican Black Bean Soup

This is a fairly speedy soup made of several convenience foods you should keep on hand for emergency meals. Any kind of salsa will be fine, as will chipotle puree (page 221). But only the canned black soybeans from Eden and the Muir Glen tomatoes, available at natural foods stores, will work here, and they're such good products you should keep them around in any case.

SERVES 6

2 tablespoons olive oil

I small onion, chopped

I teaspoon ground cumin

I teaspoon dried oregano

Salt and pepper

I tablespoon salsa or chipotle puree (optional)

2 (14½-ounce) cans low-sodium chicken or vegetable broth

I cup Muir Glen organic canned tomatoes with green chilies, with juice

15-ounce can Eden black soybeans, well rinsed

Grated Jack or Muenster cheese for garnish

Heat the oil in a large saucepan and add the onion, sautéing over medium heat until soft but not brown. Add the cumin and oregano, and season to taste with salt and pepper. Sauté lightly to release the aroma of the spices, then stir in the salsa.

Add the chicken broth, tomatoes, and soybeans and bring to a simmer. Serve in warm bowls with a garnish of grated cheese.

PER SERVING:

Carbohydrate: 5.9g plus 5g fiber   Protein: 15.8g   Fat: 14g

Quick and Creamy Bean Soup with Mushrooms and Leeks

Although this is a from-scratch soup, you can make it in no time. It's essential to use the canned black soybeans from Eden, available at the natural foods store and many supermarkets. Ordinary black beans will be far too high in carbs.

Serves 4

15-ounce can Eden black soybeans
1 large leek, trimmed and carefully washed
3 tablespoons butter
½ teaspoon dried thyme
Pinch of cayenne pepper
Salt and black pepper
½ pound cremini mushrooms, stemmed, wiped clean, and
    chopped
14½-ounce can low-sodium chicken or vegetable broth
1 cup heavy cream
Chopped fresh parsley for garnish (optional)

Dump the soybeans into a colander in the sink and rinse off the gelatinous juice. Drain well.

Quarter the leek lengthwise, including the light green parts, and slice thin. Melt the butter in a medium-size saucepan and add the leeks, thyme, cayenne, and salt and pepper to taste. Sauté gently over medium heat until the leeks are soft.

Raise the heat to medium-high and add the mushrooms, stirring in well. Sauté until the mushrooms collapse.

Dump the drained beans into the workbowl of a food processor along with half the chicken broth; process to a smooth puree. Scrape the beans into the saucepan and add the remaining broth and the cream. Stir in well and adjust the seasoning. Bring the soup to a bare simmer and serve hot in warmed bowls, sprinkled with parsley if you like.

Per serving:

Carbohydrate: 10g plus 8.1g fiber   Protein: 23.2g   Fat: 40.9g

Hearty Portuguese Soup

This soup seems to have everything in it — except the usual ingredients. This is bracing fare for a cold winter's night.

SERVES 8

2 pounds beef shank

1 ham hock

2 pounds cauliflower, cut into 1-inch pieces

2 carrots, peeled and cut into 1-inch pieces

1 large cabbage, cut into chunks

1 pound turnips, peeled and cut into 1-inch pieces

1 pound smoked sausage, such as kielbasa if Portuguese
     sausage (linguiça) is unavailable

13-ounce can garbanzo beans (chickpeas), drained and rinsed

Salt and pepper

Place the beef shank and ham hock in a soup kettle and cover with cold water by a couple of inches. Bring to a boil, reduce the heat to a simmer, partially cover, and let cook 2 hours, skimming off any foam on the surface.

Add the cauliflower, carrots, cabbage, and turnips and continue cooking, partially covered. When the vegetables are just beginning to soften, after about 15 minutes, slice the sausage and add it along with the garbanzos. Add more water to cover if necessary. When the vegetables are tender, the soup is done.

Remove the beef shank and ham hock and slice off the meat. Scoop out the vegetables and sausage and remove to a bowl. Measure the broth; you should have about 10 cups; if you have more, boil it down until you have 10 cups.

Season the broth with salt and pepper to taste. Return the meat and vegetables to the broth and let the soup simmer a few minutes. Serve in warm bowls.

PER SERVING:
Carbohydrate: 19.7g plus 10g fiber   Protein: 40.8g   Fat: 22.7g

177

Serious Soup

Another hearty soup, this one is sort of a cross between pot roast and minestrone. It's good for what ails you and it's very consoling on a cold winter night. Make it a day ahead for the best flavor, and add the last four ingredients shortly before you serve it.

If your butcher has beef bones, by all means throw one into the pot with the brisket.

SERVES 8

2 pounds beef brisket
8 cups beef broth, preferably unsalted
½ teaspoon dried thyme
1 tablespoon salt (omit if you're using salted beef broth)
1 tablespoon olive oil
4 cloves garlic, minced
1 cup chopped onion
1 cup chopped celery
1 green bell pepper, cored, seeded, and chopped
1 cup chopped green beans
2 medium turnips, peeled and diced
2 medium zucchini, diced
14½-ounce can Muir Glen diced organic tomatoes, including the juice
2 tablespoons tomato paste
¼ cup chopped fresh herbs, such as parsley and basil (optional)

Trim any visible fat from the brisket. Put the brisket in a heavy soup pot and pour the broth over it. Add the thyme and salt if the broth isn't already salted, cover, and bring to a boil. Skim off any foam and lower the heat to a simmer. Let the brisket cook 3 hours, partially covered, or until the meat is cooked through. Remove the pot from the heat and refrigerate overnight or long enough for the fat to congeal on the surface for easy removal.

Return the defatted soup to the heat. Heat the olive oil in a skillet and add the garlic, onion, celery, bell pepper, beans, and turnips. Sauté vegetables until lightly browned, then add to the soup, along with more water if necessary to cover. Simmer covered 1 hour, or until the vegetables are tender (remove the soup bone at this point). Remove the brisket, dice it, and return it to the soup. (The soup may be made ahead up to this point. Store covered in the refrigerator and reheat before continuing.)

Return the soup to a simmer and add the zucchini, tomatoes, and tomato paste. Simmer uncovered 10 minutes and taste for seasoning. Serve immediately in warm bowls, scattered with fresh herbs if you like.

PER SERVING:
Carbohydrate: 9g plus 3g fiber   Protein: 26g   Fat: 32.7g

Simple Scallop Stew

You could do all sorts of interesting things to this very basic dish to make it more exotic, but I think this irresistibly simple way of cooking it may just be the best. Besides, it's ready in less than 10 minutes — just add a nice sharp salad and whatever passes for bread at your house (Wasa fiber rye crackers, low-carb tortillas, etc.) and you've got dinner. You may not even need salt, since the scallops may be salty enough on their own.

SERVES 4

1 pound bay scallops
3 cups half-and-half
Salt and pepper to taste
4 tablespoons (½ stick) butter

Place the scallops in a heavy saucepan and add water to barely cover them. Heat gently 3 to 5 minutes, just until they turn opaque; don't let them boil or they'll be tough. Add the half-and-half and heat thoroughly. Taste for salt and pepper and adjust the seasoning.

Ladle the stew into warm bowls and top each bowl with a tablespoon of butter. Serve immediately.

PER SERVING:
Carbohydrate: 8.7g   Protein: 25.2g   Fat: 30.5g

Main Dishes

Omelet Cake

This traditional French stack of omelets with various flavors is called a *crespou*. Although it seems like a bit of a fuss, it's quite simple to make, and you can do it well ahead and serve it at room temperature. It makes an impressive brunch or lunch in spring, or whenever asparagus is around in your area.

In France the *crespou* is served unadorned, but it would also be delicious with a red pepper sauce or a simple tomato sauce.

SERVES 4

¼ cup olive oil

12 large eggs

Salt and pepper

4 medium zucchini, thinly sliced

¼ pound asparagus, cut into 1-inch lengths

20 kalamata olives, pitted

2 garlic cloves, minced

Handful of fresh basil, torn into small pieces

1 teaspoon fresh thyme, chopped, or ½ teaspoon dried thyme

4 tablespoons (½ stick) butter

Preheat the oven to 375°F.

Line a baking sheet with foil and grease it with a little of the olive oil.

Set out 4 bowls and break 3 eggs into each one. Season the eggs with salt and pepper to taste.

Heat the rest of the olive oil in a skillet and sauté the zucchini slices until they're just tender, about 5 minutes. Drain well and add to the first bowl.

Boil the asparagus for 2 minutes in salted water, drain well, and add to the second bowl.

Add the olives and garlic to the third bowl.

Add the basil and thyme to the fourth bowl.

Now start making the omelets; each one will use half a bowl of egg mixture and they should be cooked in order, so that the flavors alternate. Add half a tablespoon of butter to the pan each time and stack the omelets on the foil-covered pan as you finish them.

Flip the last omelet on its back, so that the cooked side is facing up.

Bake the omelet stack for 15 minutes, then let it stand for 15 minutes before serving. Or serve later, at room temperature.

PER SERVING:

Carbohydrate: 8.6g plus 3.2g fiber   Protein: 27.6g   Fat: 49g

The Cheese Lunch

This little repast is somewhere between antipasto and dinner. But it's a great low-carb meal, good for any season, and greeted with enthusiasm by guests, whether they're into the low-carb lifestyle or not. Arrange it all on platters and in small bowls. Here are the elements:

- Several kinds of cheese — see "The Cheese Course," page 320, for possibilities
- Cured meats, such as prosciutto, Black Forest ham, salamis
- Trimmed radishes
- Cherry tomatoes
- Low-carb pickles
- Celery sticks
- Assorted olives
- A big green salad
- Sesame breadsticks for low-carbers, sliced bread for the rest
- Lots of red wine

Arugula Omelet
with Walnut Salad

You can do this trick with any omelet — cutting it into strips and serving it over salad — but it's especially appealing with arugula and walnuts.

Good for lunch and equally good for a fast supper.

Serves 2

¼ cup walnut pieces
¼ cup olive oil
1 tablespoon red wine vinegar
Salt and pepper
4 large eggs
2 tablespoons butter
2 handfuls chopped arugula
3 cups baby salad greens such as mesclun

Toast the walnuts in a toaster oven at 350°F for 2 minutes. Whisk the oil and vinegar together, and add salt and pepper to taste.

Whisk eggs with salt and pepper to taste. Add a splash of water and whisk again.

Heat the butter in a large skillet. When it's bubbling, add the arugula and stir until it's just wilted.

Pour in the eggs and let them cook over medium heat, lifting up the edges with a spatula to let the uncooked egg reach the bottom of the pan.

Toss the salad greens with the vinaigrette and the warm walnuts.

When the eggs are just set, cut the finished omelet into skinny strips and arrange, cooked side up, over the salad on individual plates.

Per serving:
Carbohydrate: 4g plus 2.3g fiber   Protein: 21.7g   Fat: 60.6g

Welsh Rarebit

If you're not of a certain age, you may never have eaten this classic dish, which was more or less banned after the dawning of the low-fat era. Almost certainly you don't have a chafing dish to cook it in. But it's great just made in a heavy pan; use the sharpest cheese you can find and serve it with a zesty salad of winter greens and a bottle of low-carb beer.

SERVES 4

12-ounce can Miller Lite beer
1 tablespoon butter
1 pound very sharp Cheddar cheese, grated
1 tablespoon Colman's dry mustard
1 tablespoon Worcestershire sauce
Cayenne pepper to taste
4 slices low-carb bread, toasted and cut into 4 triangles each
Paprika

Pour the beer into a pitcher and let it sit while you make the rarebit.

Melt the butter in a chafing dish or a heavy pan over low heat. Add the cheese and melt it slowly, stirring in one direction with a wooden spoon. As the cheese melts, add the beer gradually as well as the mustard, Worcestershire sauce, and cayenne, continuing to stir. Keep the heat low — if the cheese gets too hot, it will seize up and become stringy.

When the mixture is completely smooth, arrange 4 toast triangles on each plate and pour the cheese sauce over them. Sprinkle with paprika and serve immediately.

PER SERVING:
Carbohydrate: 13.3g plus 2.9g fiber   Protein: 35.3g   Fat: 24.5g

Poblano Cheese Tacos

No Mexican in his right mind would ever concoct anything like this, but there are times when you just crave something simple and earthy — and this will satisfy that craving. The tacos are a little leathery by ordinary tortilla standards, but never mind, they taste good.

If you live in a poblano-free area, you could conceivably use canned chilies — just be sure to blot them thoroughly dry.

SERVES 2

2 poblano chilies, roasted and peeled (see page 122)
2 low-carb tortillas (see Sources)
4 large slices Muenster cheese
2 tablespoons salsa

Carefully cut out the stem from the chilies, leaving the flesh as intact as you can around the shoulders. Scrape out the seeds and cut the chilies lengthwise, opening them out like a book.

Toast one side of the tortillas directly over an open flame or an electric burner, very briefly, just until they take on a little color. Place them toasted side down on a baking sheet.

Preheat the broiler. Arrange the chilies over the tortillas and cover them with cheese.

Broil the tortillas just until the cheese melts and the edges of the tortillas are golden brown. This is pan-to-mouth food: Fold the tortillas around the filling, add salsa, and enjoy immediately.

PER SERVING:
Carbohydrate: 7.8g plus 13.7g fiber   Protein: 6.5g   Fat: 8.5g

Border Quiche

Quiche doesn't seem like quite the right word for a Mexican dish — but quiche this is, with a zesty attitude that's very appealing to those who are getting a little tired of plain eggs. If you have access to a Mexican market, use roasted poblano chilies and *queso fresco*.

SERVES 6

Butter for the quiche pan
6 large eggs
I cup heavy cream
Several drops of hot pepper sauce, or to taste
Salt and pepper to taste
3-ounce can diced green chilies
¼ pound chorizo, crumbled, fried, and drained
I cup diced Muenster cheese
⅓ cup chopped fresh cilantro
⅓ cup chopped scallions, including the firm part of the green

Preheat the oven to 350°F. Have ready a buttered 8-inch quiche pan.

Beat the eggs in a bowl with the cream, hot pepper sauce, and salt and pepper. Add the remaining ingredients, mix well, and pour into the quiche pan. Bake 40 minutes, or until golden brown on top. Serve hot, warm, or at room temperature.

PER SERVING:
Carbohydrate: 3.8g plus 0.6g fiber   Protein: 21.9g   Fat: 42.7g

Redneck Quiche

This duded-up version of Wheezer's Cheese Pie (*More White Trash Cooking,* Ten Speed Press, 1998) is really just a reorganized quiche. But its crust is made of cheese, a great idea, and of course you can leave out the vegetables if you'd rather, or substitute others, such as broccoli or spinach. You can also use almost any cheese you have lying around.

Serve the quiche with a sharp, refreshing green salad to counter the richness — try watercress, radicchio, endive, escarole, radishes, or whatever else appeals to you.

SERVES 4

1 tablespoon butter

1 tablespoon olive oil

2 shallots, minced

1 pound mushrooms, wiped clean, trimmed, and diced

Salt and pepper

1 cup grated Cheddar cheese

1 cup grated mozzarella cheese

1 cup grated Monterey Jack cheese

4 scallions, chopped

2 tablespoons flour

4 large eggs

1 cup milk

½ teaspoon salt

1 teaspoon Colman's dry mustard

1 teaspoon Worcestershire sauce

Hot pepper sauce to taste

Shake of paprika

Butter for the pie plate

Preheat the oven to 350°F. Heat the butter and olive oil in a large skillet and when they're bubbling, add the shallots. Cook over medium heat until soft, about 3 minutes, then add the mushrooms, stirring from time to time as they cook. Once they've released their liquid, cook until they're dry and beginning to brown. Add salt and pepper to taste.

Meanwhile, mix the cheeses together in a bowl and add the scallions and flour, combining well. In another bowl, whisk the eggs lightly, then add the remaining ingredients except the butter for the pie plate.

Butter a 9-inch pie plate. Spread the cheese mixture inside the pie plate and up the edges, pressing down to make a crust. Spread the mushrooms over the cheese and pour the egg mixture on top.

Bake 35 to 40 minutes, until golden brown on top.

PER SERVING:
Carbohydrate: 13.4g plus 2.2g fiber   Protein: 31.2g   Fat: 41g

Border Beanburgers

These might be called soyburgers, since they're made from black soybeans, but that sounds so grim and these are so tasty. The mayo is the secret ingredient here, a great idea from *Good Housekeeping* magazine.

SERVES 4

15-ounce can Eden black soybeans, rinsed and drained

1 garlic clove, pressed or minced

2 scallions, minced

1 slice low-carb bread, in crumbs

½ teaspoon ground cumin

2 tablespoons mayonnaise

¼ cup grated Parmesan cheese

½ teaspoon salt

Pepper to taste

Generous shake of hot pepper sauce

½ cup chopped fresh cilantro

Olive oil

Salsa, guacamole, and shredded romaine lettuce for serving (optional)

Dump the beans, which will still be a bit gelatinous, into the food processor and puree, leaving a little chunky texture. Spoon the puree into a bowl and mix in the remaining ingredients except the olive oil and optional ingredients.

Cover with plastic wrap and refrigerate 1 hour to firm a bit.

Heat a large skillet and film the bottom with olive oil. When the skillet is hot, make 4 burgers, flatten if necessary, and cook about 3 minutes, until browned and crisp on the bottom. Flip over carefully and cook 3 more minutes, or until the second side is browned. Serve with salsa or guacamole in a low-carb tortilla or over romaine lettuce if you like.

PER SERVING:

Carbohydrate: 7.2g plus 7.6g fiber   Protein: 21.2g   Fat: 25g

Eileen Weinberg's Roasted Chicken Tenders

These very tasty chicken bits have a nice little crust that you'd swear is breaded — but it's not. Try them for a buffet or a picnic, since they're great at room temperature. They're also delicious spiced up with smoked paprika or chipotle puree (page 221) in place of the tarragon.

Eileen Weinberg is the owner of one of Manhattan's top food shops, Good & Plenty to Go.

SERVES 6

24 chicken tenders or 6 skinless chicken breast halves, cut into
   4 strips each
2 cups mayonnaise
I tablespoon dried tarragon
I tablespoon minced garlic
½ teaspoon salt
½ teaspoon pepper
I tablespoon fresh lemon juice

Set the chicken aside. Mix the remaining ingredients together. Add the chicken strips and mix well to coat them. Marinate the chicken at room temperature 1 hour or up to 4 hours in the refrigerator. Return to room temperature before cooking.

Preheat the oven to 350°F. Arrange the chicken strips on a foil-covered baking sheet. Bake the chicken 20 to 30 minutes, turning once, or until it's crusty and golden brown.

PER SERVING:
Carbohydrate: 1.6g plus 1g fiber   Protein: 20g   Fat: 59.7g

Russian Scientist
Roast Chicken

I heard about this unusual roasting technique from a listener call-in on National Public Radio. The subject was vertical poultry roasters, and the caller claimed she'd learned a superior technique from a Russian scientist. All you do, she said, is perch the chicken on an open jam jar that has been filled with water and various seasonings. Chicken roasted this way, she claimed, is incredibly moist and delicious — and so it is. Many experiments later, I discovered that (a) a tall, skinny olive jar works well, and (b) a 12-ounce seltzer or beer can is best of all. You may not believe that a great big chicken can perch on a flimsy can for more than an hour in the oven, but it can. I've yet to have a chicken topple over, but even if it did, it wouldn't be a disaster. So be brave — give this a try. I can't roast a chicken any other way now.

Here's the technique: Choose a chicken with the broadest breast you can find. Use a shallow, sturdy roasting pan large enough to hold the chicken if it does fall over in the oven. Fill the ovenproof jar or can half full of a tasty liquid: chicken broth, broth mixed with white wine, Miller Lite beer, or just plain water. Add seasonings and the clipped wing tips from the chicken and perch the chicken on the can or jar in the roasting pan. The chicken looks quite decorous as it cooks, sitting on its throne with legs modestly pointed inward and its wings tucked over its chest.

The only trick here is removing the chicken from the can or jar. Two people can do this easily; if it's just you in the kitchen, be sure to use a can rather than a jar and give it a good squeeze before you slide it out of the chicken. Impale the chicken on a cooking fork at the top of its back and lift it up slightly; grab the can, using a wad of paper towels, give it a good squeeze, and remove it carefully, preferably without spilling any of the liquid. That will be the basis of your sauce, a delicious bonus for making this oddball chicken.

SERVES 8

Chicken, 4¼ pounds, preferably organic, rinsed and patted dry
¾ cup chicken broth, white wine, Miller Lite beer, or water
1 tablespoon chopped herbs: parsley, thyme, rosemary, sage, or
 a combination
2 garlic cloves, roughly chopped
Zest of half a lemon (save the lemon to squeeze into the
 sauce, if desired)
Salt and pepper

Preheat the oven to 450°F.

Snip off the chicken's wing tips and put them in the can or oven-proof jar. Fill the can half full of chicken broth. Add the herbs, garlic, and lemon zest. Place the filled jar in a sturdy shallow roasting pan. Carefully fit the chicken on top of the can, pulling it down so it rests securely in the pan. Sprinkle the chicken with salt and pepper to taste.

Carefully place the roasting pan in the oven on a lower rack. After 15 minutes, reduce the oven temperature to 400°F. Roast 1 more hour, or until the breast registers 160° on an instant-read thermometer.

Remove the pan from the oven and impale the chicken through the back with a cooking fork. Raise the chicken up slightly, then carefully, protecting your hand with a wad of paper towels, squeeze the can and remove it from the chicken, saving the liquid inside the can. Let the chicken rest on a warm platter while you make the sauce.

Strain the reserved liquid in the can into the roasting pan and mix with the degreased roasting juices, scraping up the caramelized bits from the bottom of the pan. Pour the juices into a small saucepan and reduce over medium heat until you have a sauce. Spoon off any surface grease. Add salt if necessary and perhaps a squeeze of lemon juice, to taste.

Carve the chicken by removing one breast half and slicing it on the diagonal. Repeat with the remaining breast, then remove the wings and the legs. Serve the chicken with the warm sauce on the side.

Any leftovers will be delicious as chicken salad.

PER 5-OUNCE SERVING:
Carbohydrate: 0.5g   Protein: 32.3g   Fat: 35.9g

Moroccan Chicken

Just the spices are Moroccan, not the way of cooking this chicken, which is incredibly easy and produces crisp-skinned, very tasty morsels. If you have pomegranate molasses on hand (available at Middle Eastern groceries), you can drizzle a tiny bit over the chicken before it goes into the oven — just a few extra carbs, but a huge flavor dividend.

Marinate the chicken in the refrigerator for at least 3 hours or as long as 24. Bring to room temperature before cooking.

SERVES 4

1 tablespoon paprika
1½ teaspoons ground cumin
Pinch of cayenne pepper
8 chicken thighs
Salt and black pepper
¼ cup olive oil
3 garlic cloves, pressed
3 tablespoons fresh lemon juice
Drizzle of pomegranate molasses (optional)
Chopped fresh cilantro for garnish (optional)

Mix the paprika, cumin, and cayenne in a small bowl. Arrange the chicken thighs in an ovenproof baking dish and sprinkle them with salt and black pepper to taste. Rub the paprika mixture into the chicken pieces.

In a small bowl, whisk together the oil, garlic, and lemon juice. Pour the marinade over the chicken and turn with tongs to cover completely. Set aside to marinate, from several hours to overnight (if longer than 2 hours, cover and refrigerate it, bringing the chicken to room temperature before baking).

Preheat the oven to 400°F. Drizzle the chicken with pomegranate molasses. Roast the chicken skin side down about 20 minutes, turn, and bake another 20 minutes or until crisp and cooked through. Serve hot, garnished with cilantro.

PER SERVING:

Carbohydrate: 4.3g   Protein: 29.8g   Fat: 24.6g

Basic Cooked Chicken

For chicken salad, chicken sandwiches (wrapped in lettuce leaves with mayonnaise or whatever else you like on them), or just plain chicken, here's how to do it. As a bonus, you get some excellent semi-homemade chicken broth.

MAKES 2½ CUPS BONED CHICKEN

4 cups chicken broth (low-sodium canned is fine)
3 pounds chicken parts

In a large pot, bring the chicken broth to a simmer and add the chicken parts. There should be enough broth to cover them; if not, add water to cover. Cook, partially covered, over low heat 25 minutes, then let cool in the broth.

Remove the chicken from the broth and discard the skin and bones. Shred the meat or cut it into cubes, and save the strained broth for another use.

PER ½-CUP SERVING:
Carbohydrate: 0.1g   Protein: 45.1g   Fat: 23.2g

A Great Roast Turkey

My favorite turkey of all is deep-fried, as they do it in the South. But that's not practical for most of us, so here's the next best alternative. Lightly brine the turkey and let it cure several days before roasting for a particularly delicious and succulent bird.

It's hard, in fact, to say just how many carbohydrates this turkey picks up from its flavored bath, but it's certainly minimal.

SERVES 10 TO 12

NOTE: *Start 3 days ahead*

   1 tom turkey, about 15 pounds, preferably organic, giblets
      removed
   7 cups water
   1 cup apple cider
   ¼ cup apple cider vinegar
   ¼ cup sea salt
   Thyme sprigs (optional)
   Softened butter
   Salt and pepper

Rinse the turkey and set it inside a large plastic bag (use a garbage bag if you have to).

Bring the water to a boil, then add, cider, vinegar, and sea salt. Stir to dissolve the salt and let cool to room temperature. Pour the brine carefully around the turkey in the bag, being sure to cover all the skin with brine. Secure the bag with a twist-tie, set it in a shallow pan or a large stockpot to catch any leaks, and refrigerate 2 to 3 days, turning it over every now and then. (If you have absolutely no room in the fridge, you can marinate the turkey in a cooler, surrounded with several packs of blue ice.)

The night before you plan to cook and serve the turkey, remove it from the brine and rinse it carefully. Pat it dry inside and out, cover loosely with plastic wrap or another plastic bag, and return it to the refrigerator (so you'll have crisp skin). An hour before roasting, remove from fridge and allow to come to room temperature.

Preheat the oven to 350°F. Pat the turkey dry again. Place the turkey on a rack in a roasting pan and put several sprigs of thyme in the cavity. Smear the skin all over with the softened butter. Sprinkle with salt and pepper to taste.

Roast the turkey about 2½ hours to 3 hours, or until an instant-read thermometer stuck in the thickest part of the thigh registers 175°F. If the breast is browning too quickly, tent it loosely with foil. If it's not browning enough, turn the oven to 400° until the turkey is done.

Remove the bird from the oven and let it rest on a warm platter 20 to 30 minutes before carving, tented with foil.

PER 5-OUNCE SERVING:
Carbohydrate: 7.1g plus 2.5g fiber   Protein: 18.2g   Fat: 9.3g

Broccolini
(aka Aspiration Broccoli)

This new vegetable is not, as it often says on the label, baby broccoli, it's another thing altogether, a relative of Chinese sprouting broccoli. You may also find it marketed as Aspiration Broccoli. This vegetable is sweet and delicate, without any of the harshness of ordinary broccoli. You can eat it raw, you can stir-fry it (see page 200), you can steam it. Just treat it like asparagus, which its long, slender stem resembles, and it will be at its best.

Broccolini is a little pricey, but it's almost free from a carb perspective. It has two seasons, spring and fall, so grab it when you see it. Broccolini even has its own Web page: broccoli.com.

Turkey with Tuna Sauce

In the olden days, before politically correct food, this dish was vitello tonnato, made with very thin slices of veal. Delicious as it is, veal is not only under a cloud, it's also very expensive — and the dish is so good made with turkey that it hardly seems worth making it the original way. Leftover roast turkey has a whole new life under a blanket of tuna sauce. Or get turkey cutlets and sauté them in a little oil, then bring them to room temperature before saucing and serving.

This is a perfect dish for a hot summer evening. You can make the sauce earlier in the day and refrigerate until about an hour before dinnertime. Then just assemble everything at the last minute and serve it at room temperature. This piquant, flavorful sauce is one of the great Italian classics, and for good reason. It also makes a great dip.

SERVES 2

½ pound cooked turkey, sliced
3½-ounce can tuna packed in olive oil, preferably Italian or
    Portuguese
½ cup mayonnaise, preferably homemade
¼ cup fresh lemon juice
2 anchovy fillets, rinsed, drained, and chopped
Pepper
1 tablespoon capers, drained
Chopped fresh parsley for garnish

Arrange the turkey slices on individual plates. Drain the tuna and put it in the workbowl of a food processor with the mayonnaise, lemon juice, and anchovies. Process briefly to a smooth sauce, scraping down the sides if necessary.

Spread the tuna sauce thinly over the turkey and sprinkle with pepper to taste. Scatter the capers over the top and garnish with parsley.

PER SERVING:
Carbohydrate: 2.6g plus 3g fiber   Protein: 46.5g   Fat: 59.2g

Chilean Sea Bass with a Nut Crust

This sweet, succulent fish comes from the West Coast and it's in season in spring. In this version it has a nutty crust spiced up with extra-hot horseradish — but don't worry, the heat mellows out and you won't particularly notice it.

Chilean sea bass sometimes has a few large pin bones, so feel over the fish with your fingers to find and remove them before cooking. If this fish is on the endangered list for overfishing, substitute cod.

SERVES 3

I pound Chilean sea bass or cod fillet
Olive oil for the baking dish
¼ cup mayonnaise
¼ cup finely chopped pecans or almonds
I tablespoon extra-hot prepared horseradish

Preheat the oven to 400°F. Place the fish in an oiled baking dish and mix the remaining ingredients in a small bowl. Coat the fish with the seasoned mayonnaise.

Bake the fish about 20 minutes, or until the crust is golden brown and the fish is beginning to flake. Serve immediately.

PER SERVING:
Carbohydrate: 1.4g plus 0.9g fiber   Protein: 28.6g   Fat: 28.9g

Seafood Stir-Fry

You can play with this simple but tasty stir-fry almost endlessly. For the protein, you can use all shrimp or all scallops instead of a mixture, or try this with little chunks of chicken or with tofu bits (use firm, not silken, tofu, and fry it first in a little peanut oil for best flavor). The vegetables can be asparagus and red pepper or almost anything you have on hand. But don't use broccoli instead of broccolini; it's too brassy for this dish.

SERVES 4

2 to 3 tablespoons peanut oil, as needed
1-inch-thick slice of onion, very roughly chopped
3 garlic cloves, smashed and minced
3 slices of fresh ginger, each the size of a quarter, minced
Pinch of cayenne pepper
¼ pound medium shrimp, peeled and deveined
½ pound large fresh sea scallops
1 bunch broccolini, stems trimmed, cut into 2-inch lengths
8 cremini mushrooms, wiped clean and sliced
Half a medium yellow crookneck squash, cut lengthwise in half
    and chunked
3 tablespoons white wine
1 tablespoon soy sauce (not low-sodium)
1 tablespoon fresh lime juice or apple cider vinegar with
    ½ teaspoon Splenda low-calorie sweetener dissolved in it
1 tablespoon sesame oil
1 tablespoon toasted sesame seeds for garnish

Place 2 medium-size bowls near the stovetop. Heat 1 tablespoon of the oil in a wok until it's very hot but not smoking. Add the onion and toss until wilted and flecked with brown. Scrape the onions into one of the side bowls.

Turn down the heat under the wok and add the garlic, ginger, and cayenne. Sauté until the garlic is soft, then add to the onion bowl.

Add another tablespoon of oil to the wok. Turn up the heat and add the shrimp, tossing only until they turn pink. Remove the shrimp to the onion bowl.

Lay the scallops in the hot wok, not touching each other, and sauté them over high heat until they're well seared and golden brown on both sides. Add them to the shrimp and onions.

Stir-fry the broccolini stems about 1 minute before adding the florets. Stir-fry another minute. Test the stems with the tip of a paring knife; when they're barely tender, remove the broccolini to the second bowl.

Add the mushrooms and squash to the hot wok. If you need more oil, add the remaining tablespoon. Stir-fry briefly, then return the contents of the two bowls to the wok. Toss to combine.

Add the wine, soy sauce, and lime juice and let it sizzle to reduce a bit. As soon as everything is heated through, add the sesame oil and stir it in well. Serve the stir-fry immediately on warm plates. Drizzle the sauce over each serving and scatter toasted sesame seeds on top.

PER SERVING:
Carbohydrate: 7.1g plus 2.5g fiber   Protein: 18.2g   Fat: 9.3g

Skate with Capers

If you've never tried skate wings, you're in for a big treat. These delicate, rich little morsels of fish have a lot of delectable flavor. Preparing them this way, in classic bistro style, takes all of 5 minutes. Have the fishmonger remove the skin and bones to speed things along. Skate is the big exception to the fresh-fish-is-best rule. The best skate is several days old, so you can buy it ahead, unlike virtually every other fish.

SERVES 4

4 skate wings, about ½ pound each
Salt and pepper
¼ cup olive oil
2 tablespoons butter
1 tablespoon drained tiny capers, or more to taste
1 lemon, cut into wedges

Rinse the skate, pat dry, and cut each wing in half. Season with salt and pepper to taste on both sides.

Heat the oil and butter in a wide skillet over medium-high heat until the butter foams. When the foam subsides, add the fish membrane side up and sauté 3 minutes, or until the bottom is an appetizing golden brown.

Turn the fish and sauté 1 minute longer, or until cooked through. Transfer the fish to serving plates and keep warm. Add the capers to the pan and stir them around for a minute. Pour the caper butter over the fish, garnish with lemon wedges, and serve immediately.

PER SERVING:

Carbohydrate: 0.3g plus 0.1g fiber   Protein: 49g   Fat: 20.8g

Caper Oil

The wonderfully tasty caper bud has virtually no carbs and adds all sorts of flavor to both fish and meat dishes. A good trick for infusing a dish with essence of caper is one devised by Paris-based food writer Patricia Wells. All you do is drain a 3-ounce jar of regular capers in vinegar, give them a good rinse in a strainer under the tap, drain again, put them back in the jar, and cover them with olive oil. Put the lid on the jar and set them aside, refrigerated or not, for the flavor to develop.

Two weeks later you have some lovely caper oil and some delicately flavored capers to use as you please. The oil is great for sautéing fish or finishing grilled fish. The capers add a piquant crunch to tuna or shrimp salad.

Almond-Fried Cod with Fresh Herb Sauce

This succulent fish with Middle Eastern flavors is simple but exotic — just right for an impromptu summer supper with a platter of sliced tomatoes.

SERVES 4

1 cup blanched almonds
Salt and pepper

Sauce

⅓ cup extra-virgin olive oil
2 garlic cloves, minced
¼ cup fresh lemon juice (about 2 lemons)
½ cup roughly chopped fresh parsley
½ cup roughly chopped fresh cilantro
1 teaspoon paprika
1 teaspoon ground cumin

Olive oil for frying
2 pounds cod fillets, in 8 equal pieces

Chop the almonds in a food processor until they're fine crumbs — but don't overprocess or you'll have a paste. Add salt and pepper to taste and mix well. Transfer the ground almonds to a soup plate and set aside.

Make the sauce: Puree the ingredients in the food processor and set aside.

Heat 1 inch of olive oil in each of 2 skillets large enough to hold the fillets. While the oil is heating, dredge the fish in the seasoned almond crumbs. When the oil gives off a blue haze, add the fish to the sizzling oil and cook 1 or 2 minutes on each side, or until it's golden brown and cooked through. Drain the fish on paper towels. Divide it among the 4 plates and drizzle with the sauce before serving.

PER SERVING:
Carbohydrate: 4.3g plus 5.4g fiber   Protein: 48.7g   Fat: 48.9g

Zesty Salmon

This unusual way to cook a salmon fillet is also incredibly easy. The seasoned mayonnaise makes a succulent little crust that's packed with flavor.

SERVES 4

1 salmon fillet, about 1¼ pounds
Olive oil
Salt and pepper
½ cup mayonnaise
1 tablespoon minced orange zest
2 tablespoons chopped fresh cilantro
2 garlic cloves, minced
½ teaspoon ground cumin

Rub the salmon with olive oil and place it on an oiled heavy sheet pan. Sprinkle with salt and pepper to taste and let sit 30 minutes to improve the flavor.

Meanwhile, place the remaining ingredients in a small bowl and stir well to combine.

Preheat the broiler and adjust the rack so it's 3 inches from the heat source. Spread the mayonnaise in a thin layer over the salmon. Broil 7 minutes, or until the fish is opaque at its thickest point. Serve immediately or at room temperature.

PER SERVING:
Carbohydrate: 0.8g plus 0.2g fiber   Protein: 1g   Fat: 1g

Salmon Cooked in Cabbage

This is how the Phoenix chef Christopher Gross prepares his terrific baked salmon. This is a great dish for a dinner party and is relatively simple to put together. You can do everything ahead of time except bake the fish. Just reheat the sauce before serving.

Serves 4

4 whole green or Napa cabbage leaves
3 tablespoons olive oil
2 pounds salmon fillets, skin removed
Salt and pepper

Sauce

1 cup dry red wine
2 shallots, chopped
2 teaspoons freshly grated ginger
1 tablespoon butter
2 tablespoons chopped tomato for garnish

Preheat the oven to 350°F.

Bring a big pot of water to the boil. Drop the cabbage leaves into it and cook, just until they're pliable, about 1 minute. Drain and pat dry.

Using a pastry brush, lightly paint the inside of the cabbage leaves with the olive oil.

Slice the salmon into ½-inch-thick pieces and season all over with salt and pepper to taste. Wrap the fish in the cabbage leaves and place the cabbage packages on a lightly oiled baking sheet, seam side down. (Fish may be prepared several hours ahead to this point and refrigerated. Bring to room temperature before proceeding.) Bake the fish 8 minutes.

Meanwhile, make the sauce. In a small saucepan, bring the wine to a boil and add the shallots and ginger. Stir and lower the heat to a simmer. Reduce the wine by two-thirds, so the sauce is slightly thickened. Off heat, beat in the butter. Season with salt and lots of pepper.

Serve the cabbage packages on individual plates, with a spoonful of sauce around the base. Sprinkle the chopped tomato on top and serve hot.

PER SERVING:

Carbohydrate: 3.6g plus 0.9g fiber   Protein: 46g   Fat: 21g

Fish but Not Fishy

My husband once wrote a novel in which one of the characters was writing a cookbook called *Fish but Not Fishy*. Up until recently, I hadn't known many fish that weren't fishy. Then the Irish chef James O'Shea, of the West Street Grill in Litchfield, Connecticut, taught me a way of cooking salmon that's outstanding — and definitely not fishy. James serves the salmon at room temperature and does wonderful things to it with herb oil, but I wanted to try it this simple way first. Now I'm hooked; this is gorgeously rich, subtle salmon, and it's also the easiest salmon I've ever cooked.

Here's all you do: Rub some sea salt (James uses fleur de sel, the best salt in the world, but regular sea salt will be fine) into the fillet. Lightly brush a salmon fillet (skinned or not, as you like) with olive oil. Let sit at least 20 minutes or up to an hour. Place the fillet on a lightly oiled foil-lined baking pan, skin side down.

Preheat the oven to 250°F. Cook the salmon exactly 15 minutes, then check to see that it's cooked through; if not, give it a couple of minutes more. Either eat warm or serve at room temperature. This salmon is delicious with a classic green sauce or just a squeeze of lemon.

Grilled Salmon

To my taste, this is the most delectable way to cook salmon, and it could hardly be easier. The only trick is to use a hinged grill basket — unless you're very deft with a spatula, you're likely to break the fish in the course of turning it. But if you have one of these grilling gizmos, you just flip the whole thing over with no problems. One more trick: Be sure to oil the grill or the grilling basket just before you add the fish, so it won't stick.

You can cut the salmon on the diagonal into wedges or leave the fillets whole, as you wish. Be sure to use lots of oil and lots of salt and pepper, most of which will fall off during the grilling.

If you have no grill, cook the salmon on the stove top in a ridged skillet over very high heat.

SERVES 4
4 salmon fillets, ½ pound each, checked over for bones
Olive oil
Salt and pepper
Lemon or lime wedges for serving

An hour ahead of grilling, remove the fish from the refrigerator and cut away the skin: begin cutting between the fish and the skin with the point of a sharp knife, then start pulling the skin with your fingers while you scrape the flesh free with the knife blade. Save the skin.

Leave the fillets whole or cut them on the diagonal into 1-inch wedges. Rub the fish well all over with olive oil and sprinkle with salt and pepper to taste. Set aside to season while you fire up the grill. Salt and pepper the salmon skin.

When the grill is ready — i.e., the coals are gray — heat the grilling basket about 5 minutes, or until very hot. Using a wad of paper towels, oil it well — or oil the grate on your grill if you're not using the basket.

Arrange the fish on the grill and cook 3 to 6 minutes on each side for whole fillets or about 3 minutes altogether for the wedges. Turn the fish over when the outer edge begins to color. Cook the skin alongside and turn it as well.

Serve the salmon with little strips of the grilled skin — which is deliciously crunchy — on top, with lemon or lime wedges.

PER SERVING:

Carbohydrate: 0.4g   Protein: 45.1g   Fat: 12.3g

Dilled Salmon

This Scandinavian dish is one of those happily mindless recipes where quantities aren't particularly important and you can just play in the kitchen and produce a terrific entree in minutes. The important thing is to use enough dill — it should cover the fish like a lawn, not just a sprinkling.

Serves 4

1 salmon fillet, about 1½ pounds
Salt
Olive oil for the baking dish
⅓ cup Dijon mustard
1 cup snipped dill, or more to taste
½ cup mayonnaise

Preheat the oven to 400°F.

Pull the skin away from the bottom of the fillet. Salt the salmon to taste and rub the salt in with your fingertips. Lay the fish in a shallow baking dish rubbed with olive oil and let it rest 10 minutes.

Smear the top of the fish with the mustard, then sprinkle with the dill. Spread the mayonnaise evenly over everything else — it will all get mixed together to some extent.

Bake the fish about 20 minutes, or until it has a golden brown crust. Serve at once.

Per serving:

Carbohydrate: 2.8g plus 0.3g fiber   Protein: 32g   Fat: 41.5g

An Excellent Burger

It seems inevitable that we'll eat many more burgers in our low-carb era than we did in civilian life, so it's a good idea to make them as delicious as possible. There are just a few rules:

- Use chuck, at least 20 percent fat. This meat is by far the tastiest, and most of the fat will run out into the pan or onto the grill fire, leaving just its flavor behind.
- Try to get the butcher to grind the meat — chuck roast, say — for you fresh or grind it at home if you have a grinder.
- Handle the ground meat as little as possible, to avoid that dense, juiceless quality so many homemade burgers have.
- Salt and pepper the meat before you form it — gently — into patties. This won't make it less juicy; it will be *more* juicy, and infinitely tastier.
- Don't press down on the meat with a spatula as it cooks or you'll get that dense quality.
- Serve rare meat at your own risk. Yes, it's much tastier, and if the meat has been ground shortly before cooking and serving, you don't really need to worry much about it. At 160°F, the temperature recommended by the USDA to kill all bacteria, the flavor is also pretty much killed. If you're serving people who have compromised immune systems, or are very young or very old, don't take the risk of undercooking. Otherwise, it's your call.

Joe's Special

A version of this dish first came to light in San Francisco, probably at Original Joe's, sometime in the thirties. It's one of those big-mess one-dish meals you can throw together in a matter of minutes, and it's very satisfying.

You can use a box of defrosted frozen spinach instead of the fresh, but the fresh spinach is part of the dish's charm.

SERVES 2

1 ½ pounds fresh spinach

Salt

2 tablespoons olive oil

8 scallions, chopped, including the green

2 garlic cloves, chopped

½ pound ground chuck

Pepper

Hot pepper sauce, to taste

3 large eggs, lightly beaten

2 tablespoons chopped fresh basil (optional)

3 tablespoons grated Parmesan cheese

Clean the spinach thoroughly and remove heavy stems. Set a big pot of water on the stove to boil, and when it's boiling, add salt to taste. Drop the spinach in and cook it 2 minutes. Drain and let cool, then use a potato ricer or your hands to squeeze it as dry as possible. Set aside.

Heat the olive oil in a large skillet and add the scallions. Cook over medium-high heat, stirring from time to time, for a couple of minutes, then add the garlic, continuing to cook until the vegetables are soft.

Add the ground chuck, breaking it into small chunks as it begins to cook. Add salt and pepper to taste and continue to cook until the meat begins to brown and is cooked through.

Add the reserved spinach and cook 2 more minutes.

Mix the hot pepper sauce with the eggs and pour them into the pan. Let them begin to set — about 30 seconds — and then take the skillet off the heat and mix in the basil, if using, and the cheese. The eggs will continue to cook off the heat. When they are cooked through, this big scramble is ready to eat.

PER SERVING:

Carbohydrate: 15.8g plus 5.7g fiber   Protein: 45g   Fat: 48.6g

Buffalo Boys Chili

The Buffalo Boys are hearty Midwesterners, farmers actually, who turn up at our house every holiday season to ski. They're spectacular cooks, as likely to bag their own deer and make their own venison sausage as they are to whip up some great biscuits on the spur of the moment using no recipe at all. The Boys are also successful low-carb dieters — though they fall off the wagon occasionally because they're fond of obscure German beers, not to mention biscuits. They set high standards in the good grub division — and I think they'll like this chili.

If there's no buffalo roaming around your supermarket, of course you can use chuck. You may like your chili much spicier — this version is relatively mild; if so, just add a chopped jalapeño or two instead of the canned chilies, more chili powder, or a jolt of hot pepper sauce before serving. I like to serve this chili in bowls with a spoonful of sour cream to stir in and a few cubes of avocado along with a sprinkle of cilantro.

Serves 5

2 tablespoons olive oil
1 pound ground buffalo meat
1 teaspoon salt
2 tablespoons high-quality chili powder such as Gebhardt's, or more to taste
1 teaspoon ground cumin
Pinch of cinnamon
½ teaspoon oregano
1 medium onion, diced
6 garlic cloves, chopped
4-ounce can whole green chilies, chopped
14½-ounce can Muir Glen diced tomatoes, including juice
½ cup Eden canned black soybeans, including some liquid
12-ounce can Miller Lite beer
Hot pepper sauce to taste (optional)
Sour cream for garnish (optional)
Avocado cubes for garnish (optional)
Chopped fresh cilantro for garnish (optional)

In a Dutch oven, heat the olive oil, and when it's hot, add half the meat, breaking it up with a wooden spoon. Add half the salt. When the meat is brown all over, remove it with a slotted spoon to a bowl and add the remaining meat and salt, repeating the procedure. When the second batch is brown, add back the first batch of meat.

Add the spices and oregano, the onion and garlic, and sauté until the onions are transparent. Add the green chilies, tomatoes, beans, and beer, stirring well.

Cover the Dutch oven and simmer over low heat, covered, for 1½ to 2 hours — the chili should be a bit thick but still slightly soupy. Taste for seasoning, adding more salt or spice or hot pepper sauce, as needed. Skim off any surface fat and serve in warm bowls, garnished with sour cream, bits of avocado, and cilantro if you like.

PER SERVING:
Carbohydrate: 7g plus 4g fiber   Protein: 19.9g   Fat: 25.8g

Out-of-India Burgers

When you can't stand the idea of yet another burger but that's what everyone wants for dinner, try these exotic ones, which taste best on the grill (like all burgers). But they're also good cooked on the stovetop. If they're beefburgers, as they would not be in India, cook them in a little butter.

Serve these with the salad on page 144 and the cucumbers on page 347.

SERVES 4

1½ pounds ground lamb or beef, preferably chuck

½ cup coarsely chopped fresh cilantro

1 jalapeño chili, seeded and minced

2 scallions, minced, white part only

1½ teaspoons ground cumin

1½ teaspoons ground coriander

1¼ teaspoons salt

1 teaspoon black pepper

½ teaspoon garam masala

Mix everything together well and gently form the meat into 4 patties. Let season for a while in the refrigerator if possible.

Cook the patties over a hot charcoal grill, about 7 minutes a side, or until done to your taste. Or cook them in a hot skillet over medium-high heat, turning once.

PER SERVING:
Carbohydrate: 1.4g plus 1.1g fiber   Protein: 30.7g   Fat: 35.6g

Kebabs

This is how my friend Niloufer Ichaporia King makes kebabs. Niloufer grew up in south India and is a spectacular cook. These are best on a charcoal grill, but you can also cook them under the broiler. Niloufer sometimes adds ginger and garlic, but these are so good I prefer to spend the carbs elsewhere.

For best flavor, grind your own cumin seeds.

SERVES 4

- I pound ground lamb or chicken
- I large egg, beaten
- I teaspoon salt
- I teaspoon ground coriander
- ½ teaspoon whole cumin seeds, freshly ground
- ½ teaspoon ground chili, such as ancho or New Mexican
- ½ teaspoon garam masala
- Olive oil for grilling

Thoroughly mix all the ingredients except the oil and shape into 4- to 5-inch-long cigars around 8 metal skewers.

Brush the kebabs with olive oil and grill or broil until nicely browned and cooked through, about 6 minutes, turning halfway through the cooking.

PER SERVING:
Carbohydrate: 0.5g plus 0.3g fiber   Protein: 20.5g   Fat: 31.3g

Smoky Brisket

This method leaves the meat juicy and perfectly cooked. Look for the fattest brisket you can find: the deckle is the best.

The smokiness comes from both pregrilling the meat over hard-wood coals and the smoked jalapeños (chipotles) in the rub (or use barbecue sauce with a little horseradish and hot pepper sauce). You can grill the meat a day ahead if you like, then season with the chipotle puree, wrap it in foil, and refrigerate until a couple of hours before it goes in the oven.

If you have no grill, brown the meat under the broiler on both sides — it will still be delicious.

This brisket is spicy but not overwhelming; its subtle and unusual flavor makes it perfect for a dinner party. It's also terrific for a picnic, because it's delicious at room temperature.

SERVES 10

I beef brisket, about 4 pounds
Olive oil
2 fat garlic cloves, pressed
Salt and pepper
3 tablespoons chipotle puree (see page 221) *or* 3 tablespoons
    barbecue sauce combined with a little horseradish and hot
    pepper sauce

Prepare a charcoal grill; it will be ready to cook when the embers are covered with white ash. Meanwhile, rub the brisket all over with olive oil and garlic. Sprinkle with salt and pepper to taste. When the coals are ready, grill the brisket until well browned and crusty on both sides, about 10 minutes a side.

Preheat the oven to 250°F. Smear the grilled brisket with the chipotle puree — use a table knife to do this; the peppers may burn your skin. Wrap the brisket in two layers of aluminum foil, place it in a baking dish, and bake 4 hours (if the brisket is larger or smaller than 4 pounds, bake it 1 hour for every pound). Some liquid will escape during the baking, but don't worry about it.

Remove the brisket from the foil to a cutting board or serving platter, cut off any fat, and slice against the grain on the diagonal. Serve hot or at room temperature.

PER SERVING:
Carbohydrate: 9g   Protein: 30.7g   Fat: 30g

Corned Beef and Cabbage

Unless you grew up eating this delectable combination, it may never occur to you to cook it. But this is one of the all-time great satisfying dishes. We'll be using turnips instead of the traditional potatoes, but if you're having company, make some boiled potatoes for your friends.

This slightly unorthodox way of cooking cabbage was popularized by a 1930s character who called himself the Mystery Chef; the brief dunk in a baking soda bath leaves the cabbage sweet and less likely to cause digestive distress. The cabbage is so good it doesn't even need any butter.

Serves 10

1 corned beef, 4 pounds
1 head of garlic, separated into cloves and peeled
10 turnips, trimmed and peeled
1 large green cabbage
1 teaspoon baking soda
Salt
Mustard for serving
Gherkin pickles for serving

Rinse the corned beef under cold running water and place it in a large pot. Cover with cold water and add the garlic. Bring to the boil, skimming any foam that rises to the surface. Reduce the heat to a simmer and cook, uncovered, 2 hours, adding more water if needed to cover the meat.

Add the turnips and continue cooking another hour.

About half an hour before you're ready to serve, fill two large pots — one of them nonreactive — with water and bring to the boil. Cut the cabbage into 8 wedges and remove the center stalk section.

Add the baking soda to the nonreactive pot, then add the cabbage. Cook the cabbage only 3 minutes, then drain in a colander.

Refill the nonreactive pot with fresh boiling water from the second pot, adding 1 tablespoon salt per quart of water. Drop in the cabbage and boil uncovered 10 to 15 minutes, or until tender.

Drain cabbage and cut into small pieces, keeping warm until ready to serve. Remove beef to a platter, slice, and serve with sliced turnips and cabbage. Offer plenty of mustard and pickles on the side.

PER SERVING:
Carbohydrate: 9.7g plus 4.4g fiber   Protein: 29.5g   Fat: 27.8g

Chipotle Puree

One of the world's great condiments is smoked jalapeño peppers, called chipotles, in adobo sauce, a spiked tomato sauce that's a little sweet and sour. A 7-ounce can of these peppers (Herdez is a good brand, available at Mexican markets and by mail-order from Mo Hotta, Mo Betta; see Sources) can be pureed in a food processor and kept almost indefinitely in a tightly sealed jar in the refrigerator. This is spicy stuff, great for any barbecued meat or chicken, lovely stirred into mayonnaise for an interesting sauce for, say, shrimp, or simply added to scrambled eggs. The carb count listed on the can seems a little optimistic: I'm guessing that a teaspoon of puree is about 1 carb, but it goes a very long way.

Stovetop Roast Beef
with Garlic

This simple Italian way of roasting beef, which I learned from my friend
Faith Willinger, is not only fast, it's inexplicably delicious. If your cut of
beef varies at all from the weight listed in the recipe, you'll need to adjust the resting time accordingly.

It's a bit of a fuss to peel a whole head of garlic unless you have one
of the new garlic-peeling tubes, in which case it's a snap.

Serves 8

**2 pounds boneless beef roast, tenderloin or silver tip, rolled
    and tied, at room temperature**
Salt and pepper
1 bay leaf
2 tablespoons olive oil
1 head of garlic, separated into cloves and peeled

Place the beef in a heavy pot with a lid, such as a Dutch oven. Salt and
pepper it well, add the bay leaf, and sprinkle the olive oil over the meat.
Toss in the garlic cloves and turn the meat in the oil, so it's covered
with oil. Let sit 15 minutes, then remove the bay leaf.

Brown the beef over medium-high heat, turning so that it browns
completely all over. When the garlic cloves begin to turn color, remove
them and set aside. Continue cooking the beef for 15 to 20 minutes altogether, or until it's evenly browned.

Return the garlic cloves to the pot and cover it. Take the pot off the
heat and let it sit 15 to 30 minutes, or until the meat's internal temperature, tested with an instant thermometer, reads 140°F.

Remove the beef to a serving platter. Add salt to the juices in the
pan and heat them. Slice the meat thinly, sprinkle with salt, and cover
with the warm juices. Scatter the garlic cloves on top of the meat.

Per serving:
Carbohydrate: 0.9g   Protein: 23.9g   Fat: 11.7g

Insanely Easy Carnitas

These wonderfully tasty little morsels of pork go into low-carb tortillas (see pages 102–103) along with guacamole, diced tomato, cilantro, and a little green salsa. In Mexico they're usually cooked slowly in broth or lard, with garlic and herbs and other seasonings. Here they're cooked slowly all right, but with no seasoning beyond salt and pepper. Obviously you can add garlic, oregano, whatever else catches your fancy, but try them once plain. You'll need good pork for such a simple recipe. Organic pork is the gold standard, and look for a piece with some serious fat streaking the lean.

SERVES 8

2 pounds boneless pork shoulder, cut into 1-inch cubes
Salt and pepper

Preheat the oven to 200°F. Arrange the pork cubes in a single layer on a baking sheet and sprinkle with salt and pepper to taste.

Bake the pork cubes 2 hours, turning several times, or until crusty all over and done in the center. If the carnitas aren't crisp, turn up the heat to 350° and cook until they are. Blot on paper towels and serve as described above.

PER SERVING:
Carbohydrate: trace   Protein: 30.3g   Fat: 16.8g

Roasted Spicy Mushrooms
with Skirt Steak

I find this Mexican-accented dish, developed by the Mushroom Council for restaurants, almost addictive. The chipotle oil is the secret ingredient. I've deliberately made too much here, so you can keep it on hand in the refrigerator to season meats and fish, liven up vegetables such as zucchini and greens, and generally perk up whatever's cooking.

SERVES 4

¼ pound white mushrooms, trimmed and cut in half, including the stems

¼ pound portobello mushrooms, stemmed and cut into 1-inch squares

¼ pound large oyster mushrooms, trimmed and cut in half lengthwise

1½ tablespoons olive oil

Salt

1 large white onion, cut into thin strips

1 pound skirt steak, rubbed with olive oil, salt, and chile (ancho, New Mexican, etc.) to taste

Chipotle Oil (recipe follows)

¼ cup fresh white goat cheese, crumbled, for garnish

2 tablespoons chopped fresh cilantro, for garnish

Chipotle Oil

1½ tablespoons pureed chipotle chilies in adobo sauce (see page 221)

½ cup olive oil

Toss the mushrooms with the 1½ tablespoons of olive oil and add salt to taste. Preheat the oven to 500°F.

Oil a sheet pan and arrange the mushrooms and onions on it without crowding. Roast the vegetables, stirring occasionally, until they're browned and just tender, about 15 minutes. Reserve at room temperature until ready to serve. The dish may be made ahead to this point; if it's refrigerated, bring the steak to room temperature before proceeding.

Make the chipotle oil: Blend the pureed chilies with the olive oil and strain. Store covered in the refrigerator up to 3 weeks.

When ready to serve, grill or broil the skirt steak over (or under) high heat, just until medium-rare. Meanwhile, heat the mushrooms and onions in a dry frying pan for about 3 minutes or until hot. Stir in 2 tablespoons chipotle oil or more to taste.

Slice the grilled steak in thin strips and top each serving with the mushrooms and onions. Garnish with the goat cheese and cilantro.

PER SERVING:
Carbohydrate: 5.1g plus 2.5g fiber   Protein: 29.4g   Fat: 44.9g

Vinnie's Italian Pork Tenderloin

At his Manhattan restaurant, Scopa, chef Vinnie Scotto serves this lovely, juicy pork dish, which is made in a matter of a few minutes. You might think you could speed things along and increase the flavor by rolling the pork in the spice rub ahead of time, but that will backfire, drawing the juices out of the meat.

Vinnie serves the pork with a cinnamon applesauce, another great idea. I've added horseradish and cut back the sugar, of course. If your apples aren't very tart, you may not need the sugar at all.

You can make the spice mix ahead and keep it around — it's delicious on all sorts of meats.

SERVES 6

Spice Rub

3 tablespoons fennel seeds
1 teaspoon sea salt
1 tablespoon black peppercorns

Punched-Up Applesauce

2 apples, cored and diced
2 teaspoons prepared horseradish, or more to taste
2 teaspoons sugar, or sweetener to taste (optional)
Pinch of ground cinnamon

Pork Tenderloins

2 pork tenderloins, 1 pound each, at room temperature
2 teaspoons olive oil
2 tablespoons unsalted butter, softened

Prepare the spice rub by pulverizing the spices to a powder in a blender, making sure no big pieces remain. Set aside. (The mix can be stored in a covered jar for up to several months.)

Next, prepare the applesauce. In the microwave or in a small saucepan, cook the apples with a little water until soft. Puree in a food mill or food processor, including the skins, and add the horseradish, sugar, and cinnamon to taste. Set aside to reheat at serving time, or serve at room temperature.

When ready to begin preparing the pork, preheat the oven to its highest setting.

Scatter the spice rub on a platter large enough to hold the pork loins. Roll the pork loins in the spice rub to coat completely and evenly.

Heat a large nonstick skillet over medium-high heat until very hot, add the olive oil, and brown the pork loins lightly on all sides, about 2 to 3 minutes.

Arrange the pork in a roasting pan and roast 6 to 10 minutes, depending on your oven temperature (at 500°F, it will take 10 to 12 minutes to reach 140° when tested with an instant-read thermometer). Remove from the oven and let the roasts rest 5 minutes. Remove to a serving platter and cut into slices 1 to 2 inches thick. Add the butter to the roasting pan and heat briefly, swirling the butter into the roasting juices. Pour the juices over the pork slices and serve with the applesauce on the side.

PORK TENDERLOINS PER SERVING:
Carbohydrate: 0.4g   Protein: 47.9g   Fat: 15.9g

APPLESAUCE PER SERVING:
Carbohydrate: 7.1g plus 1.3g fiber   Protein: trace   Fat: trace

A Lot Like Lasagna

Let's face it, there's no real lasagna without pasta, but this version comes pretty close, and it's a super one-dish meal. Just add a salad, some good red wine, and you've got it. The recipe serves 4, but you can easily double it and bake in a shallow 2-quart baking dish. This recipe is a bit of a fuss to prepare, with all its different elements — but so is real lasagna.

SERVES 4

6 medium zucchini, ends trimmed

Kosher salt

½ pound sweet Italian sausage, crumbled

½ cup Rao's brand marinara sauce or another low-carb marinara

1 cup ricotta cheese

1 large egg, well beaten

1 cup cooked spinach, very well drained and squeezed dry

¼ cup pesto (page 349)

2 tablespoons olive oil

½ pound mozzarella cheese, grated

About a dozen fresh basil leaves (optional)

Trim a thin slice from one side of each zucchini, so it will lie flat on the cutting board. Cut the zucchini lengthwise to make ¼-inch slices and lay half the slices in a colander in the sink. Sprinkle well with kosher salt, then add the remaining slices and salt them as well. Let the zucchini sit 20 minutes to drain.

Meanwhile, sauté the sausage until it's browned, then drain on paper towels. Mix the sausage with the marinara sauce and set aside.

Mix the ricotta with the egg, the spinach, and the pesto and set aside.

Preheat the oven to 450°F. Rub a baking sheet with a little of the olive oil. When the zucchini slices have drained, rinse them and pat dry, then arrange them in a single layer on the baking sheet — you may need more than one sheet, or do them in batches if you must. Paint the tops of the zucchini slices with olive oil and bake 10 minutes, or until they start to turn golden brown. Turn them and bake until the other side is turning brown, just a few minutes.

Spoon half the tomato-sausage mixture into an 8 x 8-inch baking dish. Arrange half the zucchini slices on top and then add the ricotta mixture, using a spatula to spread it evenly over the zucchini. Add the remaining zucchini in a layer, then the rest of the tomato-sausage mixture. Scatter the mozzarella evenly over the top and arrange the basil leaves, if you're using them, over the whole thing.

Bake at 350°F 45 minutes, or until the top is golden brown. Remove from the oven and let sit 5 minutes to settle before slicing and serving.

PER SERVING:
Carbohydrate: 12.7g plus 5.6g fiber   Protein: 35.5g   Fat: 54.3g

Side Dishes

Artichokes with Pecorino and Mint

The Italian food expert Faith Willinger rattled off the idea for this dish in a taxi — she'd made it the night before and it was a big hit. The artichokes here are raw, as they are often eaten in Italy. Make sure to strip away all the green leaves, down to the pale yellow; otherwise the vegetable will be unpleasantly tough. And you do need a Benriner slicer (see page 111) or a mandoline to make the slices fine enough. Otherwise, this zesty appetizer is simplicity itself.

SERVES 4

4 artichokes
¼ cup grated pecorino (Romano) cheese
2 tablespoons olive oil
I tablespoon fresh lemon juice
I tablespoon chopped fresh mint
Salt and pepper to taste

Cut off the base of the artichokes and strip off all the outer green leaves. You should have a pale yellow bud left. With a sharp spoon, pull out the hairy choke at the center of the bud. Using a Benriner slicer or a mandoline, thinly slice the artichokes into a serving bowl.

Add the remaining ingredients and toss well. Serve immediately.

PER SERVING:
Carbohydrate: 7.1g plus 6.9g fiber   Protein: 6.2g   Fat: 8.6g

Cheesy Asparagus

When the long green stalks are in season, you'll probably be eating asparagus until it's coming out your ears, which is some compensation for the heartbreak of corn season, when you have to (mostly) abstain. Here's an interesting new way to enjoy it.

SERVES 4
- 1½ pounds asparagus, trimmed and cooked until tender
- 2 tablespoons olive oil
- Salt and pepper
- 3 ounces Gruyère cheese, grated, about ¾ cup
- 2 ounces Parmesan cheese, grated, about ½ cup
- ⅓ cup slivered fresh basil leaves

Preheat the broiler. Choose a gratin dish large enough to hold the asparagus spears in two layers and brush the bottom with the olive oil. Dry the cooked asparagus thoroughly and lay half of it in the dish. Add salt and pepper to taste.

Put the two cheeses and the basil in a bowl and stir well to combine. Sprinkle half the mixture over the layer of asparagus. Arrange the remaining asparagus over the first layer, add salt and pepper, and top with the remaining cheese mixture.

Broil the asparagus 4 inches from the heat source 3 to 5 minutes, or until the cheese is melted and golden brown.

PER SERVING:
Carbohydrate: 5.1g plus 2.8g fiber   Protein: 11.5g   Fat: 17g

Refried Beans

These have little in common with real refried beans cooked in lard, but they taste very good — and what a treat on a low-carb regime!

The secret is to use canned black soybeans and spice them up a little. If you have any of the Frontera brand salsas on hand, a spoonful would be great on top or mixed right in with the beans.

SERVES 4

15-ounce can Eden black soybeans, rinsed and drained
½ teaspoon salt
Dash of hot pepper sauce
½ teaspoon ground cumin
¼ cup plus 2 tablespoons grated Parmesan cheese
Olive oil for the pan
¼ cup minced fresh cilantro

Place the beans in the workbowl of a food processor and puree until they have just a little texture. Transfer the beans to a bowl and add the salt, hot pepper sauce, cumin, and ¼ cup of the cheese; mix well.

Heat a large skillet and film the bottom with olive oil. When the skillet is hot, add the bean puree and cook over medium heat, pushing it around with a spatula. The beans are done when they've dried out a bit and have started to brown around the edges.

Serve them in a warm bowl with the remaining cheese and the cilantro scattered on top.

PER SERVING:
Carbohydrate: 4.5g plus 6.4g fiber   Protein: 21.6g   Fat: 19.1g

Broccoli with Coconut and Almonds

This exotic South American dish is delicious with fish or chicken. Steaming the broccoli is best, so that it's a bright tropical green.

SERVES 4

2½ cups broccoli florets
Salt and pepper
½ cup canned coconut milk
2 tablespoons sliced almonds, toasted

Steam the broccoli uncovered until just tender, about 3 minutes or longer, drain well, and season with salt and pepper to taste.

Meanwhile, warm the coconut milk in a small pan over medium-high heat until it boils, then let it reduce by about half.

Mound the broccoli in a serving dish and drizzle the coconut milk over it. Scatter the almonds on top and serve.

PER SERVING:
Carbohydrate: 1.8g plus 1.9g fiber   Protein: 2.5g   Fat: 7.6g

Luxurious Cabbage Gratin

My friends Linda and Fred Griffith, authors of *Onions, Onions, Onions* and *Garlic, Garlic, Garlic,* created the mother of this dish, which is perfumed with garlic.

SERVES 6

2 tablespoons unsalted butter, softened, plus 2 additional tablespoons

1 head savoy cabbage, finely shredded

1 tablespoon instant flour

1½ cups half-and-half

½ teaspoon hot pepper sauce, or more to taste

Salt and pepper to taste

½ cup Gorgonzola cheese (about 2 ounces)

⅓ cup ricotta cheese

3 fat garlic cloves, minced

Preheat oven to 500°F.

Use the softened butter to generously grease a shallow 3-quart gratin dish. Arrange the cabbage in the buttered dish and set aside.

Melt the remaining 2 tablespoons of butter in a medium-size saucepan. Whisk in the flour and blend thoroughly. Over medium heat, slowly add the half-and-half, whisking until you have a smooth, somewhat thick white sauce. Reduce heat and stir in the hot pepper sauce, salt, and pepper.

Add the two cheeses, stirring until they've melted. Whisk in the garlic. Pour the sauce over the cabbage and stir gently to blend.

Bake the gratin 15 to 18 minutes, or until the cabbage is soft, the sauce is thick and creamy, and the top of the gratin is crusty.

PER SERVING:

Carbohydrate: 5.7g plus 1.9g fiber   Protein: 7.3g   Fat: 18.5g

Bean Breakthrough

Bean lovers are in hard luck on the low-carb diet. Even though beans have some protein and fiber, most are so loaded with starch they're completely off-limits. Enter the glamorous new queen of soybeans, the black soy. These excellent legumes are creamy and much milder than ordinary soybeans. They take about 1½ hours to cook, but Eden has produced a first-rate canned black soybean, and that's the one I recommend. These beans are organic, they have added kombu seaweed (which makes them even tastier), and they have a great nutritional profile: ½ cup has only 4 grams of carbs with 9 grams of protein.

Now we can have beanburgers (page 190), bean salsa (page 348), bean soup (page 175), and beans in our chili. We can even have black soybean hummus.

Look for these great beans at natural foods stores, gourmet stores, Asian markets, and some supermarkets.

Mashed "Potatoes"

It's our favorite potato impostor, cauliflower, that's tasting so deliciously potato-like here. You don't need to serve this dish with any apologies: it's really good in its own right, and it deserves a place on any holiday table.

I learned this method of cooking cauliflower from the California Cook, Diane Rossen Worthington. Bonus: You can make this dish a day ahead and just gently reheat it before serving.

SERVES 4

1 large head of cauliflower, tough stem removed, cut into florets
3 tablespoons sour cream or ricotta cheese
½ cup shredded Cheddar cheese
¼ cup grated Parmesan cheese
½ teaspoon salt
Big pinch of ground cumin (optional)
Chopped fresh parsley for garnish (optional)

Put the florets in a steamer basket inside a large saucepan. Add an inch of water to the pan, cover, and bring to the boil. Reduce the heat to a simmer and cook 12 to 15 minutes, or until the cauliflower is just tender. Drain it very well on kitchen towels.

Puree the cauliflower in a food processor, then add the remaining ingredients except the parsley and puree until smooth. Scoop the puree into a warm serving bowl and garnish with parsley if desired. Serve hot.

PER SERVING:
Carbohydrate: 3.9g plus 2.8g fiber   Protein: 8.7g   Fat: 9g

Cauliflower Goes to Heaven

The British have a much-beloved dish in which a whole head of cauliflower is steamed and covered with cheese sauce. Not bad, but here we're talking about something a bit more sophisticated — and pretty wonderful. It's also gorgeous, with red and green bits decorating the noble head of cauliflower.

If you can't get hold of poblano chilies, you can substitute canned New Mexico chilies for a hint of the same thing. But try for the poblanos — they make a big difference.

To forgo the drama of cutting into the whole cauliflower head, you can also break the cooked head into florets and simply heat them in the sauce. Chili lovers can add some jalapeños to this mix, which won't be terribly hot otherwise.

SERVES 6

2 poblano chilies, roasted, peeled, seeded, and deribbed (page 122)

1 cup heavy cream

½ teaspoon salt

1 head of cauliflower, about 1½ pounds

12 cherry or pear tomatoes

1 cup grated Cheddar cheese, preferably white

Tear the chilies into thin strips. Pour the cream into a small skillet, add the salt and chili strips, and reduce the cream over medium-high heat until it thickens and lightly coats the back of a spoon. Turn off the heat and slide the skillet aside.

Trim the cauliflower of all thick outer leaves, leaving three or four small tender ones to look fetching on the serving dish. Carefully cut a conical plug from the core with a sharp paring knife. Stand the cauliflower in a deep microwave-proof dish. Pour in 1 cup of water, cover the dish tightly with plastic wrap, and steam on high 12 to 15 minutes, or until the tip of a knife slides easily into the top. Remove the cauliflower from the microwave and let stand, still covered, 5 minutes.

Meanwhile, return the cream to medium-low heat and add the tomatoes. Simmer for a minute and add the cheese, stirring well. Drain the cauliflower and stand it in a shallow serving dish. Pour the creamed chilies and tomatoes over the cauliflower and serve immediately, cutting the cauliflower into wedges and spooning more sauce over the wedges as you serve.

PER SERVING:
Carbohydrate: 8.8g plus 2.5 g fiber   Protein: 8.7g   Fat: 21.6g

Voluptuous Cauliflower

The title of this dish may seem like an oxymoron, but treated right, cauliflower has an alluring personality that's quite irresistible. This dish is the inspired creation of chef Anne Rosenzweig, who serves it at her Lobster Club, a much-beloved Manhattan restaurant.

SERVES 4

1 head of cauliflower, tough stems removed and cut into florets
2 tablespoons unsalted butter
1¼ cups heavy cream
1½ cups grated Gruyère cheese
Salt and freshly ground pepper
¼ cup mascarpone cheese
½ cup grated Parmesan cheese

Preheat the oven to 450°F. Place about half an inch of water in a pot fitted with a steaming basket, and bring the water to a boil over high heat. Add the cauliflower and steam until crisp-tender, 3 to 5 minutes (or steam in the microwave).

In a heavy medium-size saucepan over low heat, combine the butter, cream, and 1 cup of the Gruyère. Heat until bubbling. Season to taste with salt and pepper. Add the cauliflower and heat 2 minutes.

Spread the cauliflower in a shallow 2-quart baking dish and sprinkle with the remaining Gruyère. Season with salt and pepper. Dot with mascarpone and sprinkle with Parmesan.

Bake in the preheated oven 10 minutes. Increase heat to broil, or remove to a separate broiler. Broil about 6 inches from the heating element until the surface is golden brown, 1 to 2 minutes. Serve immediately.

PER SERVING:
Carbohydrate: 5.3g plus 1.9g fiber   Protein: 22.3g   Fat: 63.4g

Crispy Chinese Celery

This is one of those astonish-your-guests dishes — no one will imagine it's celery that's so wonderfully crunchy. It's also fast, easy, and versatile (serve it hot, warm, or at room temperature), and all the ingredients are usually at hand in your kitchen.

SERVES 4

- 1 whole head of celery
- 1 to 2 tablespoons roasted peanut oil or regular peanut oil
- 1 to 2 tablespoons soy sauce
- Pepper to taste

Trim the ribs of celery at both ends. Stack up 4 ribs at a time and slice ¼ inch thick on an angle (so the celery will both look better and, for some reason, lose its stringiness).

Pour enough peanut oil into a wok or a large skillet to completely cover the bottom. Heat until a blue haze rises from the oil.

Carefully toss in the celery and stir it briskly over high heat 4 minutes. Sprinkle the soy sauce over the celery and continue tossing another 2 to 4 minutes, or until the soy sauce is absorbed and the celery is browned and crunchy. Add lots of pepper and toss well again.

Serve immediately or at room temperature, but don't refrigerate this dish.

PER SERVING:

Carbohydrate: 1.3g plus 1.7g fiber   Protein: 1.2g   Fat: 3.5g

And the Most Valuable Player Is . . . Cauliflower!

In the low-carber's potatoless world (except for potato skins, page 255), our sole successful potato impostor is cauliflower. If you've had only waterlogged, nasty-tasting cauliflower, you need to give this lovely vegetable another chance in your kitchen. For starters, ½ cup of cauliflower is only 1.3 carb grams, an incredible bargain. And cauliflower is also high on the list of cancer-fighting vegetables.

There are only a couple of rules for working with cauliflower. One is to buy the freshest, preferably straight from the farmers market. Look for the whitest, tightest-curled heads, with no dents or brown spots. Old cauliflower will not be tender and sweet. One medium head will produce about 6 cups of florets.

Don't overcook it, and don't let it get waterlogged. The best way to cook it is to steam it, either in cut-up florets or the whole head, as the British love to serve it.

But perhaps the most delicious way of all to serve cauliflower is to grate it, then sauté it in butter, which preserves all its sweetness and yet renders it almost unidentifiable as cauliflower. Cooked this way, cauliflower takes on yet another valuable role: rice impostor. Grated cauliflower won't need more than about 5 minutes in the skillet, and it takes to many seasonings, almost as many as rice itself. You can hand grate it, of course, but it tends to fall apart; it's much easier to grate in a food processor, using the shredding blade.

You can do almost anything to cauliflower you can do to broccoli, but here are some other ideas:

- Serve it raw, to dip in everything from guacamole to old-fashioned onion-soup-mix dip. To keep it white, soak it first for about 5 minutes in cold water with a little lemon juice added.

- Steam the florets until just tender but still a little firm (5 to 8 minutes) and then fry them in butter — brown butter is especially good with cauliflower, and you could toss in a few capers while you're at it.

- Sauté steamed florets with sliced almonds browned in butter.

- Steam a whole head of cauliflower (this will take about 15 minutes), then put it in a baking dish and drift some grated Parmesan on top. Drizzle melted butter over the whole head and sprinkle with paprika. Broil until the cheese is melted.

- Mashed cauliflower with a little cream makes a perfectly respectable mashed potatoes kind of dish (see page 237). Serve it right away, though, or the water will separate out.

- Dice steamed cauliflower and turn it into "potato" salad, using your favorite dressing and plenty of fresh herbs. This needs to be put together at the last minute or the dish will become watery.

- For the "rice" version, play around with seasonings. Cumin and chili powder are delicious, and garam masala tastes very good; or try stirring in a spoonful of prepared tapenade, or just chopped olives. Saffron adds a lovely color and a delicate flavor, while tarragon or parsley or cilantro takes it in different directions — you get the idea.

Roasted Celery with Herbs and Prosciutto

Cooked celery is an entirely different animal from celery in the raw, which is such a low-carb staple we're all a bit tired of it. This version is savory and satisfying; if you have an herb garden, you'll make this often.

SERVES 4

3 tablespoons olive oil

1 whole head of celery, trimmed and cut into 2-inch lengths

6 shallots, chopped

2 slices prosciutto, diced

2 sprigs thyme

4 sage leaves

1 sprig rosemary

1 tablespoon white wine vinegar

Minced zest of half a lemon

Salt and pepper to taste

Preheat the oven to 475°F. Have ready a 9-inch gratin dish.

In a wide skillet, heat the olive oil and sauté the celery and shallots over medium heat until they take on color, 3 to 5 minutes. Add the prosciutto and stir well to combine.

Remove the mixture to the gratin dish with a slotted spatula, reserving the juices in the skillet. Strip the leaves off one of the thyme sprigs and scatter over the celery, along with the sage leaves. Arrange the other thyme sprig and the rosemary sprig on top of the celery.

Add the vinegar, zest, salt, and pepper to the juices in the skillet. Whisk together and pour evenly over the celery.

Bake uncovered 20 to 25 minutes, until the celery is soft all through. Serve immediately.

PER SERVING:
Carbohydrate: 4.5g plus 1.9g fiber   Protein: 7.5g   Fat: 12.8g

Cucumber Noodles

The easiest way to cut these noodles is with a mandoline or a Benriner cutter with a noodle blade, but you can also make very thin wide noodles with a sharp vegetable peeler.

The idea of cooking cucumber may seem weird, but these noodles are actually very good, and they are just barely cooked in any case.

SERVES 2

1 long European cucumber, peeled
3 tablespoons butter
Half a red bell pepper, cored, seeded, and cut into tiny dice
2 tablespoons minced fresh dill
Salt and pepper to taste

Insert the noodle-cutting blade on the mandoline or the Benriner. Cut the noodles from around the outside of the cucumber, discarding the small center core. You may have to make short noodles if you use the knuckle-protecting carriage.

Melt the butter in a sauté pan and when it's hot, add the diced pepper. Cook about 30 seconds, then add the cucumbers and toss very briefly, just to heat through. Add the dill, salt, and pepper, tossing well to combine. Serve hot.

PER SERVING:
Carbohydrate: 3.5g plus 1.3g fiber   Protein: 1.2g   Fat: 17.5g

Garden Greens

This recipe may look like a joke, but morning glory leaves are quite delicious — and very pretty. Or use spinach.

SERVES 4

1½ pounds homegrown morning glory leaves (unsprayed) or
   spinach leaves
4 tablespoons (½ stick) butter
3 garlic cloves, minced
1 teaspoon minced fresh ginger
1 teaspoon mild chili powder
1 teaspoon anchovy paste
Salt to taste

Rinse the greens well and drain in a colander. In a wok or other large pan, and working in batches if necessary, cook the greens down in the water clinging to their leaves, using a wooden spoon to tamp them down from time to time. When they're completely wilted, drain them in a colander. When they're cool enough to handle, squeeze them dry and chop fine.

In the wok or a large skillet, melt the butter over medium heat and add the remaining ingredients except the salt. When the garlic and ginger are soft, add the greens and stir into the sauce. Cook 2 to 3 minutes and add salt if necessary (the anchovy paste may be enough), stirring well. Serve immediately.

PER SERVING:
Carbohydrate: 1.2g plus 4.3g fiber   Protein: 1.2g   Fat: 12.3g

Crunchy Kale

This light and crispy kale cooks in about seven minutes, but it only comes out crunchy if the greens are very well dried. You can play with the seasonings, of course; this recipe is for a basic Italian-style kale, but you can use peanut oil with a little toasted sesame oil and make an Asian version — mix in a few chopped toasted peanuts before serving. Thai sriracha chili sauce is great with kale, as is regular old American hot pepper sauce.

SERVES 2
Half a bunch of kale
1 tablespoon olive oil
2 garlic cloves, smashed
Salt to taste

Wash the kale leaves and dry thoroughly. Strip away any heavy ribs and chop the leaves roughly. You should have about 2 packed cups.

Heat the olive oil in a sauté pan and add the garlic cloves, cooking for a couple of minutes. Remove the garlic cloves and turn the heat to medium-high. Add the chopped kale and sauté until wilted and slightly crunchy, about 7 minutes. Serve immediately.

PER SERVING:
Carbohydrate: 4.7g plus 2.6g fiber   Protein: trace   Fat: 5.5g

Simplest Sautéed Mushrooms

These basic mushrooms go with roast chicken, steak, and other standard protein elements, and of course you can embellish them at will, with tarragon or thyme or cardamom, or a splash of cream. Cremini mushrooms seem to have a bit more flavor than regular supermarket mushrooms.

Serves 4

4 tablespoons (½ stick) unsalted butter
2 tablespoons vegetable oil or walnut or pecan oil
1 pound cremini mushrooms, wiped clean and chopped
2 shallots, minced
Salt and pepper

Heat the butter and oil in a wide skillet over high heat. When the foaming stops, add the mushrooms. Stir the mushrooms around constantly, shaking the pan from time to time, for 5 minutes, or until they begin to brown.

Reduce the heat to medium, add the shallots, and continue to stir for another 2 to 3 minutes, until the mushrooms are lightly browned. Season with salt and pepper to taste.

Per serving:
Carbohydrate: 2g plus 2.5g fiber   Protein: 5.2g   Fat: 18.3g

Roasted Wild Mushrooms

If you can get your hands on any wild mushrooms, such as oysters or hen of the woods, try roasting them this way. They're delicious as a simple dish or served over salad greens.

SERVES 4

½ pound wild mushrooms, wiped clean and cut into chunks
Salt and pepper to taste
¼ cup vermouth or white wine
¼ cup olive oil
2 sprigs fresh thyme *or* 1 teaspoon dried thyme

Preheat the oven to 375°F. Toss everything together except the thyme sprigs and arrange the mushrooms in a single layer on a baking sheet with a low rim. Add the thyme sprigs and roast 30 to 40 minutes, tossing occasionally, until the mushrooms are soft.

Pour the cooking juices into a small saucepan and run the mushrooms under the broiler briefly to brown them. Meanwhile, reduce the juices on top of the stove and pour them over the browned mushrooms before serving.

PER SERVING:
Carbohydrate: 1.4g plus 0.6g fiber   Protein: 2g   Fat: 13.5g

Pasta e Fagioli

No, this isn't the traditional pasta and dried white beans, which is definitely not in our ballpark. It's a way to have a little pasta with a minimal carb debt, by combining it with fresh green beans, sauced with pesto. Be sure to use an imported Italian pasta made with hard (durum) wheat for the fewest pasta carbs. The beans make a difference here too — a snappy bean from the farmers market or the natural foods store will be the tastiest.

If you're really craving pasta, a bowl of this green-and-white combo will be very cheering. You can dress it up with slivers of cherry tomatoes or snips of basil or bits of roasted red pepper or some diced prosciutto. Just remember there isn't enough protein here for a meal, so you need to serve it with some grilled sausages or chicken.

SERVES 2

3 tablespoons kosher salt
⅔ cup uncooked gemelli or other short, relatively skinny pasta
¾ pound fresh green beans, cut into pasta-size lengths
2 tablespoons pesto (page 349)
Grated Parmesan cheese for serving

Bring a large pot of water to the boil and add the salt, stirring it in well. When the water returns to the boil, add the pasta and set the timer for 10 minutes. After 4 minutes, add the green beans and stir again. Check the beans and the pasta for doneness after 4 more minutes. If they're not done, continue to cook until they are, which shouldn't be more than 10 minutes altogether. Drain the pasta and beans in a colander.

Toss the drained pasta and beans with the pesto in a warm bowl. Serve immediately, passing the Parmesan at the table.

PER SERVING:
Carbohydrate: 32.7g plus 7.2g fiber   Protein: 10.5g   Fat: 8.2g

Pea Shoots

I don't grow peas, but I do haunt the farmers market in spring, when pea shoots turn up. These sweet, sweet, sweet greens are tender and delicate — all they need is a little butter, a little onion flavor, salt, and pepper and you're done. They're wonderful with fish or chicken, or even all by themselves as a treat.

SERVES 4

2 tablespoons ghee (page 352) or clarified butter or peanut oil
I pound pea shoots, rinsed and drained
2 scallions, minced, or 2 tablespoons minced chives
Salt and pepper

Heat a wok or a wide skillet and add the butter or oil or a mixture. Add the pea shoots and cook over high heat about 3 minutes, stirring from time to time.

Add the scallions or chives and continue to stir another 3 minutes, or until the pea shoots are completely wilted and have turned an intense shade of green. Season to taste with salt and pepper.

PER SERVING:
Carbohydrate: 6.4g plus 3g fiber   Protein: 3.3g   Fat: 6.6g

Lower-Carb French Fries

That's right, folks, these are real french fries, decarbed a bit by having their starch leached out in a couple of long baths. There's no way of telling how many carbs have exited, but for sure these are better for you than any you'll find in a restaurant. Not only are they somewhat decarbed, they'll also be cooked in pure new oil that isn't full of free radicals.

And they're truly French; the secret is to cook them twice, at different temperatures (you'll need a cooking thermometer). It's enough of a chore to make these fries that I know you won't do it too often, but when you do, it's a huge treat. They're even better with Lemonnaise (page 350) to dip them into.

SERVES 4

NOTE: **Start a day ahead**

> **2 large russet (baking) potatoes**
> **Peanut oil**
> **Salt**

Scrub and peel the potatoes, saving the peels to fry later. Cover the potatoes with cold water and refrigerate 8 hours.

Cut the potatoes into matchsticks and put them in a bowl. Cover with cold water and refrigerate another 8 hours.

When you're ready to fry the potatoes, dry them very thoroughly on kitchen towels. If they're at all wet, they'll be soggy and not crisp.

Heat 2 inches of peanut oil in a wok or deep fryer. When the oil reaches 300°F on the thermometer, it's ready for the potatoes. Cook a single layer at a time for just 2 minutes — you don't want them to brown. Remove with a slotted spoon to a baking rack to drain. At this point, you can wait up to an hour before the second frying.

Raise the heat until the temperature hits 375°. Drop a batch of potatoes in again, in a single layer, and cook until crisp and appealingly brown. Remove immediately to paper towels to drain, and cook the remaining batches in the same way. Fry the peelings (be sure they're dry too). Toss the hot potatoes and peels with salt to taste and serve immediately.

PER SERVING:
Carbohydrate: 11.4g plus 1.1g fiber   Protein: 1.4g   Fat: 6.8g

The Amazing Portobello

You may be in the habit of overlooking the flying saucer–size mushrooms at the market, but they're not only delicious, they're incredibly useful elements of the low-carb diet. They can be cups brimming with breakfast eggs, "buns" to hold burgers and other savory fillings, or vegetarian suppers, stuffed with cheese and tidbits like snippets of sun-dried tomato.

To get the best out of portobellos (which are just grown-up cremini mushrooms), pull off the stem and discard it, then paint the whole cap with a marinade that's half oil and half acid, such as olive oil with balsamic or sherry vinegar (2 tablespoons of marinade will be enough for 2 mushroom caps). You can add herbs, spices, minced garlic to the marinade — whatever seems agreeable. Let this mixture seep into the mushrooms for 20 minutes or more, add salt and pepper, and grill them under the broiler 15 minutes, turning once. If you're adding cheese, drain, then add cheese and run the mushrooms under the broiler again until the cheese melts.

If you want to use them as sandwich bread, you'll need to dry them out a bit by roasting them in a 400° oven for about 20 minutes.

These succulent, sizable fungi cost just over 1 carb for an ounce, so they're well worth playing with. Almost anything that's good on pasta will be good on a portobello.

The Other Pasta

It may be true that pasta is a relatively low-glycemic food and therefore won't cause you any problems on your low-carb diet, at least when you're in maintenance. And of course there's vegetable pasta, which is quite satisfying (see "Spiral slicer," page 111). But there's another alternative, for which you'll have to visit an Asian market. Bean curd pasta is quite low-carb; it comes as noodles, as flat squares that can be cut into noodles, and giant circles, which you can stuff with something interesting and sauté in oil.

This "pasta" isn't particularly tasty; in fact, it has that blank soy taste, so it's a good canvas for other flavors. The secret of cooking it, says Asian food expert Nina Simonds, is to forget about serving it hot, which will only make the noodles tough. Just arrange the noodles in a colander in the sink and pour boiling water over them. Refresh them under cold running water. Let them drain and cool, then mix them into a cold noodle salad with very thinly sliced celery, a little bit of salt, a splash of Asian sesame oil, perhaps some peanuts or snow peas, and so forth. A cilantro vinaigrette made with peanut oil makes a perfect dressing, as does a peanut butter dressing.

Potato Skins, Roasted or Fried

In our never-ending quest for the low-carb potato, this recipe shines out as a big treat with minimal carb damage. If you feel guilty about pitching the starchy interiors of more than 2 pounds of potatoes, strike up a Jack Sprat deal with a carb-eating friend.

The skins are delicious all by themselves, with just a little salt added after they're cooked — but you can also dip them in blue cheese dressing or roast them with a sprinkling of cheese.

Russets (baking potatoes) are best for this treatment, and as with all potatoes, organically grown spuds are vastly superior.

SERVES 4

Scrubbed skins from 2½ pounds russet potatoes, left in wide
    strips
Olive oil
Salt

To roast: Preheat the oven to 425°F. Dry the potato skins well and toss with enough olive oil to coat them, making sure all the surfaces are covered. Arrange them in a single layer on a baking sheet and roast 8 to 12 minutes, until they're golden brown and crisp.

Sprinkle with salt to taste and serve immediately.

To fry: Heat 2 inches of olive oil in a wok or deep fryer until it reaches 360°F. If you have no thermometer, drop a bit of potato skin in; the oil around it should bubble and the skin should turn brown in about 15 seconds. Dry the potato skins well and drop them, a few at a time, into the hot oil. Remove with a slotted spoon when they're brown, less than 1 minute, and let drain on paper towels. When all the skins have been fried, salt and serve immediately.

PER SERVING:
Carbohydrate: 6.5g plus 1.6g fiber   Protein: 1.6g   Fat: 10.1g

Baked Potatoes

In case you missed this recipe in my first book, *The Low-Carb Cookbook*, here it is again, to satisfy your potato cravings.

Bake an organic russet potato at 400°F until it's just tender, about an hour. Take it out of the oven, cut it in half lengthwise, and scoop out as much of the white as you can bear to. Spread some soft butter in the empty shell and sprinkle with salt and pepper — or add a layer of grated cheese, sprinkle with paprika, and return to the oven to brown, 10 to 15 minutes. It's impossible to say exactly how many carbs this will turn out to be, but hardly any compared to a real baked potato.

Home Fries

In the Midwest, breakfast frequently includes potatoes. My daughter Katy, who married into a family of Midwestern trenchermen, came up with this low-carb alternative to the fried potatoes that were part of their daily diet: radishes impersonating potatoes. The trenchermen love this dish, which looks like it's made with new potatoes, and they love its crusty crunch, so satisfyingly potato-like.

If your radishes are very large, dice them so they'll cook through. You can take this in a Southwestern direction by adding a dusting of chipotle chili powder, a little cumin, and some diced green chili. If there are no radishes at hand, try making this with diced young turnips.

SERVES 2

I tablespoon bacon drippings
Half an onion, diced
I bunch red radishes, trimmed and roughly chopped
Salt and pepper to taste
½ teaspoon fresh thyme leaves *or* ¼ teaspoon dried thyme
Paprika to taste (optional)

Heat the bacon drippings in a large skillet and add the onion. Sauté until soft, then add the radishes. Cook over medium heat until crisp outside and soft inside, about 8 minutes. Halfway through the cooking, add salt, pepper, and thyme. When radish fries are done, sprinkle with the optional paprika and serve immediately.

PER SERVING:
Carbohydrate: 2.4g plus 8g fiber   Protein: 0.4g   Fat: 7g

Rapini with Garlic and Sun-Dried Tomatoes

This zesty dish is one of my favorites, with its slightly bitter edge from the rapini, the sweetness of the tomatoes, and the creamy saltiness of the cheese. Not to mention a lot of garlic and olive oil, and not to mention that it's best at room temperature, so you can make it well ahead of time. Whenever I have leftover rapini, this is what I do with it. The better the olive oil, the better this dish will be.

Ricotta salata is an Italian fresh sheep's milk cheese that's salty like feta.

SERVES 6

1 bunch rapini (broccoli rabe)
2 tablespoons olive oil, plus additional olive oil to sprinkle over the dish
6 garlic cloves, chopped
6 oil-packed sun-dried tomatoes, slivered
Coarse salt to taste
¼ cup ricotta salata or feta cheese, crumbled

Peel the broccoli rabe stalks and chop into 1-inch pieces. Drop into a large pot of boiling salted water for 2 minutes to blanch. Drain well.

Heat the 2 tablespoons olive oil over medium heat in a wide skillet and add the garlic. Sauté until the garlic just begins to color, then add the chopped rapini. Continue to stir and sauté for several minutes or until the rapini is cooked, then add the tomatoes and salt. Stir well to combine.

Transfer the mixture to a shallow serving dish and sprinkle with olive oil. When the mixture is cool, crumble the cheese over the top. Serve at room temperature.

PER SERVING:
Carbohydrate: 4.3g plus 0.2g fiber   Protein: 3g   Fat: 10.7g

Spinach Bake with Pesto

This Italian twist on the classic Greek spinach-ricotta baked dish is even more zesty and inspired. You can use frozen spinach, but fresh will be tastier, as usual.

SERVES 4

1 ½ pounds fresh spinach, cooked, drained, squeezed dry, and chopped (see page 212)
1 cup ricotta cheese
¼ cup pesto (page 349)
¼ cup grated Parmesan cheese

Preheat the oven to 350°F.

Mix the spinach, ricotta, and pesto in a large bowl and spoon into an 8-inch soufflé dish or casserole. Sprinkle with the Parmesan and bake 25 minutes, or until the cheese is melted and golden brown.

PER SERVING:
Carbohydrate: 5.3g plus 4.3g fiber   Protein: 17.1g   Fat: 17.5g

Spicy Spinach with Peanuts

When you think you can't bear to take yet another bite of spinach, that essential low-carb green, try it this way.

SERVES 4

2 pounds fresh spinach, well washed and stemmed
2 tablespoons olive or peanut oil
2 garlic cloves, minced
Pinch of dried hot red pepper flakes, or to taste
½ cup chopped peanuts
Salt and pepper

Cook the spinach in the water clinging to it in a wok or a large soup pot, pressing down with a wooden spoon and turning the greens from time to time — you may have to do this in batches.

When the spinach is completely wilted, drain it well in a colander; when it's cool, press as much water out of it as possible with the wooden spoon. Squeeze the spinach again with your hands and chop it.

Heat the oil in a large skillet over medium heat and add the garlic and pepper flakes. Add the spinach and mix well. Cook several minutes, or until the spinach is warmed through. Add the peanuts and sprinkle with salt and pepper to taste. Mix well and serve immediately.

PER SERVING:

Carbohydrate: 2.9g plus 4.8g fiber   Protein: 7.3g   Fat: 10.5g

Spaghetti Squash with Butter and Parmesan

If you have a microwave oven, you can have spaghetti squash in no time. It won't taste a great deal like pasta, but on the other hand, it's pretty good in its own right, especially with lots of butter and grated Parmesan.

SERVES 8

1 spaghetti squash, about 3 pounds
3 tablespoons butter
Salt and lots of freshly ground pepper
½ cup grated Parmesan cheese

Cut the squash in half lengthwise and put it in a baking dish cut side down, adding a little water. Cover the dish with plastic wrap and microwave 8 to 10 minutes, or until the squash is tender.

Turn the squash halves over and carefully pull out and discard the seeds — some may be lurking in the strands. With a fork, scrape out the strands until you have about 3 cups.

Toss the strands in a bowl with the remaining ingredients and serve immediately.

PER SERVING:
Carbohydrate: 9.5g plus 2.6g fiber   Protein: 3.5g   Fat: 5.7g

Southwest Squash with Mushrooms

In Diana Kennedy's *My Mexico,* she gives her all-time favorite recipe, *calabacitas con hongos,* a delectable zucchini with wild mushrooms, chilies, cilantro, and cheese. I can hardly stop cooking and eating this sensational dish, which alone is worth the price of the book. On a recent trip to Santa Fe, I volunteered to re-create it from memory for a dinner party. But I couldn't quite remember it, and besides, some key ingredients weren't available. So I came up with this version. Of course it isn't as good as the original, but it's still plenty delicious, and great dinner party fare.

SERVES 6

3½ tablespoons olive oil
½ pound cremini mushrooms, wiped clean and cut into small dice
2 portobello mushrooms, wiped clean and cut into small dice
Salt to taste
3 tablespoons finely chopped white onion
2 New Mexico chilies, roasted, peeled, seeded, and cut into strips, *or* 1 (4-ounce) can green chilies, chopped
1 pound zucchini, cut into small dice
½ cup coarsely chopped fresh cilantro
¼ pound Muenster cheese, thinly sliced
¾ cup crème fraîche

Heat 1½ tablespoons of the oil in a large skillet, add the mushrooms, and sprinkle with salt. Stir-fry about 5 minutes, or until the juices make a kind of sauce. Transfer the mushrooms and their juices to a bowl and return the skillet to the heat.

Heat the remaining 2 tablespoons oil and add the onion and chilies. Sprinkle with salt, stir well, and heat 1 minute. Add the zucchini, cover the pan, and cook over medium heat, shaking the pan from time to time to avoid sticking, about 10 minutes, or until the zucchini is almost tender.

Remove the cover and stir in the mushrooms and their juices. Sprinkle the cilantro over the vegetables, place the cheese slices over the surface, and spread with the cream. Cover the pan and cook over gentle heat about 5 minutes, or until the cheese has melted.

PER SERVING:

Carbohydrate: 5.1g plus 2.4g fiber   Protein: 8.9g   Fat: 22.2g

Roasted Pumpkin with Sesame Seeds

Get a little sugar pumpkin to make this side dish; they taste the best and are a manageable size. Although pumpkin is a reasonable carb bargain — 4 grams for ½ cup — you probably won't be using up a huge pumpkin in any case.

SERVES 4

Olive oil

4 chunks of pumpkin, 4 x 4 inches each, peeled

Salt and pepper

¼ cup sesame seeds

Preheat the oven to 425°F. Oil a baking sheet and place the pumpkin chunks on it. Add salt and pepper to taste, drizzle with olive oil, and sprinkle with the sesame seeds.

Roast the pumpkin 30 minutes, or until it's tender and the sesame seeds are golden brown.

PER SERVING:

Carbohydrate: 7.7g plus 1.9g fiber   Protein: 2.5g   Fat: 10.7g

Buttery Turnips

I learned this interesting way with turnips from my friend Gene Opton, who's the queen of mandoline prep (see page 112). You can also use kohlrabi for this dish, which is much prettier and a bit carbier. If you don't have a mandoline or a Benriner cutter to slice the turnips, of course you can painstakingly do it by hand.

SERVES 6

6 medium turnips, about 1½ pounds total
1 cup water
Pinch of dried thyme
4 tablespoons (½ stick) butter
½ teaspoon salt

Trim and pare the turnips, slicing off the root end so you have a flat surface for slicing.

Using a mandoline or Benriner cutter, set the blade for ⅛ inch and cut the turnips into uniform slices.

Put the water, thyme, butter, and salt in a large sauté pan with a lid and add the turnips. Bring to the boil, cover, and steam over moderate heat 10 to 15 minutes, until the turnips are tender — giving the pan a good shake a couple of times during the cooking.

Using a slotted spatula, remove the turnips to a serving dish. If any liquid remains in the pan, raise the heat and boil it down, then pour the butter sauce over the turnips. Correct the seasoning if necessary before serving.

PER SERVING:
Carbohydrate: 5.4g plus 2.2g fiber   Protein: 1.1g   Fat: 7.7g

Roasted Roots

Unlike most root vegetables, which are carbohydrate storage centers, turnips and radishes are clean and sharp and full of flavor. Roasted, they have a surprising sweetness.

SERVES 4

1 pound small turnips
1 bunch red radishes
2 tablespoons olive oil
Salt and pepper
2 sprigs thyme *or* 1 teaspoon dried thyme, crumbled

Preheat the oven to 450°F. Trim the turnips and scrub them, but don't peel. Trim and scrub the radishes.

Arrange the vegetables in a single layer on a baking sheet with a low rim. Drizzle the olive oil over them and add salt and pepper to taste. Stir well and rearrange in a single layer. Place the thyme sprigs on top of the vegetables or scatter the dried thyme over them.

Roast about 45 minutes, or until the vegetables are tender, stirring from time to time. Serve hot.

PER SERVING:
Carbohydrate: 5.3g plus 2.3g fiber   Protein: 1.1g   Fat: 6.9g

Sweetly Spiced Sweet Potatoes

These great-tasting tubers aren't usually on the low-carb menu, but they're so good for us, so loaded with beta-carotene and minerals, that it seems worth making a little exception for them. If you buy organic sweet potatoes — Jewels or Garnets are particularly good varieties — you can scrub them up and eat the skin as well, for more fiber.

SERVES 4

2 medium-size organic sweet potatoes, scrubbed and dried
2 tablespoons olive oil
2 garlic cloves, pressed
1 teaspoon whole cumin seeds
½ teaspoon sweet paprika
Salt and pepper to taste

Preheat oven to 500°F. Cut the sweet potatoes in half lengthwise and cut the halves in half again. Cut each piece lengthwise into 4 pieces — you'll have a total of 32 pieces now.

In a large bowl, toss the sweet potato sticks with the remaining ingredients until well coated. Put them on a baking sheet and roast them on the top shelf of the oven 20 to 30 minutes, or until they're golden brown. Serve immediately.

PER SERVING:
Carbohydrate: 12.8g plus 1.8g fiber   Protein: 1.2g   Fat: 6.9g

Slow-Roasted
Cherry Tomatoes

Sweet little cherry tomatoes actually have fewer carbs than the big guys — they're about 1 gram each. They're especially sweet when they're roasted, and they make a very nice bite on the side for a summer barbecue.

SERVES 4

4 cups cherry tomatoes, cut in half horizontally
Salt and pepper
Olive oil to sprinkle on top
Pinch of sugar
Scattering of chopped fresh herbs — thyme, parsley, basil, etc.

Preheat the oven to 200°F. Arrange the tomato halves on a baking sheet and season to taste with salt and pepper. Drizzle with olive oil, add a pinch of sugar, and scatter the herbs on top.

Roast the tomatoes 2 hours. Scoop them into a bowl and serve warm or at room temperature.

PER SERVING:
Carbohydrate: 5.4g plus 1.6g fiber   Protein: 1.2g   Fat: 7g

Fried Zucchini Strings

If you're craving french fries and you don't want to dip too far into the carb allowance, try these crispy little treats. You'll need a cutting machine for these — either a mandoline, the deluxe French variety, or a less expensive Benriner, the plastic Japanese version. You're looking for something as close to shoestrings as you can get. If you have neither of these tools, you can still make this recipe — just cut the zucchini into matchsticks, as skinny as possible, by hand, which is a bit of a pain but worth it.

Each person gets a whole zucchini to himself, because they frizzle up to nothing in the pan.

For a quite different flavor, try sprinkling the zucchini with just a little cumin before you fry them.

SERVES 1
1 medium zucchini
Olive or peanut oil for frying
Salt

Cut the zucchini in half lengthwise and scoop out the seeds. Cut the zucchini halves into skinny shoestrings and blot thoroughly on paper towels.

Heat 3 inches of oil in a wok or skillet. When the oil reaches 375°F — a blue haze will be rising from the surface — it's ready for the zucchini. Drop them in without crowding the pan. The strings will cluster and quickly turn golden brown; turn them over. When the other side is golden brown, remove them to paper towels to drain, and sprinkle with salt. Serve immediately — this is pan-to-mouth food.

PER SERVING:
Carbohydrate: 3.2g plus 2.3g fiber   Protein: 2.2g   Fat: 27.2g

Greek Baked Zucchini
with Mint

This is one of those endlessly versatile dishes that can be an appetizer, brunch, lunch, or just a side dish. It's as good at room temperature as it is hot — maybe even better — so you can make it well ahead of serving. If you don't have any mint, basil will work too.

SERVES 4

1 teaspoon olive oil for the baking dish
1½ pounds zucchini, in large dice
Salt and pepper to taste
4 large eggs
¼ cup crumbled feta cheese
1½ tablespoons chopped fresh mint or basil
Pinch of freshly grated nutmeg
Big pinch of salt

Preheat the oven to 375°F. Oil a medium-size baking dish.

Microwave the zucchini for 3 minutes; drain and dry on paper towels. (If you have no microwave, steam the zucchini for 5 minutes.) Scatter the zucchini in the baking dish and toss with salt and pepper.

Crack the eggs into a bowl and whisk until nearly smooth. Add the cheese, mint, and nutmeg and whisk again until nearly smooth. Add a big pinch of salt and whisk again.

Pour the egg mixture over the zucchini and bake until set and beginning to brown on top, about 30 minutes. Serve hot or at room temperature.

PER SERVING:
Carbohydrate: 3.8g plus 2.1g fiber   Protein: 9.5g   Fat: 8.3g

Zucchini with Herbs

I simply love this way of cooking zucchini — it's speedy, it goes with almost everything, and it's just delicious. It takes a bit longer if you don't have a food processor to grate the zucchini — but just a couple of minutes longer. Any of the herbs will be delicious, even just fresh parsley.

SERVES 2

1 tablespoon butter
1 tablespoon olive oil
2 medium zucchini or 3 small zucchini, ends cut off
Salt and pepper to taste
Handful of chopped fresh herbs: parsley, mint, cilantro, or basil

Melt the butter with the oil in a nonstick skillet over medium heat. Meanwhile, grate the zucchini.

When the oil and butter are hot and foaming, add the grated zucchini and cook until it wilts down and softens. Season to taste and toss in the herbs, mixing well. Serve hot.

PER SERVING:
Carbohydrate: 6.6g plus 4.8g fiber   Protein: 0.1g   Fat: 11g

Desserts

A Philosophy of Dessert

The longer I eat low-carb, the less enchanted I am with the idea of artificially sweetened desserts and tarts. They're not always very satisfying, they keep your sweet receptors active and begging for more, and we don't yet have a low-carb sweetener that tastes great and works perfectly. For all those reasons, I'm much happier eating just a little something sweet if I feel I need it — a little square of chocolate with a cup of coffee, or a few toasted coconut chips, or a couple of chocolate-covered almonds. Then every now and then, for a birthday or some other special occasion, I just eat as little as possible of a real dessert. If I've been sticking to the low-carb lifestyle, there's usually no problem.

But I didn't feel this way when I started. For at least the first three months, I had to have sugar-free Jell-O at least once a day. Then I graduated to the kinds of desserts in this chapter perhaps once a week. But I also know low-carbers who eat some sort of low-carb dessert every day and thrive.

As with everything else about low-carb eating, you're the only one who can decide what you need and what you'll eat. But it's best to *have* a philosophy — that way you're not open to all possibilities at all times, and you'll feel much more in control.

Margarita Melon

This slightly naughty melon dessert is incredibly refreshing on a very hot day. It's important to have the melon balls chilled at least half an hour and the tequila quite cold. Pass salt and pepper at the table for those who like their melon well seasoned.

SERVES 4

I medium cantaloupe, about 3 pounds, scooped into balls
½ cup tequila, well chilled
I tablespoon orange-flavored liqueur, such as triple sec
I lime, cut into 8 wedges
Salt and pepper for serving

Chill the melon balls for 30 minutes before serving. Arrange the melon balls in a glass bowl and pour the chilled tequila and the liqueur over them. Toss gently.

Serve with lime wedges to squeeze over the fruit and pass the salt and pepper at the table.

PER SERVING:

Carbohydrate: 12g plus 1.3g fiber   Protein: 1.5g   Fat: 0.5g

Strawberries with Orange and Lemon

It's hard to say why this combination is so blissful — it's just one of those simple, perfect things. If you use regular lemon sorbet the carbs can run up precipitously; the Monterey Lemon Light brand has half as many carbs. You can also leave out the sorbet altogether and just toss in some grated lemon zest. If the strawberries are perfectly ripe, you shouldn't need any added sweetening, real or fake.

SERVES 4

I quart strawberries, sliced in half
Sweetener to taste (optional)
½ cup fresh orange juice or tangerine juice
I cup light lemon sorbet (Monterey brand)

Combine strawberries with sweetener, if using, and refrigerate until shortly before serving time. When you're ready to serve, divide the berries among 4 dessert dishes. Add 2 tablespoons orange juice to each dish, then top with ¼ cup lemon sorbet.

PER SERVING:
Carbohydrate: 15.1g plus 3.3g fiber   Protein: 1.1g   Fat: 0.5g

Summer Berries
with Mascarpone

The brilliant vegetarian cook Deborah Madison invented this dish for a late summer dessert one starry evening in Santa Fe. It's the easiest dessert imaginable, elegant and delectable. If you can't find mascarpone — Italian cream cheese — use cream cheese beaten with a little cream to the consistency of mayonnaise.

SERVES 6

1 pint blueberries

1 pint blackberries

1 tablespoon triple sec or other orange-flavored liqueur

1 pint raspberries

1 cup mascarpone

Heat the blueberries and blackberries in a large sauté pan over medium-low heat, just until they begin to release their juices. Add the triple sec and stir in well. Add the raspberries and cook just until they begin to soften. Stir well.

Spoon a mound of mascarpone in the center of each dessert plate. Surround the mascarpone with the berries, including their juices, and serve immediately.

PER SERVING:

Carbohydrate: 13g plus 6.6g fiber   Protein: 3.7g   Fat: 18.1g

Berry and Mango Compote

This is delicious warm, especially with a little scoop of vanilla ice cream, or at room temperature. It's great for breakfast or brunch, it's good in winter — made with defrosted frozen fruit — and as long as you don't eat all the mango yourself, it's not too high in carbohydrates. You may not need any sweetener at all, depending on how sweet the fruit is and your own taste.

SERVES 4

 1 pint blueberries
 ½ pint blackberries
 1 cup diced mango (frozen is fine)
 1 tablespoon Consorzio Fat-Free Mango Dressing
 Sweetener (optional)

Gently mix the fruits together in a saucepan and cook them over low heat just until the berries begin to burst. Stir in the mango dressing and taste for sweetness, adding the sweetener of your choice if necessary. Serve warm or at room temperature.

PER SERVING:
Carbohydrate: 18.1g plus 4.6g fiber   Protein: 0.9g   Fat: 0.5g

Berry Crisp

This isn't a dessert to serve guests, but rather a homey treat that's just as good for breakfast as it is for dessert. There's a secret ingredient, which is Protein Crunch cereal (from Nutritional Assistance, 800-965-9008).

SERVES 4

1 pint raspberries

1 pint blueberries

1 tablespoon plus 1 teaspoon sugar-free maple syrup

1 pack or ⅓ cup Protein Crunch cereal

1 tablespoon soft butter

Dash of cinnamon

¼ cup nuts, such as almonds or walnuts

Combine the raspberries and blueberries in a small saucepan and heat gently just until they begin to burst. Remove from heat and stir in 1 tablespoon of the syrup. Spread the berries out in a gratin dish or pie plate.

Put the remaining ingredients in the workbowl of a food processor fitted with the steel blade and chop well. Scatter the topping over the berries.

Heat the broiler. Broil the dish about 6 inches below the heat, just until the top is lightly browned; watch carefully, this goes very quickly. Serve warm with cream, if you like, or at room temperature.

PER SERVING:
Carbohydrate: 14.3g plus 7g fiber   Protein: 9.1g   Fat: 9.1g

Zabaglione

This airy, evanescent, old-fashioned Italian dessert can also be used in spoonfuls to sauce raspberries. Be sure to use a double boiler and watch the zabaglione carefully, so it doesn't overheat and curdle.

SERVES 4

4 large egg yolks
2 tablespoons superfine sugar
½ cup dry Marsala wine
2 tablespoons Splenda low-calorie sweetener

Off heat, mix the egg yolks and the sugar in the top part of a double boiler, using a wire whisk. Continue beating until the mixture is lemon yellow and has a creamy consistency.

Meanwhile, add about 2 inches of water to the bottom pot of the double boiler and bring just to a simmer. When the water is about to simmer, fit the top of the double boiler onto the bottom. Add the Marsala and continue beating. When the mixture begins to foam and swell, add the Splenda and beat in well.

Scoop the zabaglione into ramekins and serve warm, or serve as a sauce at room temperature.

PER SERVING:
Carbohydrate: 3.8g   Protein: 1.8g   Fat: 3.4g

Root Beer Wiggle

No, this isn't a joke. Actually it's pretty good, though the Jell-O folks probably aren't going to be rolling out a root beer flavor anytime soon. Try it on a hot day, with a little cream or a pile of whipped cream on top. Since you're going to be concentrating on the taste of the root beer here, it's worth looking for a good variety. My favorites are Stewart's and IBC, but you may have a local old-time sugar-free root beer that's delicious.

Serves 4

¼ cup water
1 (¼-ounce) envelope unflavored powdered gelatin
1¾ cups diet root beer
Cream or whipped cream (optional)

Pour the water into a small saucepan and sprinkle the gelatin over it, letting it sit 5 minutes or until no dry spots are visible. Heat the gelatin over low heat, stirring constantly, until it dissolves, about 3 minutes.

Remove the pan from the heat and add the root beer, mixing well. Pour the mixture into a 2-cup mold or soufflé dish. Cover with plastic wrap and refrigerate 4 hours, or until set.

To serve, stir the gelatin a bit with the serving spoon to break it up, then scoop into clear glass dishes. Top with cream or whipped cream if desired.

Per serving:
Carbohydrate: zero   Protein: 1.5g   Fat: zero

Rummy Pumpkin Mousse

This easy dessert is creamy, pretty, and delicious enough to make for Thanksgiving dinner. You can also serve the mousse frozen; just take it out of the freezer about 10 minutes before serving to soften slightly. For a higher-protein, lower-fat version, substitute 1 cup of pureed silken tofu for the crème fraîche.

The dark Jamaican-style rum is sweeter than the light Puerto Rican kind, but in this case you're burning off some of the alcohol and sugar before you use it, and the dark rum has more flavor.

SERVES 4

½ cup dark Jamaican-style rum, such as Myers's
1 (¼-ounce) envelope unflavored powdered gelatin
1-pound can pumpkin pie filling
1 cup crème fraîche
5 tablespoons Splenda low-calorie sweetener
2 teaspoons pure vanilla extract
⅛ teaspoon ground ginger
½ cup whipping cream
¼ cup chopped pecans, toasted

In a small saucepan over high heat, reduce the rum by half and set aside to cool to room temperature. When it's cool, dissolve the gelatin in it. Set aside.

In a large bowl, combine the pie filling, crème fraîche, Splenda, vanilla, and ginger, stirring well.

Whip the cream until stiff and fold into the pumpkin mixture. Fold the gelatin into the pumpkin mixture and spoon into dessert bowls or goblets. Cover with plastic wrap and refrigerate to set, about 2 hours.

Bring to room temperature and top with a sprinkling of toasted pecans just before serving.

PER SERVING:
Carbohydrate: 24.4g plus 10g fiber   Protein: 5.4g   Fat: 33.2g

Sparkling Summer Jelly
with Fruit

At some point in every low-carber's life there comes a summer or early fall celebration — a graduation, a major birthday — that requires an elegant, delectable, low-carb dessert. Here it is, a sparkling showstopper inspired by the champagne jellies created by legendary Bay Area pastry chef Lindsey Shere and Italian maestra Anna Tasca Lanza.

Feel free to splurge and use real champagne instead of less-pricey prosecco, the Italian sparkling wine. For your non-low-carb guests, use real sugar, obviously. And when tiny champagne grapes are in season, layer them through the jelly — they'll look like giant champagne bubbles.

SERVES 6

NOTE: *Start the recipe the day before serving*

I (¼-ounce) envelope unflavored powdered gelatin
I cup water
¾ cup Splenda low-calorie sweetener
I (750 ml) bottle prosecco or dry champagne
I pint strawberries, hulled and thinly sliced lengthwise, *or* I cup
    champagne grapes
I tablespoon sugar if you're using berries

In a medium-size saucepan, sprinkle the gelatin over the water and let soften until no dry spots are visible — about 5 minutes. Melt the gelatin over low heat, stirring with a wooden spoon just until no lumps remain; do not overcook.

Remove from the heat and stir in the Splenda until thoroughly dissolved. Stir in the wine. Pour the mixture into a shallow bowl or plastic container, cover, and refrigerate until set, at least 6 hours or overnight.

To assemble, toss the strawberries with the sugar. Scramble the gelatin with a fork. Spoon a scant 3 tablespoons of gelatin into each of 6 wineglasses and top with a layer of berries or a sprinkling of grapes;

repeat two more times. Drizzle a little juice from the berries over the top and serve cold.

PER SERVING:

Carbohydrate: 5.6g plus 1.1g fiber   Protein: 1.4g   Fat: 0.1g

Intense Custard

I discovered this dessert, which is silky and almost indecently rich, quite by accident one day when I had too many egg yolks hanging around. I decided to toss them into the custard I was making, and voilà, there it was. Since you're always making desserts with egg whites on a low-carb regime, you'll have lots of chances to make this simple but satisfying dessert — which also serves as breakfast on a summer morning.

SERVES 4

5 large eggs
3 egg yolks, beaten
½ cup Splenda low-calorie sweetener
1 tablespoon pure vanilla extract
2 cups milk or half-and-half
Pinch of salt
Freshly grated nutmeg

Preheat the oven to 325°F. In a 4-cup soufflé dish, whisk the eggs together well and mix in the egg yolks. Add the remaining ingredients except the nutmeg and whisk together well. Sprinkle the top of the custard with a little freshly grated nutmeg.

Bake the custard on the middle shelf of the oven 30 minutes, or until set and just slightly soft in the center.

Remove from the oven and let cool to room temperature before serving.

PER SERVING:
Carbohydrate: 7g   Protein: 13.9g   Fat: 14.2g

Lemon Mousse

The first time I tasted this classic dessert, it was served in a big bowl, decorated with crystallized violets. Sensational, but it's also very good with just a few raspberries on the side to cut the richness.

SERVES 8

2 large eggs
2 egg yolks
¼ cup sugar
2 tablespoons grated lemon zest
Scant ½ cup fresh lemon juice, strained
9 tablespoons (1 stick plus 1 tablespoon) unsalted butter, chilled and cut into bits
¼ cup Splenda low-calorie sweetener
2 cups whipping cream
Raspberries or candied violets for garnish

In a heavy pan, whisk the eggs and egg yolks together well, then stir in the sugar, lemon zest, and lemon juice. Place over medium heat and gradually stir in the bits of butter. Stir about 4 minutes, or until the mixture begins to thicken — don't let it boil.

When it's thick, remove from the heat and stir in the Splenda. Pour the mixture into a bowl and cover with plastic wrap, punching the wrap a few times with a fork so that steam can escape. Chill thoroughly.

When the lemon mixture is cold, whip the cream and fold it into the cold lemon mixture. Serve in a big bowl with raspberries on the side or decorated with candied violets.

PER SERVING:
Carbohydrate: 9.5g   Protein: 3.7g   Fat: 37.5g

Lime Mousse

This tart, airy, creamy dessert is perfect after Mexican or Indian meals. You can also freeze it in an ice cream maker for a summer sorbet. And it couldn't be easier to make, especially if you have a rasp.

When key limes are in season in early spring, or when you see the little Mexican limes in the market, snap them up and make this marvelous mousse. It's so good, in fact, that I can happily eat the entire thing by myself, so be warned.

SERVES 4

¼ cup warm water

1 (¼-ounce) envelope unflavored powdered gelatin

1 tablespoon grated lime zest

½ cup fresh lime juice, strained (about 4 limes or 18 key limes)

⅓ cup Splenda low-calorie sweetener, or more to taste

1 cup sour cream

3 egg whites, at room temperature

Put the warm water in a glass bowl and sprinkle the gelatin over it. Let sit 5 minutes, then microwave on high 20 seconds, or until dissolved. Stir to be sure no lumps remain; if they do, microwave until they disappear.

In a 4-cup soufflé dish, combine the gelatin, the lime zest, and juice and stir well. Add the Splenda and the sour cream and stir again.

Beat the egg whites just until you have soft peaks, adding a few drops of lime juice from one of the squeezed limes to stabilize the whites. Fold the egg whites into the lime mixture.

Cover the dish with plastic wrap and refrigerate 4 hours before serving.

PER SERVING:

Carbohydrate: 5.4g plus 0.2g fiber   Protein: 6.1g   Fat: 12.1g

Chocolate Mousse

I purloined this recipe from my fellow low-carber and e-mail buddy Dana Carpender, who's written her own low-carb book (see Sources). It takes about 2 minutes to make, and it's one of those great recipes you'll use all the time. Supposedly it feeds 4, but that's 4 restrained people.

SERVES 4

1.3-ounce package sugar-free chocolate pudding mix
1 package soft tofu, about 10 ounces, drained
1 heaping tablespoon unsweetened cocoa powder
¼ to ½ teaspoon instant coffee granules, or more to taste
1 cup whipping cream

Using an electric mixer, beat everything but the cream together until smooth. In another bowl, beat the cream until it's almost stiff. Turn the mixer to the lowest setting, add the chocolate mixture, and quickly combine. Don't overbeat this or you'll have chocolate butter.

Spoon the mousse into 4 dessert dishes. If you're serving it later, cover the dishes with plastic wrap and refrigerate until ready to serve.

PER SERVING:
Carbohydrate: 8.7g plus 0.8g fiber   Protein: 5.5g   Fat: 24.1g

Orange Crème Brûlée

This delectable dessert is usually made in an elongated oval dish, to allow maximum surface for the crunchy burnt sugar topping. But make it in modest ramekins, little ovenproof cups that look like miniature soufflé dishes, and you have just a little sugar topping, nothing to set off the carb alarms.

You can omit the orange and instead infuse the scraped seeds from a vanilla bean in the cream as it warms. You can also put a couple of teaspoons of grated coconut, fresh or dried unsweetened (from the natural foods store), in the bottom of each ramekin before adding the hot custard.

SERVES 6

2 cups heavy cream
Grated zest of 2 oranges
Pinch of salt
¼ cup Splenda low-calorie sweetener
½ teaspoon pure vanilla extract
3 large egg yolks, lightly whisked
6 half-teaspoons light brown sugar

Preheat the oven to 300°F. Place the cream and orange zest in a saucepan over medium heat. Heat until steam begins to rise from the pan. Off heat, beat in the salt, Splenda, and the vanilla.

Slowly pour the hot cream into the egg yolks, stirring constantly. Strain the hot custard into six 4-ounce ramekins. Put the ramekins into a baking pan and pour boiling water around them to come halfway up the sides of the ramekins.

Bake the custards on the middle shelf of the oven 25 minutes, or until they're nearly set. Remove from the water bath and let cool.

Cover the custards with plastic wrap and chill at least 2 hours or overnight.

To caramelize the tops of the custards, scatter the sugar evenly over them and set them 4 inches under a hot broiler. Broil until the sugar is brown and bubbly, about 2 minutes. Let sit several minutes until the sugar hardens before serving.

PER SERVING:

Carbohydrate: 8g plus 1g fiber   Protein: 3.4g   Fat: 31.9g

Peachy

If you allow yourself to check out the labels on ice cream containers, sooner or later you'll come across Breyer's Natural Peach, which contains just milk, peaches, sugar, and cream. And ½ cup is only 10 grams carbohydrate (plus 4 grams fat and 2 grams protein), as compared to the usual 22 to 32 carb grams for the premium ice creams. This product is sort of like ice milk, but still, at 10 grams you might find it worth a try. For less than half an additional carb, you can improve the taste considerably by spinning your ½-cup serving in the food processor with a tablespoon of heavy cream. Either eat it right away as soft ice cream or put it back in the freezer for 20 minutes to firm up a bit.

Don't cheat when you measure your ½ cup, which is hardly what a dessert lover would call a serving of ice cream. You don't want to cancel out the low-carb advantage of this treat by underestimating how much you're actually eating.

Extremely Rich Ice Cream

Eggs seem to be the secret to making ice cream successfully without sugar — lots of yolks to give a silky texture and the whites to keep ice crystals from forming. This ice cream almost counts as a meal, it's so substantial. It's also really delicious, but only when it's freshly made. You can store it in the freezer, with plastic wrap directly on the surface, but it will almost immediately harden up and lose its charm.

For chocolate ice cream, add 2 squares (2 ounces) of semisweet chocolate, melted, to the custard before you add the cream, vanilla, and Splenda.

SERVES 4

7 large eggs, separated
1½ cups half-and-half
¼ teaspoon salt
1 cup heavy cream
1 tablespoon pure vanilla extract
1 cup Splenda low-calorie sweetener

Beat the egg yolks in a medium-size bowl until they're thick.

Heat the half-and-half over low heat and bring it just to a simmer. Remove from heat and slowly whisk into the egg yolks.

Pour the mixture into a heavy pan and set it over low heat, stirring constantly until the custard is slightly thickened. Strain into a bowl and let cool.

Beat the egg whites with the salt until they form soft peaks. Stir the cream, vanilla, and Splenda into the custard, then whisk in the egg whites.

Refrigerate the mixture at least 2 hours to develop flavor. Pour into your ice cream maker and freeze according to the manufacturer's directions. Serve immediately.

PER SERVING:
Carbohydrate: 6.1g   Protein: 15.1g   Fat: 39.8g

Chocolate Cupcakes

The recipe for these tasty cupcakes — made with real food, except for the artificial sweetener — comes from low-carb dieter Susan Fischer. At a fraction over 5 carb grams per cupcake, these are a satisfying indulgence for a minimal carb price. The frosting recipe makes enough for a double batch, but you'll think of things to do with the leftovers, which cost only 1.75 carb grams per serving (enough to cover a cupcake).

MAKES 12 CUPCAKES

Cupcakes

5 large eggs, separated
⅛ teaspoon cream of tartar
6 tablespoons (¾ stick) butter
I teaspoon pure vanilla extract
30 packets Equal or I scant cup Splenda low-calorie sweetener
2 cups ground almonds
5 tablespoons unsweetened cocoa powder
2 teaspoons baking powder

Preheat the oven to 325°F. Have ready a 12-cup cupcake pan, lined with paper cupcake cups.

Beat the egg whites with the cream of tartar until they form soft peaks. In a separate bowl, cream the egg yolks with the butter, vanilla, and Equal until fluffy. Add half the egg whites to the yolk mixture to lighten. Add half the nuts and all of the cocoa and baking powder, folding in well.

Fold in the remaining egg whites and nuts. Fill the cupcake cups halfway and bake 15 to 20 minutes, or until cracked on top. Let the pan cool on a baking rack while you make the frosting.

Vanilla Frosting

8 ounces mascarpone
I cup heavy cream
I½ teaspoons pure vanilla extract
3 tablespoons Splenda low-calorie sweetener

Whip the mascarpone in the workbowl of a food processor until smooth. Add the cream, vanilla, and Splenda and blend smooth.

When cupcakes are cool, frost with this mixture. Store leftover frosting in the refrigerator, tightly covered; it will keep several days. Stir well before using.

PER CUPCAKE:
Carbohydrate: 3g plus 3.1g fiber   Protein: 7.4g   Fat: 19.4g

Capri Chocolate Almond Torte

Of the dozens and dozens of versions of this wonderful nutty creation from southern Italy, this is the best one I know. The recipe comes from Jo Bettoja, a superlative American cook who lives in Rome. It's hardly low-carb, but it does cost far less in the carb division than most cakes do because it has no flour. So it's a great choice for a celebration. You can use Splenda for half the sugar, but use any more than that and you'll regret it.

This is delicious served with whipped cream.

SERVES 10

Butter and flour for preparing the pan
1½ cups almonds with skins
5 ounces semisweet chocolate
1 cup unsalted butter minus 2 tablespoons (1 stick plus 6 tablespoons)
1½ cups sugar *or* ¾ cup sugar plus ¾ cup Splenda low-calorie sweetener
5 eggs
Pinch of coarse salt
Unsweetened cocoa powder for dusting the top of the cake
Whipped cream for garnish (optional)

Preheat the oven to 350°F. Line the bottom of a 10½-inch round cake pan with wax paper, then butter and flour the paper.

In a food processor fitted with the metal blade, chop half the almonds at a time but don't pulverize them — there should be a little texture. Set the almonds aside in a large bowl.

Add the chocolate, in pieces, to the workbowl and chop very fine. Remove the chocolate to the bowl with the almonds.

Add the butter, in chunks, to the workbowl and process until creamy. Pour in the sugar through the feed tube and process until lemon-colored. Separate 1 egg; add the yolk to the butter mixture and process. Repeat with remaining 4 eggs, reserving the whites. When mixture is smooth, remove to the bowl with the chocolate and almonds and combine thoroughly.

Beat the egg whites with the salt until stiff but not dry. Fold 1 tablespoon of the egg whites into the batter to lighten it, then add half the remaining whites and fold in carefully. Add the remaining egg whites — the batter will be difficult to mix.

Pour the batter into the prepared pan and bake 45 minutes, or until a toothpick inserted in the center comes out slightly moist. Cool on a rack 10 minutes before unmolding.

When torte is completely cool, dust lightly with cocoa powder. Serve with whipped cream if you like.

PER SERVING (MADE WITH SUGAR):
Carbohydrate: 41g plus 3.9g fiber   Protein: 9.5g   Fat: 37.6g

Flourless Chocolate Cake

There are many, many versions of this delectable, intense, puddinglike cake, but this one is not only the most delicious I've found, it's also — amazingly — the easiest one to make. It comes to us from the charming and brilliant Los Angeles chef Michael Roberts, who found it when he went off on a pilgrimage to Paris in search of the real French food.

You can play around with sugar substitutes here, using up to half fake sugar, but it's so much better made with the real thing that I think it's best to simply indulge — as cakes go, it's still a low-carb treat.

If you have no espresso machine, get takeout espresso from a good café (you'll need 1 cup, which is more than a double espresso), or use powdered espresso in a pinch.

The French are too adult to serve this with vanilla-flavored whipped cream, of course, but it's pretty delicious that way. For guests, this cake will not be sweet enough. Add ¼ cup sugar and you'll still have only 13g carb per serving.

SERVES 16

Unsalted butter and unsweetened cocoa powder or flour for
    preparing the pan
10 ounces unsweetened chocolate, cut into bits
1 cup brewed espresso
8 tablespoons (1 stick) unsalted butter
½ cup sugar
4 large eggs
Unsweetened cocoa powder for dusting

Preheat the oven to 350°F. Butter a deep 7-inch fluted tube pan and dust with cocoa. Set aside.

Heat the chocolate, espresso, butter, and sugar in the top of a double boiler over simmering water, stirring a few times, until the chocolate and butter are melted, about 10 minutes. (You can also do this step in the microwave, zapping the mixture briefly then stirring, continuing this process until chocolate and butter are melted.) Remove the chocolate mixture from the heat and keep it warm in the double boiler or just leave it in the microwave, covered.

Beat the eggs with a hand mixer at medium-high speed in a large bowl until they are thick and pale and have quadrupled in volume (or use a stand mixer with a balloon whisk).

Turn the speed to medium-low, add the chocolate mixture, and mix until incorporated.

Pour the batter into the prepared pan and set in the center of the oven. Bake 40 to 45 minutes, or until a toothpick inserted in the center comes out slightly moist and the top is cracked.

Let the cake cool in the pan on a rack 30 minutes before unmolding; then let it cool completely. Dust with cocoa powder before serving.

PER SERVING:

Carbohydrate: 9g plus 3.1g fiber   Protein: 3.7g   Fat: 19.8g

Intense Chocolate Cake

This is a lower-carb version of chef Rozanne Gold's Chocolate Climax — one of those chocolate experiences that drive people mad with pleasure. There's more chocolate here than I've ever seen in a single recipe, but it goes a long way.

It's a little tricky to make this cake, and the timing is very precise, so be sure you're not distracted at all when you're putting it together. If you don't have a 10-inch springform pan, a standard 9-inch cheesecake pan with a removable bottom will be fine — just increase the cooking time by another 2 minutes.

SERVES 12

Butter for greasing the pan
20 ounces bittersweet chocolate
1¼ cups (2½ sticks) unsalted butter, chilled
8 extra-large eggs, at room temperature
Big pinch of salt
½ cup Splenda low-calorie sweetener
½ cup chopped peeled hazelnuts, toasted (optional)

Preheat oven to 425°F. Butter a 10-inch round springform pan and line the bottom with wax paper. Cover the outside of the pan completely with foil and crimp it tightly around the pan, so there will be no leaking into the water bath as the cake bakes.

Chop the chocolate into small pieces and the butter into cubes. Melt them together in the microwave, using short bursts of power. Check frequently and stir the pieces around inside the dish so they melt evenly. When the chocolate and butter are melted, stir until smooth and set aside.

Beat the eggs, adding one at a time, in a large warm bowl. Add salt and continue beating until you have soft peaks, about 6 minutes. Gently stir in the Splenda.

Scrape the chocolate mixture into a mixing bowl and stir again. Fold half the egg mixture into the chocolate, stir well, and then add the rest of the eggs. Fold in the hazelnuts if you're using them.

Pour the batter into the prepared pan and cover the pan with a piece of foil that's been buttered on the inside. Set the cake pan inside a roasting pan and carefully fill the roasting pan with boiling water up to the level of the cake batter. Bake 5 minutes, remove the foil on top, and bake 12 more minutes.

Remove the cake from the oven — it won't quite be set — and let cool in the pan 4 hours. Serve at this point or cover and refrigerate to serve later, bringing it to room temperature first.

PER SERVING:
Carbohydrate: 24g   Protein: 5.7g   Fat: 26.7g

What Is It About Chocolate?

It's the most common craving of all — 40 percent of American women and 15 percent of men are mad for it — yet beyond the fact that chocolate tastes so good to most of us, its pharmacology remains something of a mystery. It does contain phenylethylamine, a chemical some researchers think mimics the brain chemistry of a person in love (one reason chocolate is known as both an aphrodisiac and a heartbreak remedy), but so do a lot of other foods, like salami.

Chocolate is also a good source of phenols, the antioxidants present in red wine too. Phenols prevent the oxidation of dangerous LDL cholesterol. And that may be why a study of Harvard alumni found that men who eat chocolate, 1 to 3 bars a month, live almost a year longer than abstainers from sweets. Men who ate much more, 3 bars or more, still lived longer than abstainers, with a 16 percent decreased risk of death, even after other lifestyle factors such as weight, smoking, and exercise were taken into account. In the phenol world, a 1-ounce piece of chocolate equals a glass of red wine; dark chocolate is more effective than milk chocolate. The fat in chocolate is also heart friendly.

Even women who get migraines can eat chocolate; a definitive study got it off the hook. The assumption now is that premenstrual craving for chocolate may naturally lead to much higher consumption of sugar, triggering a hormone-related migraine.

(White chocolate is just cocoa butter, and doesn't do the trick).

Choosing a Chocolate

There are some fierce-minded low-carbers who happily chew up baking chocolate, but for most of us that's not an option; it's just too bitter. But their instincts are right: Except for the added sugar, chocolate is a relative carb bargain, and if you know how to find the lowest-carb versions, you can enjoy it frequently, albeit in small amounts.

Americans love milk chocolate, which is quite sweet and high in carbohydrates, while Europeans love dark chocolate, which has a slightly bitter quality. But that more sophisticated taste is beginning to take hold here as well, and there are a number of dark chocolate bars on the market (usually at gourmet stores, not the drugstore candy counter) to choose from, all of them lower-carb than milk chocolate and good for baking.

The best dark chocolate weighs in at upward of 75 percent cocoa solids, whereas milk chocolate is 51 percent cocoa. It's relatively easy to find 70 or 71 percent, however, and that's where the carb bargains lie. Sorting out the carbs in a given bar or comparing them from brand to brand is a bit difficult, since the labeling is based on grams, usually 40g (about 1⅓ ounces), which often works out to 2½ servings per bar, an inconvenient way of looking at it. The bars are also various sizes, from 3 ounces to 4 or even 5, which makes it all the more confusing.

The chocolates listed below, all of them more or less bittersweet (semisweet is just 1 carb sweeter per ounce, usually), are good to use in baked desserts and to make chocolate treats such as chocolate-coated nuts. A small square of chocolate also makes an elegant, simple dessert with a cup of espresso or a glass of pinot noir and a few roasted hazelnuts. Valrhona makes individually wrapped tiny squares, which makes it harder to overindulge.

Lowest-Carb Chocolate Bars (carbs per 40g/1.4 ounces)

- 11 grams — Lindt Excellence, 70 percent cocoa. This chocolate is complicated and delicious, wonderful to use in baking. One generous square runs a little over 2 carb grams.
- 16 grams — Valrhona Noir Amer, 71 percent cocoa. A lot of chefs swear by Valrhona.
- 17 grams — Guylian sugar-free dark chocolate. This one is sweetened with maltitol, a grain-derived sugar alcohol that's supposedly not metabolized as sugar. Of the dark chocolates listed here, this tastes the most like milk chocolate. Warning: If you eat a lot of this chocolate, it can have a laxative effect.
- 18 grams — Scharffen Berger, 70 percent cocoa. This is the first American dark chocolate in the European style, and it has a fruitiness that many bakers like very much. For eating, it's an acquired taste.
- 18 grams — Ghirardelli bittersweet. To most palates, more appealing than Scharffen Berger.
- 21 grams — Lindt Swiss bittersweet. Not as intense as the 70 percent cocoa bar.
- 25 grams — Droste dark chocolate. Lots of carbs and a more milk chocolate taste than most bittersweets.

Spanish Lemon Cake

This cake is really a torte, and like the Capri torte on page 294 it's the specialty of a fabulous island, in this case Majorca. There the cake is so common its name is just *gato,* i.e., cake. You can make the cake with orange zest instead of lemon if you like. If you can afford the carbs, using all sugar will make a big difference to both the taste and texture.

SERVES 8

Butter to grease the pan
1½ cups almonds
2 tablespoons grated lemon zest
¼ cup sugar mixed with ¼ cup Splenda low-calorie sweetener
4 large eggs, separated
¼ teaspoon almond extract
½ teaspoon cinnamon
Pinch of salt
Whipped cream for garnish (optional)

Preheat the oven to 375°F. Butter a 9-inch cake pan with low (1½-inch) sides and cut a circle of wax paper to fit into the bottom of the buttered pan.

Grind the almonds with the lemon zest and ⅓ the sugar-Splenda mix in the workbowl of a food processor until you have fine crumbs.

In an electric mixer, or by hand, beat the egg yolks together with another ⅓ of the sugar mix, the almond extract, cinnamon, and salt until the mixture is light and smooth, about 2 minutes. Stir the almond mixture into the egg yolk mixture.

Beat the egg whites until soft peaks begin to form. Beat in the remaining sugar mix — don't let the egg whites get to the stiff-peak stage.

With a rubber spatula, fold a big cloud of the egg whites into the batter, which will be quite stiff. Mix well, then fold in the remaining egg whites.

Spoon the batter into the prepared pan and bake 35 minutes, or until the top springs back when you touch it and a cake tester inserted in the middle comes out clean.

Let the cake cool in its pan on a rack. Turn out onto a flat platter and remove the wax paper. Serve with dollops of whipped cream if you like.

PER SERVING:

Carbohydrate: 9.3g plus 3.7g fiber   Protein: 7.3g   Fat: 15.8g

Strawberry-Almond Pie

This is one of those retro icebox pies your aunt might have made, great for a summer backyard dinner. The better the strawberries, of course, the better the pie, so make this in strawberry season. There's a little sugar here to make the crust work, but not enough to get frantic about.

SERVES 8

Almond Crust

Butter for the pie plate
1¾ cups almonds with skins
1 tablespoon sugar
1½ tablespoons Splenda low-calorie sweetener
3 tablespoons butter, softened to room temperature

Preheat the oven to 350°F. Butter a 9-inch pie plate. Place about 6 almonds in a food processor and grind to dust; sprinkle the dust over the prepared pie plate. Grind the remaining almonds along with the sugar and Splenda but not too finely — it's best to do this in short bursts.

Put the ground sugared almonds into a bowl with the soft butter and mix them together with your fingertips. When you have a sort of dough, press it into the bottom and sides of the pie plate, using the back of a soup spoon to make it as even as possible.

Bake the crust 15 minutes — it should just be beginning to brown at the edges. If not, continue baking a few more minutes. When the crust is done, let it cool to room temperature.

Strawberry Filling

1 quart strawberries, halved
Pinch of salt
1 tablespoon flour
Splenda low-calorie sweetener to taste, about ¼ to ½ cup
8 ounces cream cheese
Heavy cream, as needed
¼ teaspoon pure vanilla extract

In a saucepan, cook the strawberries with the salt and flour over medium heat, breaking them up a little with a wooden spoon to release their juices. Don't let them scorch. Cook until they're thick, like jam, about 10 minutes. Add Splenda to taste and remove from the heat. Set aside.

In a food processor, break up the cream cheese and beat until it's smooth, adding a little cream as needed. Mix in the vanilla.

To assemble the pie, pour the cream cheese mixture over the almond crust and spoon the strawberries on top. Refrigerate the pie at least 1 hour and up to 4 hours.

Per serving:

Carbohydrate: 9.4g plus 5.8g fiber   Protein: 7.9g   Fat: 32.8g

Dacquoise

This classic French dessert (nutty meringues with cream), though something of a fuss to make, is worth it for a dinner party or special occasion. The only tricky part is removing the meringues from the pan; using parchment paper helps a lot, but you still need to be careful.

This recipe will make one 10-inch torte or 6 individual servings on small meringues, which may be easier to work with. You can use almonds or hazelnuts, whichever you prefer, or you can skip the nuts altogether. Bonus: You can make the meringues and the filling a day ahead and assemble the dessert just before serving.

SERVES 8 (THE LARGE TORTE) OR 6 (INDIVIDUAL SERVINGS)

Meringues

½ cup blanched almonds or peeled hazelnuts (optional)
3 large egg whites, at room temperature
1 tablespoon sugar
⅛ teaspoon cream of tartar
½ cup Splenda low-calorie sweetener

If you're using the nuts, toast them first (about 8 minutes in a 350° oven), then let them cool. Chop them in a food processor until they have a very fine texture, but don't let them turn into nut butter. Set aside.

Preheat the oven to 250°F and line two baking sheets with parchment paper.

In a deep mixing bowl, beat the egg whites, sugar, and cream of tartar together with a mixer or a whisk until the whites begin to mound up lightly. Add half the Splenda and continue beating, gradually adding the rest, until the whites are shiny and hold stiff peaks when the beater is raised. Be careful not to overbeat; if the whites begin to separate, start over with new egg whites.

Gently fold in the nuts, if you're using them, and distribute them in the egg whites as evenly as possible.

For the large torte, draw a 10-inch circle in the center of each parchment sheet. Or make six 3-inch circles on each sheet if you're making individual servings. Smooth the meringue evenly over the circles with a spatula.

Bake the meringues 1¼ to 1½ hours, switching the pan positions halfway through. The meringues should be firm and dry but not actually colored. Turn off the oven and let the meringues cool inside until the oven cools off or overnight.

Very carefully remove the meringues from the parchment paper using a spatula. Wrap them in plastic wrap or seal in an airtight container if you're not going to be serving them very shortly.

Chocolate Filling

2 cups whipping cream, very well chilled
½ teaspoon pure vanilla extract
½ cup Splenda, or more to taste
¾ cup unsweetened cocoa powder *or* ¼ cup plus 2 tablespoons instant espresso powder

Whip the cream with the vanilla until it starts to mound softly. Add the Splenda and cocoa or coffee; whip to combine, and taste for sweetness — you may want to add more Splenda. Continue whipping until the cream is very stiff, almost on the brink of separating into butter.

If you're making the filling well ahead of time, line a fine mesh strainer with a double layer of cheesecloth, place it over a small bowl, and leave the whipped cream in it to drain — this will take at least 1 hour. Tent the cream loosely with plastic wrap and place it in the refrigerator to drip (you can leave it this way overnight if you wish). Discard the liquid in the bowl. The thickened cream will spread better, and removing excess liquid will also keep the meringues from getting soggy.

To Assemble the Dacquoise:

Unsweetened cocoa powder or instant espresso powder for garnish

To fill the meringues, gently dot heaping spoonfuls of the cream over one of the large meringues or six of the small ones, coaxing the mounds together with the tip of a spatula. Be sure to save half the cream for the second layer. Place the remaining meringue(s) on the filled layer and press down just enough to distribute the cream more evenly.

Cut the large torte into servings before spreading on the second layer of cream, so you can repair any splinters or breaks. Spread the top of each serving with the remaining cream and garnish with a very light dusting of cocoa or espresso powder through a fine sieve.

PER SERVING FOR 8:

Carbohydrate: 3.7g plus 1.8g fiber   Protein: 5g   Fat: 27.2g

Wet Walnut Sauce

If you make this with sugar-free syrup — Log Cabin's isn't half bad — it's a very affordable luxury, in small quantities. The sauce is good over ice cream, obviously, but also over cottage cheese and yogurt. The recipe makes just a small quantity, so you won't be endlessly tempted. Tightly covered, it keeps for several days in the refrigerator.

SERVES 4

½ cup walnut pieces, lightly toasted
3 tablespoons sugar-free maple syrup

Stir the syrup into the nuts well, making sure they're completely covered. Store in a glass jar in the refrigerator but bring to room temperature before serving.

PER SERVING:
Carbohydrate: 3.3g plus 0.7g fiber   Protein: 3.8g   Fat: 8.8g

Raspberries on a Pool of Chocolate

These little treats fall into the tidbit category, something you serve after dinner with coffee that isn't quite dessert but satisfies a moderately sweet tooth — roasted nuts, toasted coconut chips, chocolate-covered coffee beans, and other small treats.

Supermarket raspberries usually won't cut it here because they're too old and too soft. Try the farmers market or a backyard berry patch, if you have access to one. You want plump, very fresh berries that will stand up and beg to be plucked.

MAKES ABOUT 40

3 ounces bittersweet chocolate
1 ounce unsweetened (baking) chocolate
1½ pints raspberries

Have ready a baking sheet lined with plastic wrap. Chop the chocolate into small pieces and put it in a microwave-safe shallow bowl. Microwave 1 minute, stir with a wooden spoon, then cook for another minute. Stir again; the chocolate should be melted, but if not, continue to cook in short bursts until it is. Beat it vigorously with the wooden spoon when it's entirely melted.

Using a teaspoon, make little round dollops of chocolate, about ¾ inch across, on the baking sheet. Top each chocolate blob with a raspberry as soon as possible. When all the raspberries are perched on their chocolate rounds, refrigerate the baking sheet 15 minutes, or until the chocolate is dry.

Remove the chocolate raspberry mounds carefully with a small spatula and arrange them on a plate. Cover with plastic wrap; they'll keep for up to 2 days in the refrigerator.

Remove from the refrigerator about 10 minutes before serving — any longer, and the chocolate will get sticky.

PER 4-PIECE SERVING:
Carbohydrate: 1.9g plus 0.7g fiber   Protein: 0.2g   Fat: 1g

Walnut Bonbons

For an after-dinner treat, these are pretty tasty — and pretty good for you, all things considered. The only challenge is finding perfect walnut halves (if you're serving them to company). All you do is stick two lovely walnut halves together, flat side in, with melted chocolate or cream cheese flavored with lemon and ginger. The chocolate nuts will keep for a day or so, but the cream cheese version should be made right before serving. You can make the cream cheese mixture well ahead, though, and just refrigerate it until an hour or so before you're ready to serve.

Walnuts with Chocolate
Melt several squares of bittersweet chocolate in the microwave or in a double boiler. Cover the flat side of a walnut half with about a teaspoon of melted chocolate and stick another walnut on top. (Carbs: about 2g per bonbon)

Walnuts with Lemon-Ginger Cream
Mince a cube of crystallized ginger into about ¼ cup cream cheese. Add coarsely grated lemon zest to taste. Mix well with a fork and spread about a teaspoon of the mixture onto the flat side of a walnut half. Top with another walnut half. (Carbs: about 2g per bonbon)

Toasted Coconut Chips

These are great as after-dinner tidbits, along with nuts and chocolate, or just for a snack when you want something chewy and interesting. You can chop them up in a food processor and add to a curried chicken or shrimp salad. Or dip one end of a chip into melted bittersweet chocolate for a big treat.

Makes 2 cups chips

1 coconut

Preheat the oven to 250°F. To crack the coconut open, give it a whack around its middle with a hammer or a meat mallet. Drain off the milk. Pry the meat away from the shell — you may have to whack the pieces again — leaving the brown skin intact.

Using a mandoline or a Benriner cutter, make skinny chips of the coconut meat. Arrange the chips on a baking sheet in a single layer and bake 30 minutes, stirring several times.

The chips are done when they turn a very pale blond — take them out of the oven to check the color.

PER ¼-CUP SERVING:
Carbohydrate: 1.2g plus 1.8g fiber   Protein: 0.6g   Fat: 6.7g

Chocolate Coconut Bites

These have some of the appeal of a Mounds bar — an adult version if you use the rum. The foil candy cups can be found in some supermarkets and in gourmet stores — a little fussy, yes, but if you want a treat that's a little elegant, this is it.

SERVES 6

¼ cup grated unsweetened dried coconut

2 teaspoons Splenda

Dark rum, to taste (optional)

About 1 tablespoon unsweetened coconut milk

2 ounces bittersweet chocolate, broken up into pieces

12 foil candy cups

Toast the coconut in the oven or toaster oven at 325°F for just a few minutes. Watch carefully, it can burn easily. Let it cool.

Put the coconut in a small dish and sprinkle with the Splenda, the optional rum, and only as much coconut milk as it takes to stick it together slightly.

Melt the chocolate and pour it into the foil cups, filling each one about halfway.

Pinch together about a teaspoon of the coconut and drop it into each foil cup. Drizzle the remaining chocolate on top.

To store, cover and chill the candies.

PER SERVING:

Carbohydrate: 6.5g plus 0.6g fiber   Protein: 0.7g   Fat: 5.1g

Snap Dragon

This somewhat startling post-dessert idea turns up in old New Orleans cookbooks. Certainly it will make any small dinner party a memorable occasion — and it's not really dangerous, just fun, in that perverse New Orleans way.

Get the biggest, most delicious raisins you can find — which will probably require a trip to the gourmet store or the natural foods store — and put about a cup of them on a heavy heatproof platter, earthenware or silver. Pour about ¼ cup of brandy — an airline-size bottle is fine — over them and let them soak about 10 minutes. As you serve coffee (and brandy, if that's your style), light the brandy and invite your guests to "snap" at the raisins while the flames dance around them. Timid diners can wait until the flames are gone.

PER RAISIN:

Carbohydrate: 10.8g plus 0.5g fiber   Protein: 0.4g   Fat: trace

Brandied Hot Mocha

This luscious after-dinner treat can be served with some toasted hazel-nuts and other tidbits such as toasted coconut chips (page 312). You can make it ahead and just heat up the brew in the saucepan at the last minute. It's also good chilled, with a scoop of vanilla ice cream or a little cloud of whipped cream on top.

This amount will serve 2 people, but you can easily multiply the recipe.

SERVES 2
½ cup brewed espresso or strong black coffee
½ cup half-and-half
1 ounce bittersweet chocolate, cut into small bits
1 tablespoon brandy
2 teaspoons Splenda low-calorie sweetener
Cocoa powder for dusting
Whipped cream for garnish (optional)

Put everything except the cocoa powder and whipped cream in a small saucepan and heat slowly over medium heat until the chocolate melts and the liquid is hot, whisking constantly.

Pour the hot liquid into two 4-ounce after-dinner cups and top with a dusting of cocoa and/or the whipped cream.

PER SERVING:
Carbohydrate: 11.6g   Protein: 2.7g   Fat: 9.7g

Chocolate Almonds

One of my favorite sweet treats is almond bark, an old-fashioned candy hardly anyone makes anymore. But these easy-to-make confections are an approximation of the same taste: golden toasted almonds, still in their skins, with a generous dollop of intense chocolate that's not at all sweet. You can make them in single-almond size or clusters of three for your guests. Even just one is a very satisfying indulgence for a small carb investment.

MAKES ABOUT 100 NUTS OR 35 CLUSTERS
I cup almonds with skins
4 ounces bittersweet chocolate
I ounce unsweetened chocolate
Unsweetened cocoa powder (optional)

Preheat the oven to 350°F. Line a small baking sheet with foil and scatter the almonds over it. Toast the almonds about 10 minutes, or until they smell delicious and are golden brown, stirring occasionally. Remove from the oven and let them cool.

Chop both kinds of chocolate into small pieces and place them in a microwave-safe shallow bowl. Microwave 1 minute, then stir with a wooden spoon and microwave for another minute, or until the chocolate is melted. Stir vigorously with the spoon to restore the gloss to the chocolate.

Mix the cooled almonds into the chocolate and stir well to cover the nuts completely. Drop the chocolate almonds onto the foil-covered baking sheet in clusters of three or almond by almond, or do both. Put the baking sheet in the refrigerator and let almonds harden completely before eating. These will keep several days tightly wrapped in the refrigerator — at room temperature, the chocolate begins to soften after about half an hour.

If you're serving these to company, they'll look prettier dusted with a little cocoa powder. Just pass the cocoa through a sieve over the nuts, stirring the almonds a couple of times as you do so, to coat them on all sides.

PER ALMOND:

Carbohydrate: about 1g   Protein: 0.3g   Fat: 1g

Minimalist Dessert

Oregon is the mother lode of both hazelnuts and pinot noir, one of the most enchanting wines ever devised. And in Oregon they know how to put these elements together: with chocolate. The combination is supremely satisfying and couldn't be simpler: just toast some hazelnuts, pass them and a plate of bittersweet chocolate (Valrhona wrapped tiny squares, bits of Lindt 70 percent, or California's Scharffen Berger), and pour each guest a glass of the best pinot noir you can afford. A glass of wine, a few hazelnuts, and a square of chocolate will be well under 10g carb.

Two Hot-Day Coolers

When the dog days hit, there can't be too many interesting things to drink. Here are two favorites at our house. Both of them require a little advance planning, but hardly any actual work.

Root Beer Granita

This one (an idea I found in Gale Gand's *Butter, Sugar, Flour, Eggs*) requires a food processor or an ice-grinding blender and several hours' forethought. Serve in tall glasses, with more cold root beer poured over the frozen and cream poured over the top — or just mix the cream with the frozen root beer in the food processor. Or skip the cream.

SERVES 2

2 (12-ounce) bottles diet root beer, such as IBC
¼ cup heavy cream (optional)

Pour one bottle of the root beer evenly into an ice cube tray and freeze. Chill the other bottle.

When you're ready to serve, process half the ice cubes in the food processor until you have small shards of frozen root beer. Be careful to get all the syrup out of the ice cube tray; some of it will sink to the bottom and melt. If you're mixing in the cream, add half of it now.

Repeat the procedure with the remaining frozen root beer and cream, if using.

Pile the frozen root beer into tall glasses and either pour the cream, if using, over it, followed by the chilled root beer, or just pour in the chilled root beer. Serve immediately.

PER SERVING:

Carbohydrate: 0.4g   Protein: 0.1g   Fat: 1.4g

Rhubarb-Ginger Shrub

Rhubarb drinks were an early-American treat that seems to have vanished from our repertoire. But they're particularly refreshing, especially when fresh ginger makes a contribution, as it does here.

Serves 4

1 pound rhubarb, fresh or frozen, cut into ½-inch pieces
2-inch piece of fresh ginger, peeled and smashed
4 cups water
Sweetener to taste

Bring the rhubarb, ginger, and water to a boil in a saucepan, then reduce heat and simmer 15 minutes or until the rhubarb has fallen apart. Let cool 15 minutes, then strain and sweeten to taste.

Chill the rhubarb juice for several hours until thoroughly cold. Add fresh or sparkling water to make 4 cups. Check for sweetness and serve over ice.

Per serving:
Carbohydrate: 3g Protein: zero Fat: zero

The Cheese Course

For all us turophiles — that's cheeselovers — the heart beats a little faster when the cheese platter comes to the table. Cheese *is* dessert, especially if you offer sweet wines such as port with it, as well as some interesting tidbits, such as dried fruit and nuts. There are several ways to go with the cheese course, both sweet and savory, all of them appealing and — big bonus — work-free.

After dinner, a single cheese and a salad polish things off perfectly. It could be a great Roquefort, a perfect Stilton, or a gorgeous hunk of Parmesan, possibly served with a very aged balsamic vinegar to drizzle over it at the table. Serve red or white wine alongside, plus a basket of sliced bread for your carb-eating friends. The salad can be just greens or something more complicated — with celery and nuts, for instance.

Celery is superb with cheese; it cuts the richness and freshens everything. Serve some tender inner ribs of celery, including the leaves, along with the cheese. Try this with a round of Brie: Slice off the top rind horizontally. Place the cheese on a serving dish. Sprinkle with ¼ cup minced celery and tender celery leaves, then sprinkle on a couple of tablespoons of very good olive oil. Grind a little pepper over it before presenting the cheese at the table. This is knife-and-fork food, so offer small plates to your guests. (The original version of this idea is from Venice, made with taleggio, as reported in Faith Willinger's *Red, White, and Greens*.)

Other good cheese companions are olives, nuts (toasted almonds, walnuts, or pecans), and radishes. For your carb-eating guests, along with the sliced bread, add some dried fruits — figs, dates, apricots — and some fresh fruit as well. Grapes and pears not only look great, they taste great with cheese.

Another option: Dress up a cheese with a nut oil. The late Catherine Brandel, a brilliant chef at Chez Panisse in Berkeley, liked to serve thin slices of manchego cheese drizzled with a little first-press hazelnut oil (see California Press, page 98); she added some very thin apple slices on the side (dipped in lemon juice beforehand to keep them from discoloring), as well as a few toasted hazelnuts.

If you're going beyond the one-great-cheese formula, you can serve as many as four cheeses that are either all different or all related. You could offer a goat's milk, a sheep's milk, and a cow's milk cheese, ranging from mild to sharp. The cheeses could all be from one country, served with a wine from the same country. Or they could be all blue cheeses from different countries, more of a tasting.

Take the cheese out of the refrigerator 2 hours before you plan to serve it, but leave it wrapped. Each cheese should have its own knife, if that's possible, and they should be arranged in the order they should be tasted, i.e., mild to strong. To cut the cheeses, just follow their shapes unless it's a round (cut in wedges) or a pyramid, in which case it's best to cut it in quarters. Be sure to leave the rind on; many turophiles swear the rind is the best part. If you're unsure at the table, taste the cheese first, then taste the rind; if they don't taste good together, either eat them separately or just skip the rind. The rind changes as the cheese develops, so how it will taste will vary with each individual cheese.

However you serve cheese, be sure to serve wine with it. These are both living foods, full of enzymes and changing constantly — together they're absolutely brilliant. And since your cheese has almost no carbs, you can well afford 3 or 4 carb grams for a transforming glass of wine.

A Big Fat Surprise

According to Steven Jenkins, cheese maven and author of *The Cheese Primer,* cheese has about half as much saturated fat as everyone thinks it has. When you see that a cheese is 50 percent butterfat, for instance, you think the cheese is half saturated fat. But that's not true; butterfat is about half the volume of the cheese (most of the rest is milk solids), and within that half, 60 percent is saturated fat, with a sizable 40 percent unsaturated fat. It gets even more interesting: Brie isn't actually as rich as Cheddar. Yup — because its moisture content is so much higher, it has considerably less butterfat.

Breakfast

Dealing with Breakfast

This meal comes up number one on the gripe list of virtually every low-carb dieter. Where are the bagels, the cereal, the French toast and waffles? And we're really tired of eating protein bars all the time. . . .

I'm not at all immune to this problem, but I tend to grab a fast breakfast.

The good news is that you have a slightly higher carb budget at breakfast than at other meals, because your overnight fast has made your insulin receptors much more efficient. And you have a whole active day ahead of you to burn off the calories. So if you're going to go wild, breakfast is the time to do it. This might mean a waffle, some low-carb pancakes, even juice (though I think that's a waste of carbs; real fruit is lower-carb and gives you more fiber). You can have half a bagel, if that's your dream (though I'd strongly recommend saving it for weekends). Or it might mean ice cream, if that's your passion. Whatever carb sins you commit at breakfast, they'll be forgiven by your body as long as you take in an appropriate amount of protein at the same time. It could be sausage, bacon, smoked salmon, custard, cottage cheese, hard-cooked eggs, whatever appeals.

This rule is especially true when you're traveling, and tempted by the high-carb croissant-muffin-cereal "continental" breakfast. Be sure you always have a protein bar (see page 326) with you for such occasions — as long as you have the protein, a few extra carbs shouldn't hurt.

Breakfast is the time I go for fruit in season, since my body's best able to handle the extra carbs first thing in the morning. Fruit offers you vitamins and other nutritional elements you just can't find in capsules, and it's so delicious it's hard to believe we weren't meant to have it. Breakfast is also the time for the tasty low-carb toast with the butter toasted right in (use a toaster oven) and a little sugar-free fruit jam on top.

If you're up for dinner leftovers at breakfast, that's great. A little pasta wouldn't be out of place, as long as you consume some protein at the same meal.

Breakfast should be as enjoyable as possible, a good setup for following the program the rest of the day with as much energy as possible. Whatever you do, don't skip it — you really need that protein to keep you going, and those extra carbs will burn right off.

Breakfast in a Hurry

When you're eating your first meal of the day on the run, as so many of us do, you need a little arsenal of possibilities at hand — assuming you're not going to have leftover dinner or lunch for breakfast, as some low-carbers routinely do.

Here's what I keep in the kitchen.

Protein Source If you like chocolate, this is the breakfast for you. Designed by the Doctors Eades, authors of *Protein Power,* this shake mix made of whey, egg, and soy protein has only 3g carb, a tiny amount of fat, and an impressive 22g protein per serving. And it actually tastes really good. Just be sure to use ice cold water — or even crush some ice with it in the blender. This excellent drink leaves you many carbs to play with, so you can add some fruit or yogurt or whatever your favorite breakfast treat is. You'll have to mail-order this from 800-480-9554. You can also order on the Web at eatprotein.com. One container provides 16 servings, so you might as well order several at once.

Ultimate Whey Designer Protein This shake mix tastes best in the vanilla praline flavor. A serving has 2g carb, a trace of fat, and 16g protein, from whey peptides. There's also a scattering of vitamins and minerals. This product has very high quality protein, but it needs a little help in the taste department. I add Splenda, a dusting of nutmeg or cinnamon, a little vanilla extract, and a spoonful of sour cream. This one also leaves you extra carbs in your breakfast budget. You can mix in some blueberries or raspberries, half a banana, whatever you like. Available in virtually all natural foods stores.

Protein Bars There must be about ten new protein bars introduced every week, or so it seems every time you check them out at the natural foods store. And yet, to date there's only one bar that tastes very good, has very few carbs, and offers lots of protein — which may be why so many new hopefuls are always springing up.

Taste, of course, is idiosyncratic, but the bar I prefer (aside from Energy Protein, which tastes like a Mounds bar and has a measly 8g protein along with a hefty 15g carb) is the Protein Power bar, with 30g protein and 8–10g useable carb. The new Ultra Low Carb bar is delicious and has only 2g carb. Even though it has some glycerin, the effect on blood sugar is minimal.

Protein 21 Nutrition Bar is another good portable low-carb, seriously low-carb, breakfast. These bars have 10g carb, 7g fat, and 21g protein. They contain the trendy medium-chain triglycerides (good guys) and no trans fats. Considering how much sugar they have — 8g, but no sucrose — it seems they ought to taste better than they do. Cinnamon tastes best to me, followed by almond and fudge. These bars are much improved by a smear of cream cheese (1 more carb gram). See Nutritional Assistance in Sources.

Going higher up the carb scale, there's Zone Perfect, Barry Sears's bar, which is incredibly sweet but otherwise inoffensive and has no fishy flavor despite containing fish oil. This one will set you back an expensive 18g carb, with only 14g protein.

A better choice might be Burn-It, with 25g protein and 19g carb, still quite high.

Prozone bars, which I find completely inedible, have 13g carb (but 15g sugar according to the nutrition label, so we know something's wrong) and 14g protein.

Beware a group of bars with very low carb levels but disturbing effects on blood sugar — you can feel the sugar rush from them, though they're listed at 2 or 4g carb. The culprit is glycerin, a polyol that's supposed to be listed on labels as a carbohydrate but frequently is not. Glycerin sometimes appears on labels as glycerol or polydextrose. (The Atkins bar doesn't list it, for example.) It takes only two molecules of glycerin to make glucose, according to Dr. Ron Rosedale, so it makes perfect sense that these bars do in fact have the same effect in the body, though supposedly glycerin doesn't raise blood sugar levels. (That was not the case with my son, Ben, a Type I diabetic who ate a Keto-Bar — 4g carb, 19g protein — and got a dangerous 75-point spike in his blood sugar level. We know from experience that 4g carb, when taken as glucose tablets, will raise his blood sugar by only 20 points.)

So I'd advise you to stay away from any protein bar that lists glycerin as its first or second ingredient, especially if you're diabetic. FDA labeling should take care of this problem soon, but in the meantime it looks like once again there's no free lunch — or breakfast.

Yogurt Organic full-fat yogurt clocks in at about 13g carb, 9g protein, and 8g fat per 8-ounce serving. That means you'll need an extra source of protein to get your full requirement, and there's a lot of carb here as well. If your yogurt contains live cultures, however, 8 grams of lactose per cup will disappear because they turn into lactic acid, says Jack Goldberg, co-author of *The GO-Diet*. That leaves just 5 active grams of insulin-raising carb. Either add some protein shake powder or eat a couple of hard-cooked eggs. Be sure to buy yogurt that has active cultures, both acidophilus and bulgaricus (see page 344). A little fresh fruit won't hurt with your yogurt, unless you're seriously dieting.

Cottage cheese Half a cup of creamed cottage cheese has 4g carb, 14g protein, and 5g fat. Using lowfat cottage cheese drops 3g fat but doesn't change the carb number, so choose whichever you like better. Look for organic cottage cheese with active cultures of acidophilus and bulgaricus (see above) — and try it with a spoonful of apricot or berry preserves.

Cereal My morning life has changed since Nutritional Assistance brought out Protein Crunch, a very satisfying cereal. With only 4g carb and 25g protein, this is a huge bargain, even with a little milk or cream to wet it down. The texture resembles that of Grape-Nuts (one of the all-time highest-carb cereals) and it has a slightly nutty cinnamon taste.

The editors of the (now defunct) *Diabetes Reader* like to crumble up Fiber-Rich (aka Bran-a-Crisp) crackers (about 3g carb; tastes like horse chow) and pour cream over them for a cereal-like effect. This tastes better than it sounds, especially if you add a little cinnamon and a sliced-up finger banana.

So that's a little fun for the cereal-deprived (as are Crowdie and Granola in the following pages), but it doesn't answer your protein needs: Unless you're eating Protein Crunch, you still need to eat something like hard-cooked eggs, a low-carb bar, or a shake.

Hot Cereal My readers Susan Fischer and Maggie Cekayak make a kind of Wheatena out of Quaker's Unprocessed Wheat Bran, about ⅔ cup to a cup of water. Cook about 10 minutes on the stovetop or 2½ minutes in the microwave. Maggie uses half soy flour and half bran, then adds half a carton of Egg Beaters once it's cooked. Back to the microwave for a couple of minutes, then thin with water to the right texture.

Susan adds a scoop of whey protein to the cooked cereal. I like it plain, with salt, pepper, and butter — or cream and a little sugar-free maple syrup. The cereal alone is just 6g carb, plus plenty of fiber.

Hotcakes

This recipe is a lower-carb version of the cookbook author Marion Cunningham's famous Heavenly Hots. You can mix the batter in the blender and just pour it directly onto the griddle. You can also beef them up, so to speak, by adding a packet of Protein Crunch cereal (see Sources) to boost the protein content. But do try these; they're irresistible.

SERVES 3 TO 4

4 large eggs
½ teaspoon salt
½ teaspoon baking soda
2 tablespoons cake flour
2 cups sour cream
3 tablespoons Splenda low-calorie sweetener

In a bowl, beat the eggs until well blended — or whirl them in a blender. Add the remaining ingredients and mix well.

Heat a griddle or skillet until a drop of water skips on the surface. Add butter and when it's bubbling, make small (2½-inch) pancakes. Turn the pancakes when the edges have bubbles and cook briefly on the other side, just until speckled with brown. Serve immediately with butter and sugar-free syrup.

PER SERVING (PANCAKE ONLY):
Carbohydrate: 10.4g   Protein: 13.5g   Fat: 38.9g

No-Brainer Pancakes

These are based on Atkins Diet Bake Mix (available in most natural foods stores or from the Dr. Atkins Web site, atkinsdiet.com), an astronomically expensive (about $12 a 20-ounce can) low-carb product that's mostly soy powder and oat bran, plus something called Litesse, a carbohydrate that's supposedly minimally absorbed. Still, if you're stumbling around in the morning and pancakes would be a big treat, it's worth having this product on hand to make them. You'll have enough carbs left over for fruit syrup or a blend of maple syrup and sugar-free syrup or a cappuccino.

I've used sour cream — Atkins uses heavy cream — and more sweetener than he does, and to cook the pancakes I use just a little butter instead of the very large amount of oil he recommends. If you don't have seltzer on hand, plain old water will be fine.

SERVES 2

2 large eggs, beaten well
½ cup Atkins Diet Bake Mix
⅓ cup seltzer water
4 packets Splenda low-calorie sweetener, to taste
¼ teaspoon salt
1 tablespoon sour cream
1 tablespoon butter

Mix everything but the butter together, using a whisk. Heat a griddle and when it's hot, add the butter and swirl it over the griddle. When the butter is bubbling, make the pancakes — silver dollar pancakes are particularly appealing.

Flip the pancakes over when they're just golden brown, about 30 seconds. They'll have little bubbles on the edges, just like regular pancakes. Cook them only long enough to turn golden brown on the other side and serve immediately, with butter and sugar-free maple syrup or with Berry Butter (page 353).

PER SERVING (PANCAKE ONLY):
Carbohydrate: 3g plus 1g fiber   Protein: 24.5g   Fat: 15g

Russian Pancakes

Although these delicate pancakes are traditionally served for dessert, they make excellent breakfast fare. They're actually fried in butter; you can cook them either in a large pan or on a griddle, but be sure to be generous with the cooking butter. Serve them garnished with sour cream and pass a little pitcher of the raspberry sauce to drizzle over them.

SERVES 4

Raspberry Sauce

1 pint raspberries
Splenda low-calorie sweetener, as needed

Put the raspberries in a small saucepan, cover, and gently heat until they release their juice. Break up the berries with a wooden spoon to release all their juice. If the liquid is very thin, you may need to cook it down briefly to a more saucelike consistency. Pass the berries through a sieve and taste the sauce; if it needs sweetening, add a little Splenda to taste. Set the sauce aside in a small pitcher.

Pancakes

½ cup (1 stick) butter, melted
1 cup farmer cheese or dry pot cheese or lowfat cottage cheese
2 large eggs, lightly beaten
1 tablespoon Splenda
¼ teaspoon salt
½ cup sour cream, plus 1 additional cup for garnish
3 tablespoons flour

Put 1 tablespoon of the melted butter into the workbowl of a food processor and add the remaining ingredients except the sour cream garnish. Process until well combined.

Keep the rest of the melted butter next to the stove to cook each batch of pancakes, and have a platter ready to keep the cooked ones warm under foil.

Set the pan or griddle over medium-low heat (not hotter) and generously butter the surface. When it's hot, drop rounded tablespoonfuls of batter on the surface, letting them cook until bubbles appear on top. Turn the pancakes and cook briefly on the other side, just until lightly browned. Repeat with the rest of the batter, keeping the cooked pancakes warm.

Serve the pancakes with a spoonful of sour cream and a drizzle of raspberry sauce.

PER SERVING:

Carbohydrate: 10.3g plus 4.3g fiber   Protein: 12.4g   Fat: 32.5g

The Pancake

This carb-lean version of Dutch babies, an old-fashioned American oven pancake, is really a sort of Yorkshire pudding made with butter. It puffs up dramatically in the oven and comes to the table fragrant with the aroma of hot melted butter.

I like this without syrup, but you can pour some diet maple syrup over it if you'd like. You can also sweeten it by dropping in a handful of blueberries or raspberries once the batter's in the skillet. A savory version, with little bits of ham and cheese, and an herbed version are also delicious. You can cut the carbs even further by using only ¼ cup flour, but that's a little stingy.

Remember that there isn't enough protein here for breakfast, so you'll need a side of sausages or ham to make it work.

SERVES 4

4 tablespoons (½ stick) butter
2 eggs, lightly beaten
½ cup milk
⅓ cup flour
Pinch of freshly grated nutmeg

Preheat the oven to 425°F. Put the butter in an ovenproof 9-inch skillet, preferably cast iron, and let it melt in the oven. Meanwhile, combine the remaining ingredients in a bowl and beat lightly, leaving the mixture a little lumpy.

When the butter is hot, pour the batter in, tilting the skillet to cover the bottom completely with batter. Bake 15 to 20 minutes, or until the pancake is puffed and tinged with golden brown. Serve immediately.

PER SERVING:
Carbohydrate: 9.4g plus 0.3g fiber   Protein: 5.3g   Fat: 15g

Roasted Spiced Apples

I learned this simple recipe from my friend Carver Blanchard, a lutenist who scavenges abandoned apple orchards in New York's Catskill Mountains for the tart little apples the deer have missed to make this dish. Humble as it is, it reminds me of tarte tatin, the wonderful French upside-down apple tart. You can have this for breakfast, with yogurt or just plain, or for dessert with cream or a scoop of vanilla ice cream. The apple peel gives it a somewhat chewy quality, which I like very much, and of course it's extra fiber. You can add nuts, grated lemon zest, freshly grated nutmeg — but here's how Carver does it.

SERVES 4

4 tart apples, cored and cut into small chunks
2 tablespoons butter, in small dice
1 tablespoon dark brown sugar
Cinnamon to taste

Preheat the oven to 400°F. Arrange the apple chunks in an 8-inch square glass baking dish. Dot with the butter and sprinkle with the brown sugar. Dust on a little cinnamon to taste.

Bake the apples 30 minutes, stirring once, or until done. Serve in small bowls with yogurt, cream, or ice cream if desired.

PER SERVING:
Carbohydrate: 19.6g plus 3.7g fiber   Protein: 0.3g · Fat: 6.2g

Crowdie

The Scots love oats so much that they actually eat them raw — an acquired taste, maybe, but quite delicious. And obviously full of fiber and other good things. The standard liquid for crowdie is buttermilk or thinned yogurt, but it's also good with soy milk or almond milk. If you like, add some berries and a little Splenda and you're set, oatmeal with no cooking.

Or you can ignore the Scots and make a softer, spiced-up crowdie: Add a little grated orange zest and a pinch of cinnamon to the oats and buttermilk, cover, and refrigerate overnight. Add a few crushed nuts on top before serving.

SERVES 1
½ cup rolled oats
½ cup buttermilk or thinned yogurt
Handful of raspberries (optional)
Splenda low-calorie sweetener (optional)

Mix the oats and buttermilk in your cereal bowl, topping with berries and Splenda.

PER SERVING:
Carbohydrate: 29.3g plus 4.2g fiber   Protein: 10.9g   Fat: 3.8g

Granola

This is about as close as you'll get to granola on the low-carb regime. But it's really quite good, and you can play with it endlessly, adding a few currants or diced dried figs or apricots if you have the carbs to spare. You can extend it even further by adding crumbled Fiber-Rich crackers, which will give you a lot more volume — and fiber. Freshly ground flaxseeds are good, too.

Make up a bunch of this glorified version and keep it in a big glass jar, tightly sealed. Just scoop out ½ cup for your morning breakfast — and try it with almond milk.

MAKES 6 SERVINGS
2 cups Protein Crunch cereal (see Sources)
I tablespoon unsweetened dried coconut
¾ cup chopped nuts, such as walnuts, almonds, pecans
I tablespoon nut oil, such as walnut or almond
Sprinkle of cinnamon

Preheat the oven to 300°F. Mix all the ingredients together in a bowl and pour them out in a single layer on a baking sheet. Toast 5 minutes or until the cereal starts to smell good. Let cool before eating or storing.

PER SERVING:
Carbohydrate: 6.1g plus 1.9g fiber   Protein: 28.8g   Fat: 14.6g

Scrambled Tofu

Sometimes the idea of more eggs for breakfast is just unappealing but you can't think of anything else. Tofu is lighter and has a nice texture. If you want an eggy yellow look, add a pinch of turmeric.

SERVES 2

1 tablespoon olive oil

2 scallions, minced, including some of the green

10-ounce box silken tofu, drained

Big pinch of turmeric (optional)

Salt and pepper

Hot pepper sauce

½ cup grated Cheddar or jack cheese (optional)

Paprika

Heat the oil in a skillet and sauté the scallions until they're soft, about 3 minutes. Meanwhile, crumble the tofu. Stir the tofu into the pan with the turmeric, if you're using it. Add salt, pepper, and hot pepper sauce to taste. Cook over high heat until the tofu is firm, about 2–3 minutes.

Add the optional cheese and sprinkle with paprika. Serve hot.

PER SERVING:

Carbohydrate: 4.5g plus 0.8g fiber   Protein: 10.2g   Fat: 10.6g

Exquisitely Scrambled Eggs

This old French way of scrambling eggs over extremely gentle heat is labor-intensive — but think of all those endlessly stirred polentas and risottos you aren't making anymore. Besides, this little bit of labor really pays off; these are the best scrambled eggs you'll ever taste. You need a double boiler to cook these eggs, but if you don't have one, you can make the eggs in a heatproof glass bowl perched on top of a saucepan half full of barely simmering water.

If this seems like way too much kitchen work for breakfast, serve the eggs for a light supper. Or add some snipped chives, a scrap of cheese, or even a dollop of caviar and serve these as a first course. But try them first the plain way, just to see how heavenly eggs, butter, and cream can taste all by themselves.

SERVES 4

10 large eggs, well beaten
8 tablespoons (1 stick) unsalted butter
½ teaspoon salt
Pinch of white pepper
2 tablespoons heavy cream

Have ready the bottom part of a double boiler half filled with barely simmering water. Pass the eggs through a fine wire sieve to remove the albumen "strings."

Melt a little of the butter in the top of the double boiler and swirl it all around to cover. Add the eggs and 2 tablespoons of the butter and cook 2 minutes, stirring constantly with a wooden spoon or rubber spatula in a figure-8 pattern, stirring around the edge of the pot from time to time to pick up the coagulated egg.

Add the salt and pepper and continue to cook another 8 minutes, stirring all the time and adding the remaining butter, 1 tablespoon at a time.

When the eggs are beginning to hold together but are still creamy, add the cream and stir a bit faster for 1 more minute. Serve immediately.

PER SERVING:

Carbohydrate: 1.8g   Protein: 16g   Fat: 38.2g

Baby Frittatas with Wild Mushrooms

There seem to be hundreds of varieties of frittatas (Italian open-face omelets), most of them quite good. But this version is truly extraordinary, not only because they're so delicious (the touch of cream cheese works wonders) but also because their creator has had the wit to make them miniature size, so they're perfect for brunch, with drinks, or as an accompaniment to salads or light meals. They're the work of Manhattan cook-to-the-stars Eileen Weinberg, owner of Good & Plenty to Go, a cheerful takeout shop where you're likely to see Steve Martin standing in line when he's in town.

You can make this recipe as a regular large frittata if you prefer — bake the frittata in a large skillet for 1 hour, then run it briefly under the broiler to brown.

You can also make the mini-frittatas the day ahead, then just reheat them in the oven at the last minute — or make the mixture and store it overnight in the refrigerator, ready to bake the next day.

MAKES 3 DOZEN MINI-FRITTATAS

Olive oil to grease pans, plus ¼ cup
2 cups minced cleaned wild mushrooms or a mix of shiitakes
    and portobellos
8 large eggs
Pinch of salt
Pinch of pepper
½ cup cream cheese, in small pieces
¾ cup grated Muenster cheese
¾ cup grated mozzarella cheese
¾ cup grated Swiss cheese
¾ cup grated Parmesan cheese
¾ cup grated white Cheddar cheese
½ cup heavy cream

Preheat the oven to 350°F. Spray two mini-muffin pans with nonstick cooking spray or rub them with some olive oil.

Heat the ¼ cup olive oil in a skillet over medium-high heat. Sauté the mushrooms in the oil until they brown and begin to reabsorb some of the cooking juices. Set the skillet aside.

Beat the eggs well in a large mixing bowl and add the salt and pepper. Mix in the cheeses, the cream, and the sautéed mushrooms. Pour the mixture into the pans and bake 30 to 40 minutes, until the tops are slightly golden brown and firm.

PER FRITTATA:

Carbohydrate: 0.6g   Protein: 4.9g   Fat: 8.2g

Old-Fashioned Egg Coddlers

Unless you had a British childhood, you probably don't have one of these porcelain gizmos lurking in your kitchen cupboard. But they're charming and ingenious, and they produce delectable eggs with a minimum of fuss. It's hardly worth getting anything but a king-size coddler (Royal Worcester makes them, and they're widely available), since the smaller ones hold only one egg, hardly enough protein for us.

Here's how they work: You paint the inside of the cup with melted butter, crack in your eggs, add salt and pepper, maybe some more butter, and whatever else catches your fancy: little bits of cheese, snipped chives, ham slivers, almost anything. Screw the metal top on loosely and set the coddler in a pan of boiling water, to come halfway up the side of the coddler.

Let the eggs cook 7 minutes for a soft, "three-minute" egg, another minute if you'd like it more set. Don't lift the coddler out of the water by its ring; use a potholder and grasp it by the porcelain part to remove it. The porcelain part of the coddler can go right in the dishwasher.

There are also microwave plastic egg coddlers from France in bright jellybean colors — very cute, but they don't really work. To poach an egg in the microwave, put 2 tablespoons of water in a ramekin or shallow glass dish and break an egg into the water. Prick the yolk several times with a toothpick. Loosely cover with plastic wrap and microwave 30 seconds. Let rest one minute, then remove with a slotted spoon.

Green Eggs and Ham

Lighter than bacon and eggs or eggs with cheese, this zesty combination is particularly appealing on a summer morning — or for a light supper.

SERVES 2

6 large eggs
Salt and pepper to taste
Dash of water
Dash of hot pepper sauce (optional)
2 tablespoons butter
2 scallions, minced, including the firm green part
I cup chopped fresh cilantro
2 tablespoons chopped fresh dill
2 ounces ham, diced

Whisk the eggs in a bowl, adding the salt and pepper, water, and hot pepper sauce and mixing well.

Melt the butter in a skillet and when it's foaming, add the scallions. Sauté a couple of minutes. Pour the seasoned eggs into the skillet and scatter the cilantro and dill on top. With a spatula, turn back the edges of the eggs and let the uncooked egg on top take their place. Begin to gently scramble them and scatter the diced ham on top.

Cook the eggs to the degree of wetness you like and serve.

PER SERVING:
Carbohydrate: 3.4g plus 1.3g fiber   Protein: 26.2g   Fat: 29.2g

Have Some Yogurt . . .

Because plain full-fat yogurt seems relatively high-carb at 13 grams a cup, you might think it doesn't belong in your refrigerator. But the health benefits of this ancient food are formidable, and whether you have it by the spoonful on fruit or by the cupful for breakfast, you really don't want to miss out on the unique nutrients it provides, namely, the good bacteria *Lactobacillus Acidophilus* and *L. Bulgaricus*.

In your intestinal tract there are over 400 distinct species of microorganisms, good guys and bad guys, enough of them to weigh about 4 pounds. The good guys face off against the bad ones (acidophilus, for instance, fights candida), as well as against viruses, and they also produce essential vitamins and maintain your hormone balance. They have other jobs too: They're key elements in immune function and energy production.

Your good health may depend a lot on the balance between these good and bad bacteria. James R. Privertera, M.D., editor of *Alternative Medicine Newsletter*, says many alternative doctors believe that a disrupted ecology of the gastrointestinal tract may cause up to 90 percent of illness and disease. And the balance is easily skewed, by antibiotics, stress, chlorinated drinking water, and — what else? — too much sugar. Your symptoms might include candida, allergies, vitamin B deficiencies, a sensitivity to dairy products, and chronic bad breath, as well as gastrointestinal problems. If you catch every passing cold, your immune system might need a boost; a study done at the University of California, Davis, found that the bulgaricus strain of bacteria increased the body's production of interferon (a key factor in immunity) by an amazing 400 percent.

Not all yogurt contains these beneficial bacteria; check the label for "active cultures." And of course all flavored or "light"

Make-Your-Own Ricotta

You can amaze yourself as well as your friends by making your very own ricotta — which is a snap. It's also very much more delicious than anything you'll find at the store. Made with organic dairy products, it's even better. Freshly made ricotta is wonderful for breakfast.

MAKES ABOUT 3 CUPS

2 quarts whole milk
1 cup plain full-fat yogurt
1 cup heavy cream
Pinch of salt

Have ready a large colander lined with a damp (not wet) kitchen towel — the towel should extend over the edges of the colander so you'll be able to pick up the cheese curds in it later. Combine everything but the salt in a large pot and bring to a boil. The milk should be curdled in 2 minutes; if not, cook it a little longer.

Carefully pour the curdled milk into the lined colander and let it drip directly into the sink 30 minutes. Pull up the ends of the towel and twist to squeeze out as much liquid as possible.

Empty the towel into a bowl and salt the ricotta to taste, mixing in well. Refrigerate until ready to use, up to 3 days.

PER ½-CUP SERVING:
Carbohydrate: 18g   Protein: 12.9g   Fat: 26.8g

yogurt on the market is full of sugar; organic full-fat plain yogurt with both kinds of good bacteria is what you want. Some organic cottage cheeses now contain the bacteria as well, and these are lower-carb than yogurt. If you can't find any of these, you can make your own yogurt — yogurt starter is sold at natural foods stores.

Sauces

Cucumber Raita

This cooling Indian salad/salsa is delicious all by itself but especially useful with grilled foods and spicy dishes. It's an extra step to use whole cumin seeds and toast them before grinding, but this small bit of work makes a big difference in the flavor of the raita.

SERVES 4

½ teaspoon whole cumin seeds
I cup plain full-fat yogurt
I medium cucumber, peeled, seeded, and coarsely grated
2 tablespoons finely chopped fresh mint
¼ teaspoon cayenne pepper
½ teaspoon salt or more to taste
Freshly ground black pepper

Put the cumin seeds in a small heavy skillet and toast them over medium heat, stirring constantly. When they turn several shades darker and start to smell good, they're done. Grind them in a mortar and pestle or a spice grinder.

Beat the yogurt in a bowl with a whisk until it's smooth and creamy. Add the remaining ingredients and mix thoroughly. Cover and refrigerate at least 1 hour.

PER SERVING:
Carbohydrate: 3.9g plus 0.4g fiber   Protein: 2.5g   Fat: 2g

Quick Black Soybean Salsa

This speedy salsa uses two excellent convenience products: Eden's canned black soybeans and their diced tomatoes with green chilies (Muir Glen also makes a first-rate version of tomatoes with chilies.) I can't improve on this recipe, which comes from the folks at Eden, so here it is.

MAKES 2½ CUPS

15-ounce can Eden black soybeans, drained
14½-ounce can Eden diced tomatoes with green chilies, drained
½ cup minced red onion
½ cup minced fresh cilantro
3 tablespoons fresh lime juice
¾ teaspoon salt

Mix everything together in a bowl. Taste for lime juice and salt, adding more if necessary.

PER 2-TABLESPOON SERVING:
Carbohydrate: 1.5g   Protein: 1g   Fat: 0

Pesto

In a perfect world, there would always be a little pesto in the fridge or freezer — or the makings would be on hand. If you're getting bored eating the same old vegetables all the time, give them the pesto treatment. For almost no carbs at all, just a spoonful or two will liven up that spinach, zucchini, cauliflower, green beans, a tomato half to be broiled. And even though Italian bread is off the menu for most of us, a smear of pesto and a generous grating of Parmesan on top of a slice of Alvarado Street Bakery's California Protein Bread (see Sources) bound for the toaster oven comes pretty close to the joys of bruschetta.

The lustier the olive oil for this dish, the better — I use an inexpensive Greek or Spanish extra-virgin oil.

MAKES 1½ CUPS

1 cup olive oil

2 cups lightly packed fresh basil leaves, preferably small

¼ cup walnuts or pine nuts

2 garlic cloves, minced

½ cup grated Parmesan cheese

Pour the olive oil into a blender jar or the workbowl of a food processor and add everything else but the cheese. Blend until smooth, scraping down the jar if necessary.

Transfer the pesto to a bowl and stir in the cheese. The pesto will keep a couple of days in the refrigerator or several months in the freezer. If you're planning to freeze it, leave out the garlic and cheese; add them after it's defrosted.

PER 2-TABLESPOON SERVING:

Carbohydrate: 1g plus 0.4g fiber   Protein: 2.6g   Fat: 20.7g

Lemonnaise

This condiment, available from Dean & DeLuca (800-221-7714), is great to have on hand. You can also improvise it yourself. Start with a good mayonnaise, such as Delouis Fils, Hellmann's, or Best Foods.

MAKES 1 CUP (16 TABLESPOONS)

1 cup mayonnaise
2 tablespoons fresh lemon juice
1 teaspoon Dijon mustard
Lemon zest to taste (optional)

Whisk everything together in a small bowl and taste for seasoning. Store in a tightly covered jar in the refrigerator up to several days. Whisk again before using.

PER 1-TABLESPOON SERVING:

Carbohydrate: 0.2g   Protein: 0.3g   Fat: 11g

Dressing for Smoked Fish

Very nice with smoked trout or other smoked fish. If you don't whip
the cream, it can be a salad dressing for sharp greens.

SERVES 4
½ cup heavy cream
2 tablespoons plus 1 teaspoon sherry vinegar
Salt and pepper to taste

Whip the cream just until it gets very thick. Whisk in the vinegar, salt,
and pepper. The dressing will keep, tightly covered in the refrigerator,
for a couple of days if the cream hasn't been whipped, for several hours
if it has.

PER SERVING:
Carbohydrate: 0.9g   Protein: 0.6 g   Fat: 11g

Make-Your-Own Ghee

This deliciously nutty Indian butter-oil is made by cooking the water out of butter, then heating it further so the milk solids caramelize in little clumps. Strain out the clumps and you have a delectable clarified butter that's an instant sauce for vegetables and makes fantastic pancakes. It's excellent for frying fish. Just a spoonful does wonders. Ghee keeps a very long time, best in the refrigerator, and it also freezes.

Makes 2 cups (32 tablespoons)
1 pound (4 sticks) unsalted butter

Have ready a fine-mesh strainer lined with a kitchen towel and set over a bowl.

Melt the butter in a saucepan over medium-high heat. Its water will boil off after about 15 to 20 minutes and the surface will be covered with a film over large flat bubbles. Reduce the heat to medium-low and cook another 15 minutes, or until the milk solids at the bottom of the pan turn golden — be careful not to let them turn brown, or the flavor will be spoiled.

Pour the ghee into the prepared strainer. Discard the milk solids. Store the ghee tightly covered at room temperature for a few days or refrigerated for several months.

Per 1-tablespoon serving:
Carbohydrate: trace   Protein: trace   Fat: 14g

Berry Butter

This is a sort of cross between jam and butter, good to spread on toast or on pancakes. It will keep about two weeks in the refrigerator, tightly covered.

MAKES ABOUT TEN 1-TABLESPOON SERVINGS
1 pint blueberries
½ cup (1 stick) butter, slightly softened

Put the berries in a small saucepan and heat gently just until they begin to release their juice — this goes quickly, so watch carefully. Let cool. In a small bowl, mix the cooled berries with the butter until fairly well combined. Pack into a sealed container and refrigerate. Let stand at room temperature briefly before serving.

PER SERVING:
Carbohydrate: 1.2g plus 1.6g fiber   Protein: 0.3g   Fat: 9.3g

Sources

LOW-CARB PRODUCTS (SEE ALSO "ON THE WEB," PAGE 363)
Advantage International USA, (917) 441-1038,
www.advantageintl.qpg.com: The low-calorie sweetener xylitol is
the big draw here, both powdered xylitol (a lifetime supply in a
3.63-pound jar) and gum and mints flavored with xylitol. This is
one of those mysterious polyols, compounds that supposedly
don't raise your blood sugar levels very much. Xylitol, a natural
product, has a cool, almost piney taste that's not great with
everything but is definitely good in gum and other places where a
minty taste would be welcome. Xylitol has lots of pluses of its
own: it reduces plaque, fights bad breath, and has some other
health benefits.
Atkins Products, (800) 285-5467, www.atkinsdiet.com: The bars, the
shakes, the bake mix. These things are also available at most natural foods stores and through some low-carb Web sites at a dis-
count.
Just The Cheese, (800) 367-1711, makes ingenious food products
out of pure cheese, including Frito-like chips, crackers, and crum-
bles, which can be sprinkled over salads and soups. Flavors include white Cheddar, sour cream and onion, and jalapeño.

Coming soon are salami chips and a sweet chip. Check their Web site at www.specialcheese.com.

La Tortilla Factory, (800) 446-1516. This company mail-orders low-carb tortillas and burrito wrappers, including some flavored ones. Check their Web site at www.latortilla factory.com.

Life Services Supplements, (800) 542-3230, www.lifeservices.com (see also www.lowcarbcentral.com): A low-carb site with a strong presence from Durk Pearson and Sandy Shaw, nutritional gurus from another decade. They offer a shake mix (KetoShake) that's creamy and tasty, as well as the questionable KetoBars (see page 328), a bake mix, and other low-carb products, including ersatz mashed potatoes. Relatively inexpensive.

Nature Sweet, (877) 997-9338, www.sweetbalance.com: They offer a high-price (an 80-gram bottle costs $11.95) low-glycemic sweetener made from fruit called Sweet Balance that has no bitter aftertaste and is supposedly thermogenic (supports rather than interferes with fat-burning). Sometimes called KiSweet. You use very tiny amounts of this sweetener, and though it hardens up quickly it can be easily resuscitated. You can also bake with this product, which has no carbs.

Nutritional Assistance, (800) 965-9008, www.lowcarbohydrate.com: Makers of the Protein 21 bars, Protein Crunch cereal, and Energy Burst Protein Snack Mix, this family-owned company is always coming up with new products, such as piecrust mix and snack drinks. Ask them what's new and what's coming soon.

Sugar Free Paradise, (800) 991-7888, has a number of low-carb products, including brownies, bagels (7g carb each), and a variety of crackers (4.9g for an entire box). These products are also kosher. Their Web site is sugarfreeparadise.com.

Wisdom of the Ancients, (800) 899-9908, has a variety of stevia products.

PHARMACY
Dews' 21st Century Products, (940) 382-1849: Dews stocks many body-building products and supplements, including BHB Plus (see page 58), an invention of the proprietor.

Phase'oLean starch blocker, (800) 572-8446, is available from Life Plus International.

Prolongevity perilla oil, an omega-3 oil, is available from Life Extension, (800) 544-4440.

TheraBreath, (800) 997-7999, www.therabreath.com: Try their products if nothing else works on your ketone-stinky breath.

FOOD AND EQUIPMENT

Alvarado Street Bakery, (707) 585-3293: High-protein sprouted organic breads. The California Style Protein Bread is 8 grams carb. Call for a source near you.

The Baker's Catalogue from King Arthur Flour, (800) 827-6836, www.kingarthurflour.com: You may have thought your days of perusing baking catalogs were over, but this one lists all sorts of useful things for the low-carb life. These include ClickClacks, airtight hard acrylic storage canisters that exactly fit Wasa Crackers (4×5 inches); Boyajian's excellent citrus and garlic oils; caraway, poppy, and sesame seeds; sheet gelatin; nut flours; unsweetened shredded coconut; pitted kalamata olives; and cinnamon/nutmeg mini-graters. If you like to play around with low-carb baked goods, look here for xanthan gum (to thicken batters), Betatrim fat replacer (a soluble oat starch with oat fiber that may also work as a starch replacer), toasted soy grits, and other food phenomena.

Dean & DeLuca, (800) 221-7714, New York City: The Manhattan epicures' mecca publishes a catalog offering luxury products ranging from caviar of all stripes to exotic cheeses, vinegars, chocolates; Kobe-style beef; succulent Lucques olives, Menes sardines and imported gourmet tuna.

Formaggio Kitchen, (888) 212-3224, Cambridge, Massachusetts: A shop that mail-orders truly great cheese, olive oil, vinegar, smoked Spanish paprika, amazing mustard, and other treats from all over the world. Call for a catalog.

Indian Rock Produce, (888) 302-6182: Almost any exotic produce you can think of will be found here, from herbs to Tokyo turnips to watermelon radishes to key limes and edible flowers (no carbs).

Mo Hotta, Mo Betta, (800) 462-3220: Spice, heat, and more heat.

Natural Ovens of Manitowoc, (800) 558-3535, www.naturalovens.com: This family-owned company produces good bread, some at 7 grams carb or lower per slice. If you like their bread, encourage them to offer a truly low-carb bread. They're serious about what they produce and have some interesting information in their literature.

The Spanish Table, (206) 682-2827, Seattle: So many delicacies from Spain are low-carb, including high-quality olives and olive oil, jarred piquillo peppers, smoked paprika. Marcona almonds (get these right after the fall harvest), vinegar, sardines, tuna, caper berries, Serrano ham, chorizo and lots of other sausages, plus wine and piri piri (Portuguese hot pepper sauce). Call for a catalog.

Sur La Table, (800) 243-0852: Kitchen equipment.

Williams-Sonoma, (800) 541-2233, www.williams-sonoma.com: Good for almost every kind of slicer: butcher knives, superb Matfer mandolines, Benriner vegetable slicers, Japanese bamboo vegetable graters. Williams-Sonoma also sells, in its print catalog only, Forgotten Tradition concentrated gravy bases (priced more like perfume than food), as well as meat and cheese.

SMALL FOOD PRODUCERS

Alaskan Harvest, (800) 824-6389, www.alaskanharvest.com: Wild-caught fish and seafood from the icy waters of Alaska, everything from salmon to Dungeness crab to shrimp. Party platters and gift selections are available. This is probably the freshest, tastiest, healthiest fish you'll find anywhere in the country, a very different thing from the months-old frozen and thawed mushy fish offered at most local supermarkets.

Birdsong Peanuts, (757) 539-3456: Peanut oil (made from a special peanut that doesn't go rancid easily) and peanut flour.

Bland Farms, (800) 843-2542, www.blandfarms.com: By the time it's ready for the spring harvest, a full-grown sweet Vidalia onion can pack as much sugar as another Georgia treat, a Coke. Order these little green ones instead; their harvest begins December 1, just in time for Christmas. Carb count is variable but much less than, say, a leek, and a bit more than 2 scallions.

Embudo Station, (800) 852-4707, www.embudostation.com: From the New Mexico countryside, oak-smoked turkey, boneless trout, pheasant, game hens, slab bacon, barbecued ribs, Canadian bacon, and ham.

Everything Under the Sun, (530) 795-5256: Organic dried kiwifruit, in either slices or chunks. This gnarly stuff is a tart and chewy treat.

La Española Meat, (310) 539-0455, Harbor City, California: Delectable Spanish sausages, 23 different kinds, plus dry-cured Serrano ham. Call for a catalog.

Legal Seafoods, (800) 477-LEGAL: Quite good frozen clam chowder that's 10 grams carb per cup.

Native Seeds/SEARCH, (520) 622-5561, Tucson, Arizona, www.nativeseeds.org: This Native American–owned company produces rare and delicious chili powders of all kinds, such as Aji amarillo, a yellow one, and Chimayo chili. They also sell interesting seeds to grow.

Niman Ranch, (510) 808-0330, Oakland, California, www.niman-ranch.com: There's not enough superb Niman meat to go around, and restaurant demand for this all-natural, carefully raised meat is high, so call ahead for a special occasion. Niman makes my favorite bacon, an applewood-smoked, center-cut bacon that comes in 3/4-pound packages and freezes well. Their hot dogs, however, are an acquired taste.

Original Nut House, (800) 803-1309, Wakefield, Virginia: The source for anything peanut-related, from extra-virgin peanut oil to several kinds of peanuts. Call for a catalog.

SERVICES

Personalized recipe analysis. NutriCalc, the company that analyzed the nutrient content of the recipes in this book, offers some unique services to dieters. Dr. Daniel Nelson, a Mayo Clinic–trained doctor of Internal Medicine, and his wife, Anna, a registered dietician with a Master's degree in Nutrition, will analyze your diet, screen for possible drug-nutrient interactions, and monitor your eating pattern to make sure it's appropriate for your medical condition and conforms to the diet you're trying to follow. Their Web site is www.NutritionKey.com. Toll-free phone number: (877) 422-5337.

On the web

There are literally dozens of low-carb Web sites and discussion groups you can visit, and they appear and disappear with startling frequency. If you want to hang out with scientific types who know a lot about the biochemistry of low-carbing (and talk about things like gluconeogenesis), there's a tech group for that; there are many support groups, recipe archives, and product sources. There are Atkins dieters, vegetarian groups, and even a couple of Christian groups. You can spend many happy hours browsing hundreds of sites, most of which are at least interesting.

Adiposity 101, "The World's Biggest Fad Diet" (anti low-fat) at: www.syndicomm.com/lowfat.html

A major source for low-carb lists: listserv@maelstrom.stjohns.edu. This one includes the tech group, a diabetes group, and a support group, all with great archives. If you just want to look up a specific point, you can send a message such as: search low-carb ketosis and e-mail to the address above. To join a list, send a message such as: SUB LC-DIABETES or SUB LC-TECH.

Dr. Robert C. Atkins's site has material from his newsletters, which includes lots of scientific journal citations that are comforting — the science for this lifestyle is really there. You can also order the numerous Atkins products here. www.atkinsdiet.com

The Web site of Dr. Michael R. Eades and Dr. Mary Dan Eades is heavily devoted to products at the moment, but that may change (and the products are excellent). www.eatprotein.com

For four low-carb mailing lists (lcexpert, lcrecipe, lowcarb, Atkins), send an e-mail that says "subscribe [list name]" to majordomo@cuy.net.

For interesting low-carb products, try www.low-carb.com/low-carb. They carry excellent catsup, plum sauce, cranberry sauce, and

barbecue sauce. They also have a low-carb café and market in An-
derson, South Carolina.

CarbSmart, "Smart choices for a low carb lifestyle": www.carbsmart.com

The SynergyDiet.com, "Empowering Today's Dieter": www.Synergy-
Diet.com

Expert Foods: www:expertfoods.com (which also has useful information on food labeling)

A vegetarian low-carb site and mailing list:
www.immuneweb.org/lowcarb/

A source for diabetes info and glycemic index info: send an e-mail to
mendosa@mendosa.com

For information on thyroid and other hormones:
www.brodabarnes.org

My own Web site: www.blackdirt.net/lowcarb

Bibliography

Atkins, Robert C., M.D. *Dr. Atkins' New Diet Revolution*. New York: Avon, 1997.

————. *Dr. Atkins' Vita-Nutrient Solution*. New York: Simon & Schuster, 1998.

Audette, Ray. *Neanderthin*. Dallas: Paleolithic Press, 1996. Reprint: New York: St. Martin's, 1999.

Barnes, Broda, M.D., and Lawrence Gayton. *Hypothyroidism: The Unsuspected Illness*. New York: Crowell, 1976.

Bernstein, Richard K., M.D. *Dr. Bernstein's Diabetes Solution*. Boston: Little, Brown, 1997.

Biermann, June, and Barbara Toohey. *The Diabetic's Book*. 4th ed. New York: Tarcher, 1998.

Brand-Miller, Jennie et al. *The Glucose Revolution*. New York: Marlowe, 1999.

Budwig, Johanna. *The Oil-Protein Diet*. Vancouver: Apple Publishing, 1994.

Cabot, Sandra, M.D. *The Liver Cleansing Diet*. Berkeley, Calif.: Ten Speed Press, 1997.

Carpender, Dana. *How I Gave Up My Low Fat-Diet and Lost Forty Pounds!* Bloomington, Ind.: Hold The Toast Press, 1990.

Crayhon, Robert. *The Carnitine Miracle.* New York: M. Evans, 1998.

Eades, Michael, M.D., and Mary Dan Eades, M.D. *Protein Power.* New York: Bantam, 1996.

———. *The Protein Power Lifeplan.* New York: Warner Books, 2000.

Goldberg, Jack, and Karen O'Mara. *The GO-Diet.* Chicago: GO Corporation, 1999.

Jenkins, Steven. *Cheese Primer.* New York: Workman, 1996.

McCullough, Fran. *The Low-Carb Cookbook.* New York: Hyperion, 1997.

McCully, Kilmer S., and Martha McCully. *The Heart Revolution.* New York: HarperCollins, 1999.

McDonald, Lyle. *The Ketogenic Diet.* Kearney, Neb.: Morris Publishing, 1998.

Madison, Deborah. *This Can't Be Tofu!* New York: Broadway Books, 2000.

———. *Vegetarian Cooking for Everyone.* New York: Broadway Books, 1997.

Messina, Mark. *The Simple Soybean and Your Health.* Garden City Park, N.J.: Avery, 1994.

Mitscher, Lester A., and Victoria Dolly. *The Green Tea Book.* Garden City Park, N.J.: Avery, 1998.

Montignac, Michel. *Eat Yourself Slim.* Translated by Daphné Jones, 5th ed. London: Montignac Publishing, 1996.

Robertson, Donald S., and Carol P. Robertson. *The Snowbird Diet.* New York: Warner Books, 1986.

Simontacchi, Carol. *Your Fat Is Not Your Fault.* New York: Tarcher, 1997.

Somers, Suzanne. *Suzanne Somers' Get Skinny on Fabulous Food.* New York: Crown, 1999.

Steward, H. Leighton, M.D. et al. *Sugar Busters!* New York: Ballantine, 1998.

General Index

Recipe Index

Vegetarian dishes are in *italics*.